NORTH OF THE NARROWS

Men and Women of the Upper Priest Lake Country, Idaho

PREFACE

This book is a sketch history and collection of stories about people and places in a small area of the Priest Lake country. It is about a small part of the Kaniksu National Forest for which I have a deep affection. I have attempted to bring together a diversity of information to structure a record of the people, places, and things that have been and are the area I know.

My personal interest dates back to June 14, 1936, the first time I saw Priest Lake. I was on my way to Elmer Berg's Shady Rest Resort at Beaver Creek to spend the summer on my honeymoon with my bride Catherine Diener. Catherine came to Priest Lake in 1930 as a member of the Newport High School senior class. The next summer she spent a short vacation at Elmer Berg's resort. She chose the honeymoon spot, for which I shall forever be grateful.

The idea for the title, *North of the Narrows*, came to me one day during one of my many trips to Beaver Creek from Stevens' Marina and Moorage at Granite Creek. The narrow channel of the lake between Granite and Bear Creeks separates by sight the southern two-thirds of the lake from the northern third, as one heads north by boat. Why not, *North of the Narrows?*

I will not attempt to describe either lake or how they affect me. If I did, I'm sure I would be accused of prejudice or charged with provincialism. I could describe my lakes only as the two most beautiful in the world. I will let others detail their verbal image.

J. E. "Jim" Ryan, a forest supervisor of the area, wrote in 1925, "A sapphire set in emerald, resting placidly in the Kaniksu National Forest."

"The lakes laugh at journalistic description," wrote a Spokane newspaper man.

According to a Kalispel Indian legend, "Priest Lake was a woman, gentle, calm, and kind. Pend Oreille Lake by comparison was the male, very fierce and mean with an evil spirit. The Great Spirit drew the two together and they were married at the Sacred Place, the huge rock below the caves on the Kalispel Indian Reservation."

Mrs. Rose Hurst, who lived near the lake for many years, gave a classic description of Priest Lake. "This lake is a moody lake. I have named her my Moody Lake. She is always in a different mood. To study this lake is a marvelous thing. One hour she can rise to be worse than a fretful woman and shake herself.

"I have seen her when she looked like a bunch of wild horses swimming with their tails flying backwards with the waves and the foam coming out of their nostrils. I've seen her when she went along with the ha, ha, story of laughing waters. She laughs at you when she has quieted down."

C. O. Johnson, a noted historian, called the lake, "A dark, ominous she devil," as he watched a storm-warning black streak move north between Tule Bay and Canoe Point.

Emmett L. Avery once made a choice remark about the lake. "The old lady has it in for me. Everytime I even think about going to Granite Creek by boat, she rises up and tries her best to *beat* me back to Beaver Creek!"

I have limited the Introduction to a short geological history of the area and a brief rundown on facts about the coming of the white man. This was done in an attempt to create a setting for the stories and pictures I have collected over a 44-year period.

A major task confronted me as I began writing the stories, namely, separating fact from fiction and how to write folklore, popular beliefs, and convincing yarns that the vivid imagination of various individuals stretched to exciting and popular legends.

Fig. 1 United States-Canadian border, Idaho Panhandle. (Al Piper)

I have cross- checked dates, happenings, and stories whenever and wherever possible. In some cases the information is so confusing that the facts or truth may never be known. When stories could not be checked, they are preceded by an explanatory label. Some of the true stories, almost unbelievable, are stranger than fiction.

An interesting sidelight is related below that emphasizes the problem of facts vs fiction when a historical writer is confronted with oral history. Mrs. Betsy Vitousek wrote and directed a pageant of early Priest Lake days that was presented at Priest River High School. She said that after the show many old- timers came up and said, "It was a good show but that was not the way it was, because the true story is . . . "

I have avoided altering the literary style of the personal stories in the book. It is unfortunate that the reader cannot hear the original words of the story tellers as well as see the printed words. To hear the voice inflections, feel the enthusiasm, the despair, the joy, the love, and at times the bitterness, of the interviewees has been one of the major thrills of collecting the information for *North of the Narrows*.

I owe a lot in the way of personal satisfaction to these freedom-loving people who created their own way of life on Priest Lake during the late 1800s and early 1900s. It was a way of life that no longer exists in northern Idaho. They found freedom in God's Country and lived it to the fullest.

In gratitude to these courageous, strong willed individuals, I am giving the original tapes, my notes, the pictures I have collected, and related files to the Idaho Historical Society, Boise, Idaho.

Claude Simpson

Fig. 2 Priest Lake fishing in the old days. Smoked Dolly Vardens and Silvers, 1960. Clark and Claude Simpson. (J. Jordan)

TABLE OF CONTENTS

INTRODUCTION

Priest Lakes lie in Bonner County in the Selkirk Range of mountains, an offshoot of the Rockies. The range is a rugged glacially affected southward extension of the Canadian Selkirks that extend north and northwest of Bonner County and Upper Priest Lake.

According to Edward F. Rodenbaugh in his *Sketches of Idaho Geology*, second edition, Priest Lakes owe their basins to the Wisconsin ice flow of about 30,000 years ago. The Wisconsin ice cleared the debris left by earlier ice ages of the Pleistocene period, of at least 1,000,000 years, and left the basins full of water.

Rodenbaugh wrote that the Iowan ice stage about 600,000 years ago came down from Canada and covered the Idaho-Washington border area as far south as Spokane. He stated, "The plateau-like Selkirks were covered by ice sheets except ridges such as Chimney Rock, Smith Peak, Goblin Knob, Squawman, Lookout, and perhaps Old Snowy." These ridges are called nunataks. Nunatak is a topographical term of Eskimo origin meaning the top of a mountain or hill which projects above a glacier. These nunataks were completely encircled by the Iowan glacier.

Dr. Fred Miller, geologist for the U.S. Geological Survey, Department of the Interior, stated in a personal letter that, "The lake [Priest Lake] itself is a relatively young geological feature which probably formed in one of the latter glaciation stages, most likely between 80,000 and 32,000 years before the present. At this time, the Priest Lake area was covered by an ice sheet that was probably several thousand feet thick. Most of the scenic, rugged looking mountains east of the lake achieved their present appearance during the last alpine glaciation, more than 15,000 or 20,000 years ago."

Dr. Miller published a report on the ages of rock in northeastern Washington and northern Idaho. He found biotite mineral rock on Plowboy Mountain that is approximately 87,000,000 years old. Rock he found in the Indian Creek area was approximately 90,000,000 years old. Rock in the Caribou country was assessed to be approximately 48,000,000 years old.

The early pioneers, the trappers, the miners, the homesteaders, and the loggers around Priest Lakes opened up new country for the white man for the same basic incentives that all countries were started, by seeking and acquiring wealth, and all that was connected with it. The settling of the Priest Lake area is a repeat of what happened to this nation from the shores of Virginia to the Pacific Ocean.

History has not recorded the name of the first white man who saw Priest Lake. It is an accepted fact, however, that the Kalispels, the Kutenais, the Coeur d'Alenes, and other Indian tribes, hunted, fished, and gathered berries and camas around Priest Lake and the Pend Oreille River areas many years before the white man arrived. Undoubtedly a few, and perhaps many, incomparable trappers followed the Indian trails west from the Dakotas to Priest Lake in search of beaver pelts, but no written record has been found.

David Thompson in 1808-09 built Kullyspell House on Pend Oreille Lake as a base for trade with the Indian and white trappers. He is called Idaho's first white businessman because there is a written record, dated September 9, 1809, stating that he exchanged 120-130 skins with the Indians in barter.

By 1811, Astor's hunters and trappers began crossing the Rockies through Idaho on their way to Astoria, Oregon. Within a few years trappers of the Northwest Fur Company and the Hudson's Bay Company were crossing the Rockies in search of pelts. The observations of these early frontiersmen add little, if anything, to the history of this area. They were neither interested in nor had the ability to write accounts or journals of their exploits.

The next important event of recorded history was the coming of Jesuit missionaries called Kaniksus, an Indian word meaning priests or black robes. Father Peter Jean De Smet in 1846 was the first man of the order to arrive in the Priest Lake country. He was a gifted writer with a special interest in giving names to various landmarks. He named Priest Lake, Lake Roothaan, for one of his teachers, Father J. P. Roothaan, of the Society of Jesus in Rome. Mt. Roothaan is one of the few names given to landmarks by Father De Smet that remains today. Many of the names given by Father De Smet were too difficult or foreign for the Indians and the early pioneers to pronounce. Examples are: Riviere des Robes for Priest River; Hollandoise and Lyonnaise for Reeder and Granite Creeks; Triandoise for Kalispel Creek. As would be expected, the majority of the permanent identifying names in the Kaniksus are of Indian or pioneer origin. A few examples would include: Squawman, Tepee Creek, Kaniksu, Phoebe Tip, Eddy Peak, Goblin Knob, Trapper and Gold Creeks.

The 1865 map that Captain John Mullan made of northern Idaho, when he surveyed and built the Mullan Road from Walla Walla to the Coeur d'Alene mines, carries the name Lake Kaniksu for what is now Priest Lake. In a personal letter dated October 25, 1971, written to Peggy Simpson Yates, Fred E. Bailor mentioned several landmarks of the area. Mr. Bailor was a member of the party that resurveyed the 1873 survey. The party had the original notes and put in a new post every mile. When they reached Granite Creek a large blaze was found on a white pine tree with the inscription, "Camp Friday, October, 1873."

"The last mile and a half we cut the timber off a strip 50 feet wide. I cut the last tree to finish the resurvey from Lewiston to the Canadian Border.

"It might also be of interest to you, Peggy," stated Mr. Bailor, "that my old friend, Charlie Horton, used to pole up Priest River to Priest Lake each year. It was a five- day trip going up. He would return in nine hours."

Considerable flap was created when President Grover Cleveland issued a proclamation, February 27, 1897, creating the Priest River Forest Reserve. According to Sleep's historical report, "With this 650,000 acres closed to settlers and loggers *prophets of doom* predicted the economy of north Idaho would be scuttled."

Contrary to predictions, Sleep reported, "Feverish logging activity continued on all sides of the reserve which sparked the economy into a period of growth that had not since been equalled. By 1902, north Idaho had more miles of railroad than any other part of the state."

Fig. 3 Samuel Tilden Byars. (Duffill Collection)

1

FOREST LODGE

Forest Lodge on the north shore of the Thorofare between little and big Priest Lakes was the dream of Samuel Tilden Byars. Sam came to Priest Lake as a young man from the mountains of Tennessee. He was a tall, raw-boned, powerful man of Scandinavian parentage. When he arrived in the Panhandle he filed and lived on a homestead along Lion Creek near the mouth of Lucky Creek. In May 1913, he filed on a 113- acre homestead in Section 10 near the mouth of the Thorofare and lived in his homestead cabin until he finished the first unit of Forest Lodge late in the fall of 1914. Prior to devoting full time to his business interests, Sam was a ranger for the U.S. Forest Service. As late as 1915, there were references to Sam Byars' Forest Service District above little Priest Lake.

On June 18, 1914, the *Priest River Times* reported that Samuel T. Byars, one of the best-known men in the Forest Service of the northwest, and Mrs. Grace Hamm were married in Spokane. Grace was about 5 feet tall, inclined to plumpness, a family trait. She had snappy brown eyes, dark hair, and was a very charming hostess. She was an excellent homemaker, with an eye for color, arrangement, and comfort. She was also a marvelous cook as attested by Fern Geisinger, as well as the many guests at Forest Lodge. The living room or lobby of Forest Lodge was a very comfortable place to relax. Grace was a voracious reader and she had lots of books and magazines for that time and place.

Grace Chambers Hamm was born June 14, 1886, in Ankeny, Iowa. She came west in 1911 with her husband, Edward Hamm, and daughter Madlyn, born July 22, 1908. They settled in Newport, Washington, where Edward operated a tailor shop until they divorced two years later.

When Madlyn first came to Priest Lake, she recalled that the family lived in Sam's homestead cabin and lean-to just east of where Forest Lodge was being built. "My first memories of Priest Lake centered around Sam's cabin," said Madlyn. "Sam was very good to me. I was never legally adopted by him because my father would not

15

Fig. 5 Madlyn Byars with the mounted locked deer horns. (Duffill Collection)

the lodge. The barn was on the west edge of the big meadow back of the lodge. Each year near the barn there was a big garden, which was Billy Duffill's pride and joy. It furnished welcome additions to the meals for family, friends, and guests. Madlyn remembered the barn was large enough to house two or three cows, three or four horses, as well as horses that guests would bring with them for packing and riding. It had a large haymow that was filled each year with wild hay cut from the meadow.

The story that Sam built a road from the lodge to Mosquito Bay to transport his guests at the end of their steamer trip up the lake was not true. There was no road, nor a buggy, or hack on the place. There was a good trail and many guests used it to hike to the lodge. Most of the vacationers who arrived by steamer were transported by motor boat or small launch from Mosquito Bay to the hotel.

Sam's homestead log cabin was east of the lodge. There was a good-sized frame guest cabin between it and the main building.

Below it were two small guest cabins, one with a screened sleeping porch. Up the Thorofare from the lodge were two additional guest cabins. They are still standing today.

By 1917, Forest Lodge was running full tilt. Guests were coming and going from May to November. Madlyn recalled, "The piano was a surprise to new guests. I remember Dr. George Anderson, a Spokane diagnostician, accompanying himself as he sang clever little songs with a strong Swedish accent. Everyone's favorite was 'Little Tillie Olson.' We had many doctors, dentists, and businessmen who came to Forest Lodge from Spokane and some of the surrounding towns, Colfax, Rosalia, Reardan, Pullman, and Moscow. Throughout the summer months they came with their families and in the spring and fall they often came with other men for the fishing and hunting.

"Many of these people became our good friends. There was Dr. A.A. Matthews, one of the finest surgeons in the northwest. He loved to fish and would go out to fish before breakfast. After the morning meal he would take a lunch and Billy Duffill, to act as skipper of the boat, and according to Billy, he never left the boat until it was too dark to fish any longer. He said it relaxed him after his heavy schedule of surgery. My mother catered to his whims and many evenings kept his dinner hot for him when he would come in an hour or two past the dinner hour. Mother pampered all of the guests.

"There was big Jim O'Neil, who dealt in wheat; the Heberts of Kemp and Heberts store in Spokane; Mr. and Mrs. James Cole, proprietors of a family-type printing shop in Spokane; Mr. and Mrs. Jack Barron— he later became the northwestern divisional manager for Diamond Match Co.; Mr. and Mrs. Charlie Snell— Charlie traveled for Hills Bros. Coffee and was a prototype of the old-time traveling salesman. There were also professors from Washington State College, the University of Idaho, and Cheney Normal."

One of the families that Madlyn and her mother always waited for were the Turnleys. Mr. Turnley was a traveling salesman for Red Goose shoes. He brought his entire family and usually some of his relatives from Rosalia, Washington, to the "Old Plantation" as he called it, for a three or four week outing. They were still coming each summer as late as 1931. The family was lively, talented, and out for a good time. There were always several Turnley kids about Madlyn's age. They were a real find for her, as at times she got lonesome for someone to play with.

When there were no kids around to play with, Madlyn spent a lot of time with Daddy Duffill. She would go up the Thorofare with him

19

Fig. 6 Forest Lodge, 1914. (Duffill Collection)

Fig. 7 Forest Lodge, 1915. (Duffill Collection)

Fig. 8 Forest Lodge, also called "The Old Plantation," 1921. (Duffill Collection)

and tow logs down to the sandspit where he would saw and split them for Sam's steamboat. One of Madlyn's favorite remembrances of Daddy was his cure for almost anything that was wrong with the human body. You took a quart and a pint, mixed them together, drank them before you went to bed and the next day or two he guaranteed that one would be well and happy. Billy apparently believed in the theory that the special remedy had to be mixed, regardless of the liquid used.

She also spent a lot of time picking huckleberries with Frank the Finn Algren. He would permit her to pick in his self-prescribed area so that she would listen to his stories.

Frank was in the Russian army as a young man and told a story that Madlyn never forgot. According to the story the entire camp was called to the parade grounds early one morning and ordered to stand at attention in full battle dress because the Czar was to review the troops. The soldiers had to stand there at attention all day. Dozens of the men fainted and had to be carried away. Frank was one of the men who was able to stand at attention until nightfall. The Czar never did show up. Frank didn't admit it, but Madlyn felt that was the reason he came to America.

Frank was a typical anti-social old-timer. Once in awhile he would come to Forest Lodge with a full gallon jug, rent a room, disappear into it, and wouldn't be seen for two or three days. When he finished his jug he would come down to meals as if nothing had ever happened.

Another of Madlyn's pals was Cougar Gus. He taught her to paddle the canoe that Sam bought for her on her twelfth birthday. She had heard Gus tell the story of getting his nickname for skinning a cougar at the end of main street in Sandpoint. She was convinced that the story was true because the details as told by Gus never varied.

Madlyn always enjoyed the frequent visits of Aunt Belle Angstadt. She said it was hard to believe that Aunt Belle was once a chorus girl because she had become very heavy and her enlarged goiter made her look rather scary to youngsters. In spite of that, Madlyn recalled that Aunt Belle was loved by everyone. She was talented, clever, quick-witted, wrote poetry, and could really entertain people. Her one fault was her superstitious nature.

Madlyn recalled, "One Christmas we spent several days with Aunt Belle and Harry. I wasn't tall enough to hang the towel on the high rack, so I hung it on the door knob. Belle almost went through the roof! That was bad luck to her. Mother and I gathered an armful of cedar boughs to decorate Belle's mantle. They went out faster than we had brought them in because Aunt Belle knew that disaster would strike if cedar was used for Christmas decorations. My family was not the least bit superstitious so it was hard for me to understand her phobia. It really made a deep impression on me."

Madlyn told one of her favorite stories about Alva Allen from Allen-a-Dale on the little lake. Mr. Allen was having trouble with his memory. He was taking a memory course by correspondence. One week he rowed down the Thorofare to meet the mail boat and to get his next lesson for the course. He was very embarrassed when he discovered he had forgotten to bring the lesson that he had just finished. Mr. Allen was a good sport about it and laughed with everyone else. She couldn't remember whether he ever completed the course or not.

Madlyn was a very special friend of Elmer Berg's. As far as can be learned, she was one of the two people to whom Elmer told anything about his early life. While talking with her about Sweden he showed her a picture of the girl he left in the old country. Shortly before the date set for their wedding his bride-to-be died. Elmer was 19 at the time.

When Madlyn was 10 years old she made her first trip to the top of Lookout Mountain. As she told the story, "It was a rough trip, but we all made it. Coming back down I wore holes in both shoes. Elmer insisted that I get on his back and he carried me to the bottom, piggyback style. When we got back to the lodge and my mother heard the story she said to Elmer, 'Did you carry that big lunk of a kid down that mountain? What did you do that for?' Elmer said, 'Vell, the poor little thing — her toes vere sticking out.'

"The thing I remember best about Elmer was when you got ready to push your boat away from the dock he would always say, 'Yump girlie, yump. If you can't make it in one yump, make it in two.'

"One day Billy and Elmer were over at our place and as usual Billy was making fun of Elmer's accent. Billy was mimicking Elmer and said, 'Pass the yug, Elmer!' Elmer replied, 'Billy you shouldn't say yug, say chug!" He was a fine old Swede.

"Shortly after our son John was born, George and I spent the winter in one of the small cabins just below the hotel. The cabin was so small that the only place we had to put the baby was in a trunk in the lean-to on the cabin. One evening Jack Rule and Elmer came to play cards. Every 10 or 15 minutes one or the other would get up and take a look at John. They were so afraid the lid would fall down and smother him."

The year that Nell Shipman had her crew and zoo animals at Forest Lodge, Madlyn told of how much she enjoyed taking her girl friends on a tour of the zoo. The man in charge of the animals was a veterinarian called the "Mad Russian" because he got so excited when people disturbed his animals.

Doc, as he was also called, always wore an Australian type hat with a wide brim and when he met the girls to take them on a tour he would doff his hat and make a sweeping bow. This was a dramatic sight for the ladies. If Nell was met around the zoo, Doc would jump into the air, click his heels three times and then make his sweeping bow. Madlyn said that everyone agreed that the Mad Russian was a real lover of animals and he knew how to handle them. But good as he was, he could not equal Nell's talent for handling wild animals. Madlyn said, "Once in awhile at night a wild animal would come out of the mountains and get the zoo animals all excited. The uproar would be deafening. If Doc couldn't get them to settle down, Nell would go out to the pens and you could follow her progress from pen to pen because everywhere she went the animals quieted down. It was really remarkable.

"I'd swear she had nerves of steel. I watched the filming of a scene near our barn where there were some moss-covered logs and brush. According to the script, a cougar was to attack Nell. The first thing the crew knew the cougar was really stalking her. The trainer had taken off his leash and collar so the cougar was not play acting. Nell knew she was really being stalked. She laid there and never moved a muscle while the camera ground away. The cougar got within a few inches of her before the trainer could lure him away with a piece of meat on a long pole."

Another of her friends was Barry Shipman with whom she would spend hours acting out scenes from the *Tarzan* and *Tom Sawyer* books. Between the two of them they figured out a way for Barry to climb up on the back porch and get into the kitchen to help himself to the cookie jar. Eventually, they were caught in the act and a permanent screen on the window stopped the cookie route. Another of their favorite pastimes was to entertain the guests by playing in the canoe in front of the lodge. Their favorite trick was to tip the canoe over, right it, and not ship water. Barry was an excellent swimmer and diver and he put on quite a show.

Sam started a boat business after the lodge got to be a paying proposition. The Coolin base was operated by Madlyn's grandfather. Bob Carey came into Coolin one day and wanted to rent a row boat. Granddad knew that Sam didn't like Bob but he promised to get back before Sam arrived. That night when Sam and Granddad settled up, Granddad gave Sam a dollar and told him he had rented a boat to Bob Carey. Sam threw the dollar back on Granddad's pile and told him in no uncertain terms that he would have nothing to do with Carey's filthy money and under no circumstances was he ever to rent another boat to Bob Carey.

Bert Winslow and Sam had a falling out over freight rates that ended their friendship. Bert got the better of Sam one day when Sam got stuck in the mud with his Model T on the Dickensheet road. Bert came along and offered to help but Sam ignored him. Bert didn't let it bother him and got some poles and a few boards from his pickup and helped Sam pry his Ford up to solid ground. But Sam drove off without giving a word of thanks to Bert. "That was Sam," said Madlyn. "He was just that independent. If he didn't like you he wanted to have nothing to do with you. I imagine that was part of the reason he was at Priest Lake."

Sam parted ways with Shipman Productions over a financial

dispute on the lease of his place to the company. Madlyn felt that Nell Shipman would have liked to stay at Forest Lodge but Sam had issued the ultimatum, if you can't pay, you can't stay.

Madlyn said she always felt cheated because she was not allowed to visit the company after it moved to Mosquito Bay. She missed playing with Barry as well as the excitement that went with the activities of movie making. "I'm probably the only person, except my mother and Sam, that didn't go to the Priest River band day celebration and barbecue. I remember sitting out on the front steps listening to the music, the fun, and all the noise. Sam was through with Shipman Productions, and that was that! Sam wasn't entirely to blame. He had to make a living, too.

"Nell had her odd ways. She didn't like to ride in a motor boat. She would prop herself up with pillows in a canoe and the motor boat would tow her to Coolin. Made you think of Cleopatra.

"Sam and some of the rest of us knew that Director Van Tyle liked to put up a typical Hollywood front. Occasionally, when the company made a little money Van Tyle would not take a regularly scheduled boat trip but would order a special run to Coolin and then order a special stage to get to Priest River. This type of thing was not acceptable to a lot of Priest Lakers."

While commenting on Sam's personal make-up, Madlyn told the story of Sam's toughness even dealing with members of his own family. His brother, Tom, came to Priest River as a young man and was flying high by gambling and drinking in one of Priest River's well-known establishments. The county sheriff, a good friend of Sam's, told him that the place was to be raided and suggested that Sam warn his kid brother. Sam told the sheriff that he was not going to warn him. He had repeatedly told Tom to stay clear of the place and if he didn't do it he would get what was coming to him. Madlyn said, "The raid took place and from what I heard there were men and girls going out of doors and windows in every which direction. The Byars' luck held and Tom was one of the few who didn't get caught."

During prohibition, Sam went into a business venture with Elmer Stone. Sam bought the equipment, the sugar, corn, and other supplies. Elmer ran the still and in general took care of the operation, except at batching time when Sam had to help out.

During a spring vacation when Madlyn came home from school, Sam wasn't around the lodge and when she asked her mother where he was she was told that he was with Elmer. Her mother suggested they go out to see the operation as Madlyn had never seen it. She related the following account of the incident. "Mother and I picked our way through the trees in a northerly direction from the icehouse on the Thorofare. The path was well-disguised, covered by brush and trees. We finally came to two big tents. One housed the still and the other the mash and charred oak barrels for aging the moonshine. We peeked into the tent that had the still in it. Along one side of the tent was a big long table with jugs, oak barrels, and other paraphernalia on it. When we got into the tent Sam was at one end and Elmer at the other, each with a rifle within an arm's length of their reach. Mother spoke to me and each man grabbed his rifle before they realized who we were. I thought, wow, it could be dangerous sneaking up on these two! They had their plan worked out as to what they would do if a stranger should ever show up.

"The first fall they were in operation a newcomer came to the lodge and said that he was a geologist looking for a certain type of metal. He asked for directions to Caribou Creek. Sam and Elmer sent him on a round-about way to the creek, well east and north of where the still was located. They followed him until they were sure he hadn't spotted the still site. When they returned Elmer remarked, 'That guy is a revenuer! He isn't any more a geologist than I am.' I asked him how he could tell. 'You can always tell a government man because he tucks his pants inside his high topped laced boots!'"

Madlyn saw Barney Stone on Memorial Day, 1978. She told him that Al Piper who bought the property where his dad and Sam had had their still had found a lot of copper tubing, crocks, and some remains of barrels. She asked Barney if he thought that was the site of his dad and Sam's operation. Barney replied, "Yes, it's bound to be."

In the fall of 1930, Madlyn and her mother had gone to Spokane to do some shopping before winter set in. Sam made a last trip alone up the lake to deliver supplies to various camps. He stopped at Schaefer's camp on Distillery Bay on his way up and left mail and supplies. When he passed by Distillery Bay on his way back one of Schaefer's men tried to flag him, but Sam was walking along the catwalk hanging onto the railing around the top of the steamer. He did not see the signal to stop and that was the last time Sam was seen alive.

Sam did not get back to Coolin that night. The next morning the boat was found aground on Cape Horn. No one knows how long he was in the boat. The fire was out, the boiler cold, and Sam was sitting in the pilot's seat, with his hands on the steering wheel, his body frozen stiff. He died from a heart attack which was no surprise to anyone because he had had heart trouble for several years. The legal death notice states that Sam died "on or about the 15th day of November, 1930." He was buried in the Priest River cemetery. Madlyn continued, "Mother leased Forest Lodge to Birg Pattee in March, 1931. The Pattees were from Boston. Pattee added a Delco light plant and a fireplace. He was there about 3 or 4 years. Another couple leased the place for a year or two, but they had no boat and found it impossible to make any money without regular boat service. In March, 1938, it was leased to Edward C. Klein and John R. Burton. They had it when it burned. It was believed that sparks from the fireplace set the tinder dry building afire.

"My mother put the place on the market, sold it to Mrs. Pearl Smith and bought the Courser apartments in Sandpoint. In the late 1940s she sold the apartments and bought the Peterson Hotel in Priest River which she renamed Kings Hotel. She formed a business arrangement with Buddy Moore. He took over complete management of the bar while she managed the hotel and they split the profits. The arrangement was very successful for both. Just before Idaho banned the slot machines she sold the place to the Bridgewaters. She bought a home in Priest River, but sold it after a year or two and returned to Sandpoint. She bought a home there with two apartments for rental and lived there until she entered the Riverview Terrace Rest Home in Spokane. She died September 1, 1970 at the age of 84."

Madlyn left Forest Lodge when the Pattees leased the resort. She lived in Coolin, on her grandfather's ranch, and in Priest River, for the next 30 years. While living in Priest River she worked for the *Priest River Times* and kept books for a real estate and insurance office. After she and her husband separated in 1962, she worked in the land section of the Bonner County Assessors Office. In 1971, she went to Washington, D.C. where she worked at the Navy Department until she retired in 1973.

Madlyn said, "After living all my life, except my D.C. stint, in Bonner County, I find peace and contentment in my retirement home, North 512, Pines Road, Opportunity, Washington."

Fig. 9 Steamer "W. W. Slee" leaving Canoe Point, 1915.
(Hungate Family Collection)

Fig. 10 Capt. Markham's "Tyee," built in 1925, docked at BCRS.

2

BOATS

The main link between civilization and early life on Priest Lake, north of the narrows, was a boat. There were no roads north of Granite Creek prior to mid-20th century. A pack or foot trail was in existence on both sides of the lake. The many boat stories and comments about particular boats related by old-timers and early tourists are responsible for this chapter. The author did not attempt an exhaustive study of boats on Priest Lake.

The early settlers, north of the narrows, resorted to the most favorable route as a necessity of life, the water. It took care of the problems of trail maintenance over rugged mountainous terrain, the high cost of land transport, as well as escaping the mosquitoes in the summer. In the winter months, the ice furnished an excellent route, sometimes precarious, for transport by dog sled, skates, or snowshoes.

The early boats on Priest Lakes were used for work. They were sturdy tug-like steam boats, gasoline powered launches, rowboats, and undoubtedly many canoes. At least one boat or canoe was part of the life of each permanent or semi-permanent resident on the lake. The steamers and motor powered launches were operated as commercial carriers. Some of the rowboats were large enough to have two sets of oar locks and could haul supplies as well as a number of passengers for trips from Coolin as far north as Upper Priest River.

Two of the most common rowboats were the wood-ribbed, galvanized tin, of the Can't Sinkum type, and the Thompson lapstrake wooden boat. By the 1930s, the aluminum scow type, lightweight boats gained popularity.

Cougar Gus had a canoe that carried the name, "Cougar's War Boat." Boat houses were also a part of early Priest Lake days. The boat transportation that evolved was responsible for the development and economic welfare of the area. It made possible for the early settlers a sense of community sociability, and now the recreational activities that have all developed because of boats.

29

The first powered boat on Priest Lake was Walter W. Slee's "Kaniksu." The boat was plying the clear waters of Priest in 1896. Bert Strayer of Newport, has a picture of the "Kaniksu" and the "Sacajawea" tied up at the dock in Coolin in 1905. The steam-powered "Sacajawea" was built at the Langill Shipyards one mile downriver from the east end of the bridge that crosses the Pend Oreille River at Oldtown, Idaho. Bert's father was foreman of the shipyards when the boat was built. Bert knew that the "Sacajawea" had been used as a steamer to transport tourists and to haul supplies to Shipman Productions in Mosquito Bay. The steamer was still in operation in 1930.

The name of Granddad Slee's "Kaniksu" is often confused with the Forest Service boat also called "The Kaniksu." Bert Winslow's well-known steamer, "The W.W. Slee" also has been confused with Slee's "Kaniksu."

The *Priest River Times*, July 1, 1976, carried the following story in their 50 year column, "The steamer 'Cougar,' a 45-foot boat, which has been in passenger service on Pend Oreille Lake for a number of years, is to be transferred to Priest Lake. The boat will be taken down-river to Laclede and thence by auto truck to Coolin."

The "Banshee," an ill-fated steamboat built by C.H. Wheatley, at Coolin, made only one trip up the lake and back because there wasn't enough room on the deck to store all the wood necessary to make the round trip. On the way back she rammed a submerged rock and was wrecked beyond repair. Marj Paul Roberts reported that during WW II the boat was dragged onto the beach just south of Bishop's Marina, stripped of her metal, and burned.

Construction of the "Banshee" began in 1905, and was completed in 1907. Robert Wheatley, C.H. Sr.'s grandson, has a picture of his grandmother holding his father, C.H. Jr. His dad was born in 1907, so the above date is reasonably accurate. Bob also has a letter dated 1908 from a Chicago firm that sold C.H. Sr. the engine for the "Banshee." The letter was addressed to Coolin and gave details on the "fine tuning of the mechanics" of the boat's engine.

Bob also has a 1913 photograph of the "Banshee" on the beach near Coolin with the caption "The Last of the Banshee."

Bob remarked in the letter, "I sometimes wonder how Granddad found the energy for boat building, townsite development, inventions, gold mining, trapping, song writing, script writing for plays, oil leases, ad infinitum."

The "Lady of the Lake" was a fast boat equipped with cabins. Her

Fig. 11 Northern Navigation Co. "Tyee," built in 1945.

Fig. 12 "The Kaniksu," transferred from
the Coast Guard to the USFS.

Fig. 13 "Papoose."

Fig. 14 The "Ridley," towing partner of the "W. W. Slee."
(Herrick Heitman, Heitman Marina)

Fig. 15 The "Swastika," owned by Earl and Fern Geisinger. (H. Branyan)

Fig. 16 "Tyee," built in 1945. Now in Mosquito Bay.

power source was probably a gas motor. No confirmation of power source could be obtained.

The launch "Firefly" was an inboard craft owned by the USFS. It was used in the early 1920s to transport men and supplies from the Forest Service warehouse on Kalispel Bay to Beaver Creek Ranger Station. For many years Art Moore was the pilot.

On June 28, 1978, the *Priest River Times* carried a 60- years- ago story. "Sam Byars has bought the 'Papoose' from Mose Fish and we understand will take daily trips to all parts of the lake." It was powered by a Fordson tractor motor.

Earl and Fern Geisinger owned and operated a motor powered launch called the "Swastiki." They traded fox for the boat. The Geisingers bought Dad Moulton's motor launch and named it "Old Dad." Moulton had used the launch to transport prospective buyers of lots at the platted site of Wheatley, Idaho.

The steamboat owned and operated by Captain Art Tyler, named "Constitution" was available for charter on Priest Lake.

The following item appeared in the *PRT,* August 18, 1925, "The steam tugs, the 'W.W. Slee' and the 'E.W. Harris,' set a record during the week of May 7, 1925, when the boats towed 6,000,000 board feet of logs from Mosquito Bay to Outlet in 39 hours and 30 minutes.

"Captain Graydon Winslow was at the helm of the 'W.W. Slee' and Captain Bert Winslow piloted the 'E.W. Harris.' Aubrey Overmyer and F.O. Lamb were the firemen for the trip.

"The logs in the boom were cut for Diamond Match under the general direction of Phil Flint and James Holmes. During the trip 300,000 board feet of logs blew out of the boom. They were rounded up later in another boom that was towed by both tugs."

These two tugs were the power that towed the Priest River Band and overflow passengers on a barge from Coolin to Mosquito Bay to honor Nell Shipman for her part in raising money for new band uniforms.

Another story goes that Millie Adams bought the Schaefer's houseboat and operated it between Coolin and Kalispel Bay for gambling, girls, bar, and dancing — the works, during the years of WW II. The houseboat, still docked at Coolin, had its own electric light plant, four bedrooms, and a big living room. Millie's cruises lasted from one to three days at a time.

The "Ridley" was built at Sunnyside on Pend Oreille Lake by Capt. Markham during the summer of 1937. She was 41 feet long and the construction was double-sawed frames with carvel planking. The power was a compound steam engine with a wood fired boiler. She was the most powerful tug ever to be transported to Priest Lake. She held the title until the "Tyee II" was built in 1945.

The "Ridley" slumbers beside the Herrick Heitman Marina, Glengary, on Lake Pend Oreille, P.O. Box HCR 66, Box 786, Sandpoint, Idaho, 83864. In a letter dated December 20, 1977, Mr. Heitman furnished the above information on the construction of the "Ridley." The *Ruralite* magazine issue of December, 1977, carried a story and pictures of Herrick and the "Ridley." The caption under the picture states in part: [The boat is] "... of more than casual interest to Herrick Heitman, for he is one of the last builders of handmade wooden boats." He also indicated in his letter that Russ and Mona Bishop of Coolin were good sources of boat information because Mona was the daughter of E.O. Elliot who owned the Northern Navigation Company of Coolin.

The Northern Navigation Company, owned and operated by Ed Elliot and Ralph Smith, built the "Tyee II" in Coolin and launched the hull during the summer of 1945. The "Tyee II" was powered by a compound steam engine with a six- foot propeller. She was 82 feet long and made entirely of native wood. Russ Bishop of Coolin was the chief mechanic on the job. Russ has a 12" x 18" photo of the "Tyee II." The partially sunk hull of the "Tyee II," stripped of all her brass and metal, lies in Mosquito Bay near Shipman Point. The old girl refused to die. An attempt to burn her hull failed. She just drifted into Mosquito Bay and anchored herself in the sand. She remains an object of interest to young and old as a classic relic of the past.

In a personal letter, May 30, 1979, Harold Branyan wrote ... "I was surprised about the history of the 'Tyee.' Nearly the same could be said about the other 'Tyee' of the 1920s.

"I saw Capt. Markham hook a string of boomsticks on the beach at Nell Shipman's. The logs were half buried in the sand. We were used to the power of Sam Byars' tug, so I looked at Doolittle and Earl (Geisinger) and none of us expected him to move the boom. When he took slack, the boom began to move out into the lake like a large snake. She was a powerful tug alongside of Byars' tug or Bert Winslow's tug.

"Sam's tug had a compound steam engine also. I heard it said that it came from Sandpoint and had been used for some years before coming to Priest Lake."

In 1932, Capt. Markham built a boat, "the Seneacquoteen," to run the mail and supplies on Priest Lake. It was approximately 60 feet long with a narrow beam. He powered it with a Buick engine with a marine attachment. A lot of doubters laughed at him while he was building it in his backyard at Coolin. The skeptics were convinced that he would not have enough power to push that big a boat. It turned out to be a good outfit. It was light, long, and fast. It rode the waves beautifully. Capt. Markham knew how to build boats! The author had the exciting experience of riding on this fast boat from Elmer Berg's Shady Rest Resort to Elkin's Resort in August, 1936.

The most versatile boat on the lake, prior to dredging of the shallow channels in the Thorofare, was the 18-foot, wood-ribbed metal "Can't Sinkum" rowboat. It could handle a 24-horse outboard motor. Most of the resorts had at least one boat of this type. The Forest Service had several, for they could safely transport six men with full packs, a half ton of hay or oats for the pack trains, as well as other supplies for fighting fires. They could be docked almost anywhere along the shore of either lake and could be maneuvered up the Thorofare in low water. After the building of the dam at the Outlet the water level in the Thorofare was no longer a problem.

One Forest Service ranger said, "It was almost a full time job for one man to keep the 'Can't Sinkum' boats in operation. The galvanized tin was not thick enough to withstand the beating they took when they were run up on the rocky shore to unload men and supplies or battle the waves when powered by large motors."

Large pleasure boats on the lake today have created a continuous round of pros and cons as to whether or not high powered boats should ply the waters of the Thorofare.

Prior to the late 1940s, the Thorofare channel was narrow and lined with shrubs and trees along its banks. As early as the 1950s, it was obvious that erosion from boat wakes and high water at runoff was undermining the banks. By the 1970s the width of the channel doubled and tripled in many places. Nothing of significance has been done to control the erosion, except a short strip of riprap along the north shore above the Al Piper property.

The cons moan about the loss of trees and beauty of the Thorofare. They would limit the boat traffic to canoes and boats with motors not to exceed 5 or 10 horsepower.

The pros are equally vocal about letting the Thorofare get wider so more boats can get to Upper Priest Lake.

A compromise is probably in order, but what will be the outcome is anyone's guess.

3
CAPT. MARKHAM
MASTER BOAT BUILDER AND PILOT

Fig. 17 Capt. Markham's company sign in Leonard Paul's store, Coolin. (M. Rutherford)

Melvin C. "Capt." Markham, a boat builder and pilot on Pend Oreille and Priest Lakes, was born in Oregon Territory, July 26, 1871. He came to the Idaho Panhandle from the Willamette Valley, with his parents Francis M. (1847-1915) and Elmina Biggars Markham in 1882. The family settled across the Pend Oreille River from Laclede. According to one authority, Fred "Duke" Campbell, Francis Markham built and operated the first ferry across the river at the Laclede crossing. The ferry site was about three-fourths of a mile below a long established Indian village on the south side of the Pend Oreille river.

According to information received from daughter Elsie Markham Calvert, Capt. built his first boat in 1890, a stern wheeler, the "Elmina J.," that he piloted on Pend Oreille Lake. After the turn of the century he built the "Coyote" which he sold in 1917, to the White Lumber Company. Until 1925, Capt. operated a passenger and freight business on Pend Oreille Lake. In the fall of 1925, the family moved to Coolin where Capt. began business under the title, Captain Markham Northern Navigation Company.

During the winter of 1925-26, Capt. built a steamboat, the "Tyee." The "Tyee" was built on the beach just south of where the boat moorage in Coolin now stands. It was launched in the late summer of 1926. Capt. christened this boat the "Tyee," which means, in Chinook language, a chief or anything superior. (This boat was the first "Tyee" to operate on Priest Lake. The burned hulk of the second "Tyee," built in 1945, lies half buried in the sand in Mosquito Bay.)

The second boat that Capt. Markham constructed in Coolin was his gas-powered, "Seneacquoteen." Daughter Elsie's husband, Don, was Capt.'s right-hand man on the job. They built it in the winter of 1932-33, in Capt.'s backyard. His house stood on top of the hill on the right side of the road as it enters Coolin.

"During the construction," wrote one old time Forest Service employee, "the sidewalk superintendents shook their heads in dismay at what they saw. They were sure the boat would be too long and too narrow to ride upright in the storms of Priest Lake. Capt. knew what he was doing. When she was launched, true to his faith in his boat building ability, she was a masterpiece of craftsmanship. For years it was the sleekest looking, if not the fastest, craft on the lake. The "Seneacquoteen" was powered with a Buick engine connected to a marine transmission."

Soon after WW II Mr. Markham built his last boat. It was constructed for the Forest Service. It hauled supplies and towed barges, generally loaded with a string of pack mules and hay, until the Forest Service closed the ranger stations on the lake.

The "Tyee" was piloted by Capt. as he made daily runs during the tourist season from Coolin to Mosquito Bay. He carried mail and groceries to people living around the lake. If a resident along the way wanted supplies or transport, the usual sign for him to dock was a white dish towel tied to a stick on a dock piling. Capt. would pick up the note or the passenger and if supplies were ordered, they would be delivered the following trip. The usual fee was 25 cents per stop. He operated under a mail contract with the Forest Service.

George Duffill recalled a typical mannerism of Capt.'s that never failed to amuse and entertain his passengers. George said, "Capt. Markham was a real character. I remember the tin cup that hung from the roof of his 'Tyee.' He would take the cup, spit out his tobacco, scoop up water from the lake, take a drink, and hang the cup back up."

In his spare time, Capt. ran a trap line and did a lot of hunting in the Priest Lake country. He got his early training in this art from the Indians who lived around Laclede.

A legend grew up around Capt. Markham that he got his training as a river boat apprentice and pilot of steamboats on the Mississippi River. He did look the part because he was a tall thin man with a white flowing beard and always wore a captain's cap. He could be called a distinguished looking gentleman. In one of Elsie's letters she stated that her Dad never saw the Mississippi let alone received his initial pilot training on the river. She did confirm the fact that her father was a first cousin to Edwin Markham (1852-1940) the poet and author of the famous poem, *The Man with the Hoe*. Capt.'s father, Francis M. and Edwin Markham's father were brothers. Edwin, like his cousin, was also born in the Oregon Territory near Oregon City.

One mother told the story of when she asked Capt. to put the bottles of milk that he had brought from Coolin for her small son, in a cooler place on the boat, he replied, with a twinkle in his eye, "Bob really doesn't need the milk anyhow. What he needs each day is a good shot of whiskey."

Captain Melvin C. Markham died in 1951 and is buried in the beautiful private cemetery, Seneacquoteen, along Dufort Road on the south side of the Pend Oreille river near Hoodoo Creek. There is a pilot's wheel engraved on his headstone. The land was deeded to the Markham family for a cemetery by Francis M. Markham.

Seneacquoteen is an Indian word that means "deep water crossing." The crossing played an important part in the history of the area. Long before the white man found the river, Indians had camped for centuries at the crossing. Fur traders and miners followed the Indian trails to the Kalispel, an Indian word meaning crossing. During the Kootenai gold rush of 1864, a wagon road was built from Walla Walla to the crossing. A pack trail ran from the north shore of the river to the Kootenai mines in British Columbia.

4
ALLEN-A-DALE

In 1919, Alva and Myrtle Allen filed on a 90 acre homestead in Sec. 32, T 63, N, R 4W, along the south shore of Upper Priest Lake. They built a log cabin approximately 200 yards south of what is now called Plowboy Camp Ground, along the Beaver Creek-Navigation Trail #302. Substantial remains of the cabin are still standing.

At the time the Allens selected the building site, the view up the lake extended to the mouth of Upper Priest River and the Hughes Meadow valley. By the late 1930s, the trees and underbrush had all but hidden the cabin from the casual sightseers who hiked along the trail.

Over the years, the couple completed the cabin with their own hands, using native timber. They split the shakes for the roof and hand-hewed the boards used for the floor, the trim, and front porch. Mr. Allen built all the furniture from birch limbs and cedar shakes.

A spring south of the cabin was walled with rock. The water was channeled through a filter system made from an old washing machine tub and the main boiler from an old still. The two tubs had holes punched in the bottom and were installed in the sand which produced filtered water of excellent quality.

On August 16, 1962, Mrs. Allen wrote to the R.D. Smiths, Harry Marshalls, and Donald McCalls, thanking them for the courtesies they had extended to Alva and her during their final nostalgic visit to "our beloved 'Allen-a-Dale,' the beautiful Thorofare, and Little Priest.

"I said to Alva enroute, 'Do you mind that everything in and around the cabin looked so wrecked and that this was our last trip to something we've enjoyed so much?' With a tightening of the lips and a sort of quip he replied, 'Not at all. I feel the few hand-made pieces of furniture left are in good hands and will be moved to a drier place to be enjoyed for more years by those who want to think back to the days when Little Priest almost became incorporated.'"

Mrs. Allen indicated in her letter that no two people could have cherished more the exquisite beauty of the Thorofare, the lake, the trails, the ferns, the flowers, and the hidden spot they called Allen-a-

Fig. 18 Mary Rutherford in Allen-a-Dale cabin, 1961 (L. Luck)*

Dale. She paid tribute to her husband for the artist he was, in the things he made and the immaculate condition in which he kept the place. It was not work but a joy for him, for the people who lived on the lakes, and for their many friends who shared their retreat.

The "friends" also included deer that went by their cabin almost nightly on their way to water; bears would leave their tracks and marks on nearby trees; families of grouse, chipmunks, and squirrels came by for visits.

Mrs. Allen remarked that huckleberries grew in abundance on Plowboy. Fishing was good and the trails were superb for hiking to Caribou, Gold, Lion, and Trapper Creeks, Upper Priest River, and Lookout Mountain. Their favorite was the mossy trail down the Thorofare to Beaver Creek.

She commented, philosophically, that there were many good years prior to the beginning of the disintegration of their cabin, in the early 1950s. The growth of the white pine and a dry cycle caused the underbrush to dry up and die. This removed the natural screen so that the cabin could easily be seen by hikers from the trail. Then the break-ins began. Mrs. Allen said, "It wasn't the intrinsic value of clock or dustpan or lamp that was important, but its usefulness that was hard to replace when everything had to be packed in from Granite Creek."

In 1957, high winds and snow tumbled trees all about the place and their beautiful treasure was nearly destroyed. Mrs. Allen concluded in her letter, "It was good to see that all the old buildings around the lake were gone and to see the area around the little lake so lush and green. Soon our cabin will be 'dust to dust' and that is good! A beauty spot like all the Upper Priest country should be a primitive area for the enjoyment of all people and not a hideaway as Allen-a-Dale has been. I am reminded today of a passage from the scriptures:

When I survey thy wonderous firmament,
What is man, that thou art mindful of him?

Very sincerely yours,
Myrtle Hasselberg Allen"

In another letter dated August 23, 1962, Mrs. Allen told the Smiths, Marshalls, and McCalls that Alva and she had met with District Ranger Dan Montgomery and signed the documents to finalize the deed of their beloved property back to the United States Government. She further informed the people who lived at Beaver Creek Camp and along the Thorofare that they were welcome to any of the items that had been left at the cabin because the Forest Service planned to burn everything left by November 1.

The Allens had no living relatives and rather than sell their homestead to developers, they deeded it back to the people of the United States, on October 25, 1934. They granted the deed with the proviso that they would have life tenancy. It is a shame that the Forest Service did not name Plowboy Camp, Allen-a-Dale Camp.

Articles of Alva's skill and artistry are being used and treasured by people at Beaver Creek Camp. Hammarlunds, McCalls, and Rutherfords have stools; Simpsons, a chair and table; Marshalls, a bed; and Jan Elkins Bailey of Sandpiper Shores, many birch crotch wall hangers.

The Allens gave Mary Avery, Washington State University archivist and Northwest historian, their guest book with entry dates from June, 1922 to June 25, 1957. Well known Priest Lake names that appear in the book include, Wm. Fox and wife in 1922; Fern and Earl Geisinger, 1928; Wm. "Daddy" Duffill, 1929; Les Eddy, 1931; Ann Geisinger, 1937; Frank Algren, 1943; Elmer Berg, 1944, and Rose Hawkins, 1946.

The guest book also contains various notes and comments. Some of these are as follows: "Two delightful weeks spent in a perfect bit of heaven in the wilds." "Truly the home of an artist." "Hail, Allen-a-Dale, of thee we sing; may your shadows never grow less." Mrs. Allen herself wrote, "Such healthy appetites." "Elmer Berg called yesterday. After dinner we walked with him to Armstrong Meadows — lovely !"

In June, 1957, she wrote, "Cabin has been entered — all keepsakes are gone except lamp and water pail. Many trees have fallen."

In the mid-1950s Mr. Allen retired after a lifetime with the U.S. Postal Service. He died May 6, 1976. Mrs. Allen died April 29, 1977. They are buried in Memorial Gardens, Spokane, Washington.

---

* The lovely little wood cook stove was salvaged in the late 1960s by second-generation Priest Lakers Steve Dompier and Mike Stefan.

After the cabin roof caved in the boys discovered that the stove was rusting badly. They disassembled it and carried it to Beaver Creek, piece by piece.

It is still in use by Mike in his home in San Francisco, California.

5

ROSE HURST

IN THE SHADOW OF CHIMNEY ROCK

Rose Hurst was too busy the last 20 years of her life to finish her book, *In the Shadow of Chimney Rock*. As a cattleman (in the true sense of the word), a rancher, a mother, and a friend and counselor to hundreds of people, she started her Priest Lake story at least twice. Her words on paper have been lost, as the manuscript for her book cannot be located.

This hard riding, hard working rancher loved life, her children, people, and Priest Lake. In bursts of poetic prose, Mrs. Hurst filled three hours of tape during a series of interviews in the fall of 1972. This self-reliant woman, her face tanned and wrinkled, but firm and colorful at the age of 88, told her story with wit, with philosophical insight, and with great enthusiasm for living.

"Rosie" as she was called by many, and "Tiny" by some of her close friends, was born at Hubbard Springs in the Columbia Mountains of Virginia, October 23, 1883. When she was 5 years old the family moved to Kentucky. She remarked that this early move must have put a golden touch for adventure on her. Names of far away places always sounded exciting to her. She remembered as a child continually packing her bag at play, to go somewhere.

Her public school experience was in Hubbard Springs and after graduation she attended Berea College for two years, in Berea, Kentucky. She was married March 8, 1901. She returned to Berea College after she was married to please her surrogate mother who had raised her. Her mother died when Rose was quite young. Rose told a little about this period of her life by stating, "I finished up the hard way. I came home at night exhausted, to my husband and two little ones. I didn't want to disappoint my mother. I stayed with it until I graduated.

"My husband worked for a spoke outfit. That's when automobiles first came in and as you probably know the spokes in those days were made out of hickory. We followed this outfit around Kentucky until we came to the State of Washington. My foster mother came to

Sumner, Washington, after I was married. She came by to visit and told us she saw great possibilities in the West that were not visible in the South. Two of my four girls were born in Sumner. We came to Spokane in 1917."

Shortly after the family moved to Spokane, they bought a farm on Four Mile Prairie, northwest of Spokane. After Rose's husband died in 1927, she bought a three-acre tract along the Pend Oreille highway about one half mile from the city limits of Hillyard.

Fig. 19 Rose Hurst, 1965, and the back
of her ranch home.

Mrs. Hurst continued to buy and sell livestock, as she and her husband had built up a sizeable business while operating the Four Mile farm. She built a home of Moorish design of her own creation and developed a prize winning garden around the house. She lived there until she bought the John Nordman property near Nordman, Idaho.

The Rose Hurst Garden was, in the words of Junior Lambert, "... so beautiful that people came for miles to look at it. I know, because I started to work on that garden from the time the lily pond was a mud patch until it became a sight to see."

45

In 1933, Marita Killen wrote a feature article on the Hurst garden that appeared in the *Spokane Chronicle*, entitled, "Hillyard Has Wonder Garden." Excerpts are quoted below:

"From the road one never would suspect the glory which lies beyond. But, drive in . . . and behold the remarkable work of Mother Nature and one little lady, Mrs. Rose Hurst, with the true vision of an artist, Mrs. Hurst has achieved a masterpiece.

"The first impression is that of splendor . . . a riot of color around the Japanese tea house . . .

"The heart of the garden is the lily pond . . . with a cool inviting cave filled with ferns from which a happy little wood nymph gaily emerges to fish in the pool. Lilies of rare beauty float on the pond . . . In the glen back of the pool, a remarkable reproduction of Romona's 'Wishing Well' reposes.

"Here and there about the garden are life-like affairs, which Mrs. Hurst calls "Quirks." 'I have the largest collection in the Pacific Northwest' says Mrs. Hurst. These strange formations are from gnarled and weathered roots and limbs picked up on her journeys throughout the world.

"Mrs. Hurst was not only an artist, but as a lover of nature, she was able to live closely with those things she loves and thereby have a greater understanding."

Mrs. Hurst made her first trip to Priest Lake just before the 1921 fire that swept the country. Her fourth trip was in the early 1930s when she came to buy some posts to build for her garden an old-fashioned well-housing that a bucket and pulley hangs on. Her Congregational college background was affronted when the man she was making the trip with suggested she needed a flask of brandy to take along. He said to her, "The old Swede up there will cut down the forest for you if you take a bottle along." She replied, "Well, I'm not takin' brandy up there as I want some work done when I get there and if I give him brandy, that's it! I don't go along with that brandy business. I don't condemn people, they can do as they want. I never got used to it and I'm glad I didn't from what I see of people that have."

A year or two after the big fire, the Hurst family came to Priest Lake for an outing. Rose said, "I saw so many things around the lake that were so delightful and peaceful that I had a great desire to come and stay. They all laughed at me about my lake vision. That carried on for several years. I loved to talk to my friend, Mr. Sager, who worked for the Hoffis-Ferris Company, about the wonders of the lake.

"Another time I went up there by myself. I stayed at a resort at Outlet Bay. The first morning I got into my pickup and wandered along the road to where these meadows are, the Bismarks. I got hungry and stopped at Roy Kenyon's store. He didn't have anything to eat except canned or cold stuff.

"I wandered on and stopped at a house and asked if I could get a piece of toast and some coffee. The woman said she was out of bread but she had some hotcake batter left over from breakfast. That will be plenty good, I said, and I got my fill. She wouldn't take any money from me for my big breakfast.

"I wandered on and came to a lane. I had to dodge stumps and mud holes, but at the end of the lane I came to an old log house with a big front porch. It was standing in the open without a thing around it, not even a fence. I got out to look around and I heard a rough Swedish voice say, 'Vy don't you come over?' I thought, I didn't dare, so I got into my pickup and drove off.

"Later I told my friend, Mildred Sager, about my trip. She said, 'Tiny, you had breakfast with some people we know. They are from the drought country. They came to Priest Lake with their worldly possessions, including a sow pig in a pickup. They had been completely wiped out back in the dust bowl. They are nice neighbors. Three of us up there owned a cow together.'"

In July, 1932, Mildred called Rose and said she needed help to get her son to the doctor. Her son had taken the family truck, against his father's orders, and turned it over. She didn't want to tell her husband about the boy's accident and injuries so she needed to rely on Rose's moral support.

"When I got there, the boy had a bad shinbone, a swollen hip, and was feverish. I told Mildred that I would get him to a doctor, which I did.

"When I got back I mentioned to Mildred that I was very much taken with the place at the end of the lane. Mildred said, 'By golly, Rosie, he wants to sell that place.' I sez, and I want to buy it. I started to dig in my jeans to see how much money I had on hand. Mildred did not know how much the ranch would cost but felt it would be reasonable, as land up here is nothing like it is in Spokane.

"Mildred said she would take me to see John Nordman, the Swede, who was the owner of the place at the end of the lane. When we came to the gate I saw an old man sitting on the porch. We went over there and was he crabby! He said he didn't like to be disturbed and didn't like women at all. I found out later that he did.

"After a while, when Mr. Nordman got accustomed to me, I never

47

had a better friend. He was so kind. He had come to the point in his life where he needed somebody for companionship; somebody he could tell his troubles to. He needed to recite a lot of his past troubles that were nothing serious but they bothered him.

"Well, anyway, we came to him and my friend said, 'I brought a lady to buy your farm.' 'Ha!' he said. He didn't say come in, sit on the porch, or anything. 'Vell,' he said, 'I vant to sell, but I vant the cash. You got the cash?' I said, that depends on how much you want and how much I like your farm. Of course, I was used to conditions before you make a deal.

"He said he didn't want to be bothered if I didn't want to buy it. I said, Mr. Nordman, I have never seen your farm. Would you give me the privilege of looking it over? Let me decide if I'd like it and see if we can agree on a price. You haven't told me what it was. Then I can mighty quick tell you whether or not I want it. I was getting just like he was, kinda angry. I had never had a gentleman treat me quite like that.

"He said, 'You got any rubber boots?' I said, no I don't got any rubber boots. He said, 'Down on the meadow the vater is that deep. The beaver, I don't do no more with them as they run that vater all over that field all the time.' Well, let's look at it anyway, I said, I'm used to going barefooted because I'm from the South and we go barefooted all the time down there. I said, to get my feet wet won't hurt me, if it won't hurt you.

"We went down to look at the meadow. He hopped along and didn't say much of anything, and didn't ask me anything either. He just went ahead. He showed me where he had started to clear some brush, where the government had made a mess for him. The government was bringing in boys for them gooseberries and mess up the place. (Mrs. Hurst was referring to black currant bushes that are hosts to the white pine blister rust, which kills white pine trees. In the 1920s to the early 1960s the USFS attempted to eradicate the wild black currant bushes by hiring hundreds of men to dig up and burn the bushes. In the past decade or two the project has been abandoned.)

"I don't think he was really trying to sell me his farm. I think he was really taken aback with my real interest. We came back to the house."

"I said, well, Mr. Nordman, tell me what the consideration is on your farm. He said, 'I have been vanting $5,000, but I'm going to sell it for less money than that.' I said, if you want $5,000 I haven't got that much money. I didn't tell him I wouldn't buy it. I had assets but not that much cash. Finally he agreed to come to within $500 of what I thought I wanted to pay for it. I said, Mr. Nordman, that's how much money I've got. I'm not asking you to take it. I'm not asking you to leave your home, as I know you must be very attached to this beautiful spot and you have been here a long time. But if I could, and you are willing, I would love to have this place. I will keep it in mind. Then he says, 'Vill you split the difference?' I said, yes I'll do that. I decide in a second what I'm going to do and when I said it, that is the same as if it was recorded in heaven. Yes, I will do that, Mr. Nordman. I thought if I didn't have that much in my checking account that I could easy put it there.

"He said, 'Ven are you going to give me the money?' I said, Mr. Nordman, I didn't bring that much money with me. I'll have to go back to Spokane.

"When we got back I said to Mildred, 'Do you think that old duck means what he said?' She said, 'I think he does.' I told her, when I get back to Spokane I'm going to draw that money out and bring it up here and stay all night with you.

"By the time I went to bed that night I felt I had just the same as bought the farm. I was already planning where the pasture was going to be, where the fences were going to be built, and all the other things that I was planning to do.

"The next morning after I got back to Mildred's we went over and got him and took him to Sandpoint to see about it. During the trip to Sandpoint I wanted to find out if there was a lien against the property, if he had a deed, a clear title, and all the things I needed to know. When I asked Mr. Nordman about these things he said, 'Vat you vant to know all these things for? I don't like to deal with vomen, nohow!' I said, Mr. Nordman, you listen to me. I'm going to give you my hard-earned money and you are going to give me a farm so we have to come to a decision. You have to know if the money is good, when you're going to get it, and I have to know if the farm is good for the money I'm going to give you.

"In the morning Mildred said, 'Rose, a nephew of mine told me that John had divorced his wife who still lives in Sweden.' He had told me he was a single man.

"On the way to Sandpoint I kinda tripped the old man up with this information. He said, 'That's none of your business vhether or not my vife divorced me.' I told him it would be necessary when we got ready to make out a deed. He said, 'I got everything in a paper back home that Taft sent to me, the President of the U.S. Isn't that good enough for anybody?' He was adamant about that, whether his wife had divorced him or not.

49

"He insisted the land was clear so we went on over to the bank. There were some customers in the lobby talking with the men we wanted to see. Mr. Nordman went to the little wicket door and wanted me to come on. I said that we would wait until the other people were through. He got mad at me for that!

"When the others left we went to see the banker Mr. Von Canon. Mr. Nordman said, 'Now you tell him!' I said, Mr. Nordman has agreed to sell his farm and I have agreed to buy it. We came to you as he tells me you have the papers here and he wants you to take care of the business which is perfectly all right with me. I have come to inquire about the condition of the property. 'Well,' he said, 'John owes me $1500 on the place.' I said, John you told me that the place was clear. 'Damn,' said John, 'give me the money and I'll pay it.' What do you do with a man like that? Mr. Von Canon said, 'John, I'll have to put you out of the office, you can't talk to a lady like that in front of me. You'll have to quiet down.' Mr. Nordman said, 'She's right, I shouldn't be dealing with a voman nohow!'

"I said to Mr. Von Canon, perhaps Mr. Nordman is right, you could handle the money so he could pay off the mortgage which you hold and he would receive the rest. When I brought up the divorce business Mr. Von Canon said he would make an escrow of it and get testimony from Sweden. I asked if Mr. Nordman would have to have an attorney. Then he blabbered like a big calf, so I said, Mr. Nordman, I'll pay for the attorney. So I asked the banker if he could recommend an attorney as I had never been in Sandpoint on business before. He said that he couldn't recommend anyone other than to give me the name of his own attorney, Judge Hunt. The judge and I have since become good friends. I used to call on him everytime I was in town. I enjoyed talking with him, not only on business matters, but on general things. I always felt like I'd found a new brother in him.

"Mr. Nordman agreed to get information on his divorce. He went to Mullan where he had lived when he first came to Idaho. He was going to find a Sam Olson or someone by the name of Beanbury. He said that they knew all about him. When he got there one of the men had been dead for 40 years and the other one had left and no one knew what had become of him. He came back much disgruntled, so in the long run he wrote back and forth and tried to find somebody, but to no avail.

"So I put the money in escrow and he signed the deed. In the meantime he stayed here and I took him from place to place. I took him down to Spokane with me. He was very restless. He had lost his home and had no place to go. He wanted to leave here as he couldn't stand to see anything done to the place that he hadn't done.

"I had friends that came up from Spokane to see me and they brought some carrots. I cooked them in one of Mr. Nordman's kettles. I'll be darned if I didn't let them boil dry and stick to the bottom of his kettle. I didn't dare let him see what I had done so I hid the kettle from him. This kind of thing went on all fall while he was waiting for the divorce thing to be settled.

"In the meantime he took pneumonia and when I came up in January he was in the Priest River hospital. He said, 'Ven you go back I vant to go back vith you as I don't like it anymore in Priest River. You just get moved up and down, up and down, and nobody doing nothing all the time.'

"I lived on the ranch from time to time and spent some time at my home in Spokane. Mr. Nordman was trying to contact people about his divorce so the abstract could be cleared. He wasn't having much luck because most of the people who knew about his early life were dead. I had the Swedish Consulate write a letter to a court judge in Sweden. It finally paid off."

According to the tract sheets on file in the Safeco Title and Abstract company of Sandpoint, John Nordman granted a deed for his homestead property to Rose Hurst, December 20, 1937. The tract sheet also shows John was granted a homestead patent by the U.S. Government, August 30, 1913, for the land he sold to Rose Hurst.

"John got sick January 4, 1938 and died January 10. His son, Ole, came down from the mines up north and was appointed administrator of his father's estate. He was about as high tempered as his father. I worried along with him and helped as much as I could. He told me one day that he was going to buy me a nice present when the estate was settled. I told him I didn't want a present as I loved the ranch and I did my best to be honest and forthright about the deal. I never knew anything else, I was brought up with the belief to be honest. My mother taught us if you never wasted you never would want and if you were honest, God would take care of you always. I don't want anything for what I have done. I even loaned John $500 before he died as he had run out of money before the estate was finally settled.

"Ole had signed a statement that he was the sole heir of the estate. This again was fouled up as John had three brothers and each of them thought John was an old bachelor. Eventually information was received from a high court in Sweden that released the facts needed to settle the estate."

Fig. 20 Laura Hurst and the plow handhewn
by John Nordman, 1977.

Mrs. Hurst called one of John's nephews in Spokane to come and get the things of John's that he or the family might want. The one item that everyone wanted was a trunk that Mr. Nordman had hand hewn from a solid log. It disappeared and was not located until 1978, when it was put on display at Irene Cottrell's Country Shop in Priest River. It still is in excellent condition and Mrs. Cottrell plans to give the trunk to the Bonner County Historical Society. Mrs. Hurst's daughter, Laura Lee, who was administrator of her mother's estate found a wooden plow that Mr. Nordman had broad-axed from a single log. She gave it to the museum for Bonner County. John was a master with the broad axe. He learned the art in Sweden and continued using the tricks of the trade as a hobby.

"I was lucky to get the Nordman ranch," continued Mrs. Hurst. "Banker Von Canon who handled the deal for us told me one time that I would never be able to buy the ranch. He said to me, 'I have had at least 20 people come here to buy it, but John queered every deal so far.' I told Mr. Von Canon that I would get the ranch and make John like it.

"I do believe that John finally got to like me and trusted me. After I gave him the $500 he needed when he was in the hospital he said, 'I vant to give you my copy of our contract.' I didn't want to take it, but he insisted. He said, 'You got all the stuff anyway. I have no business with that paper. You keep it.' That encouraged me to go ahead and give him all he had coming to him and more."

Rose Hurst was a very active community worker. She served on the Nordman school board for many years. She was secretary to the Draft Board during WW II. She remembered registering Elmer Berg for the draft even though he was not an American citizen at the time. In 1948, she was acting postmaster of the local post office. At that time the post office was a one-room cabin that she called Government House. As postmaster she got acquainted with practically everyone who lived in the surrounding country. She was proud of this fact.

The post office at that time, 1948, was located where Tom and Phyllis Low now live, 1979. When Tom built his new house he moved the original Government House to another location just east of where it stood. Mrs. Hurst said it was more of a hut than a building. She added a room in the back where she lived while serving as postmaster. She said it was an interesting job that she really enjoyed, but was too confining as a permanent job.

Mrs. Hurst told about two boys who came down quite frequently from Upper Priest Lake that really intrigued her. They were well-educated and reported that they were trappers. Rose remarked that they weren't any more trappers than she was. She said, "Trappers don't come out of the woods with white fur bonnets on their heads and white kid gloves on their hands.

"They stayed up at the head of the little lake for about 18 months. When they came down they had a boat load of little sacks. They stayed in one of Steve's cabins for several weeks working on their rocks that they carried in the sacks.

"When they left they stopped to say goodbye. I asked them if we might expect them next fall for another season of trapping. They told me they wouldn't be back as they weren't very good trappers. I asked them right out what they were doing up there. One of them answered, 'Just fooling around and bothering you.' They were really nice boys." She never actually found out what they were doing.

For six years Mrs. Hurst was the summer attendant in charge of the Reeder Creek campground. Throughout the remainder of her life, Reeder Creek campers would call on her at her ranch to talk to her. Many young couples would bring their children to meet her.

This pleased her. She was very proud of her southern heritage. She got a great deal more satisfaction out of being referred to as a true southern belle than she did out of talking about the English coat-of-arms that was handed down from her ancestors.

In early winter of 1970, a reporter from the *Spokane Daily Chronicle* interviewed her and his story appeared in the December 9, 1970 issue. With an impish, yet satisfied twinkle in her eyes she remarked, "He nearly embarrassed me to death when he printed the story. We have our crest and coat-of-arms. He was quite interested in that. It doesn't really mean too much to me. Women are very fickle about such things. If they would say what they really think instead of beating around the bush they would be better off. I never would believe a reporter could conjure up such a lot of stuff. Maybe some of it is based on facts but it was too flowery. I could never live up to what he wrote.

"I don't know what it means to be pampered. I would go mad if I were pampered like some women are, including my daughters.

"I am a determined woman! I never have felt a nerve in me quiver while making a decision. I know what I can do. I have always been the one who gets up and gets things going. I don't know my own strength. I've never been very large. I don't weigh 100 pounds, even today. I also know that God has been good to me and time has been kind. I'm truly grateful.

"I have never been sick or had an operation. I hit the ball every morning. I get up, make the fires and get breakfast. I get the men to work. Once in a while I will roll under the old wagon and sleep for a few minutes. It takes me less time to revive myself than it does for men to sit down and take a smoke. I do the dirty work as well as the easy jobs. I never back off for anything. In my time I could bring out a hundred head of cattle with a dog and my horse. I could drive a fence post and fix the fence. I can do anything there is to do on the farm.

"Junior has been with me for a long time and is good help. He's good with animals and I love that. I love my stock. I'm afraid I've talked too much. Whatever you are going to do with this I hope you are successful with it.

"This is a wonderful locale, you'll never find a better one. My stories roll off as if they are a part of it because I began with the early history of the country when the trappers first came in here. Then came the miners; next the loggers; then came civilization and that cluttered everything up. Before it, it was so quiet and peaceful here.

"Of course there was some romance too. When I was on the school board people would tell me about seeing so and so at the school house talking to the teacher after the children were gone. I called it spring folly! Naturally you would want to talk to people. You don't want to come up here and hibernate. I think the old proverb is right, 'Idle hands are the Devil's workshop.' God says in His holy word, 'Be impartial. You are not to judge people, lest you be judged by the same judgment.' People are not as bad in general as they are believed to be.

"We have now entered into one of the most serious climaxes in all history with this drug business that these children are indulging in and the way our colleges and that kind of thing are upholding vice and sex relations. That was made for a purpose and it's alright in its place, but it need not be demonstrated and that kind of thing. If it does, it can tear you apart quicker than anything. It can cause more heartaches and destruction than any other thing known. I think we are wavering or wandering away from the normal way that God taught with the Ten Commandments. The Ten Commandments were given us as a blueprint for our lives. We are going to fall short of them.

"When I wrote the beginning of my book, *In the Shadow of Chimney Rock*, it was my intention to write a little history or narrative on the facts of some wonderful people who came up here to live. The courage they had! The hardships they went through! I appreciate their efforts because I have gained by that. They have made it so I could live here. When I first lived on this ranch the CCCs came in and what a marvelous thing that was for the country. That was one of the things that Roosevelt did that was a good deed. He gave employment to those boys. He gave them a place to work! A place to eat! A place to sleep! He gave them a supervisor who was a man of ability. They learned from him. We still have several of them around here.

"John 'Snick' Sudnikovich is one. He will retire from the Forest Service next year. He has been with them for years and probably knows more about the forest than a lot of the rangers they have down there.

"I was kind of a mixture myself. On my father's side of the family I was Union; on my mother's side of the family I was a Confederate. I never really got to know my mother's side of the family as I was raised by my father's sister. My aunt had a family of her own but she chose me I think because as a child I was very English by nature. She apparently liked it. If I did some little trick that I should not have done, I was very seldom punished. Even when I started to school I got by with most everything. I never was real contrary though, but a child

55

should be brought to justice and right. I don't think I ever did anything really bad but I was pretty 'bridgety' from the time I was two years old. If I didn't agree with the family I would tell them. My aunt would say, now and then, 'Listen to Little Jake, the Rebel.' I was called Rebel as a nickname. I don't really know why! Things I say come right out of my heart and that's it. If I owe a dollar it is just the same as paid. I was just born like that. I never have had much trouble to live in this world because I get along with people."

One of Mrs. Hurst's grandsons wanted to buy an airplane. She purchased some land to build a landing strip for him. It lies just east of Nordman on the Granite Creek road. Part of the property is now owned by the James D. Coopers and Tom Lowe. After she cleared the strip and dozed it level, the grandson got married and flew off to California with his bride. She was philosophical about it and charged it up, in her mind, to the fact that that is the nature of young people and they will just do things like that. Not to be undone, she planted the cleared area with trees that would be suitable for sale as Christmas trees. Included in the plot are three cedar trees from Lebanon. They were brought from Lebanon in a mushroom bag by her friend, Lara. The three cedars survived the trip and are now sizable trees, 1981.

At one time Mrs. Hurst gave some thought to naming the plot the "Rose Hurst Grove," but since her farm carried the name of the "Rose Hurst Ranch" she decided to call it "Memory Lane." She envisioned letting each neighbor plant a tree. "I wanted all the neighbors to have a part in it and then everybody could share. Without sharing, I cannot embrace the Lord.

"The man and his wife from California (Jim and Marcella Cooper) to whom I sold part of the tree plant, were going to put a fish pond on the back of the property. He put in a well and built a house. I think they are wonderful people. I think his fish pond will help the country. I stayed on the lake for six years and I know how scattered the fish are in the lake. I've seen people come in here lately with a lot of gear and maybe catch one fish, or none at all. The fish are not there anymore. After they put in those fish, whatever they are called, they seem to have destroyed the fishing. We used to have good silver fishing.

"When I first came up here I was just enthralled when I went down to the lake to see the whitefish spawners coming into Granite Creek. It looked like they were a foot deep. The men would be standing there picking out fish for the spawn. I would stand around all day nearly freezing myself to death. I'd run up to Steve's, get a cup of coffee, and go back and watch some more. Oh my, how that did amuse me!

"One evening when I was getting ready to go home I thought I would take a few fish along for supper. One of the men standing there had two gunny sacks and he filled them with fish and tossed them out on the bank at my feet. The fish were all about the same size. I tell you, I had fish smoked, canned, dried, and fresh. In fact, I worked on those fish for two weeks. I got a recipe from the Indians here and canned the smoked fish in oil. One of my men would take three or four of those fish and carry them in a bread wrapper for his lunch.

"Mrs. Gregory, who lived on the Lone Star Ranch across the narrows, used to come over and watch the whitefish run with me. For the next few years I would put on my hip boots and wade out to catch my own whitefish in a can. Most of the time I would have my boots full of water as the first thing I did was to step into a hole and the water poured in the top of my boots; but I stayed right with it! How I loved to catch those whitefish!

"The whitefish didn't run up Reeder Creek very much. When they logged along the creek they put in a lot of corduroy roads and the fish couldn't get by. The beaver had a heyday up there. For years I trapped them on this meadow.

"The Flathead Indians came to Granite Creek to catch the spawners. I don't know much about them, but I can tell you about the Kalispel Indians. When they came in they followed the ridge as there was no road down Granite Creek in the early days. Up north here I can show you the stops or spots one of the old men told me about. He told me he was 102 years old at the time I talked to him. I learned from him the names of many places and why they named them what they did. He told about the good transportation from the lake to the Pend Oreille and then to the Hudson's Bay Trading Post.

"The old Indian told me about coming from Montana to sell trinkets and to catch whitefish. They brought their trappings piled on two poles dragged by a horse. They also brought furs, moccasins, and deer skin shirts with them. I have a pair of moccasins that I bought from him. I showed the old Indian a bridle I had, that at one time belonged to Charlie Russell, the famous Montana artist. The Indian knew him. A friend of mine, Mabel Rude, gave me the bridle. Mabel used to ride with Mr. Russell."

Rose had a soft spot in her heart for Frank "Huckleberry Finn" Algren. He got his nickname because he was one of the fastest huckleberry pickers in the Kaniksu. He picked berries for the commercial market for many years. She related the story about the time she and two of her hired men were stranded on the little lake during a 48-hour blow. They made it to the Forest Service cabin at Navigation, but they didn't have any food. She sent the boys to

Frank the Finn's houseboat for some food. When they returned empty handed she wanted to know the reason, for in those days anyone around the lake would give you the shirt off his back.

The boys reluctantly told her that Frank had been on a spree and had passed out completely. She told the boys to go back up there and to bring beans, flour, and anything else that could be eaten and not to worry about Frank as she would tell him the next day and send food back to him when they got to Granite Creek.

Mrs. Hurst knew the Allens of Allen-a-Dale for she used to visit with them at mail time, although she said, "I never did get around to visit them at their cabin on Upper Priest. They were very secluded people." She felt that they were sufficient in their own society up there and she understood that he was a good woodsman.

For years Rose took it upon herself to visit every newcomer that moved into the country. She would generally take a small gift of food as a welcome gesture. She recalled that many times she would take a kerosene lamp, as many people in the early days would come up to Bonner County not realizing there was no electricity.

She recalled one instance of a large group of people coming up who owned stock in the Continental Mine. The group came on a special railroad car to Priest River. They made the trip to the head of the little lake by boat and rode horses up to the mine.

Onstime "Joe" Cyr[1] was a close friend of Mrs. Hurst. Joe lived on the narrow point about where Kaniksu Resort now stands. He was a Canadian trapper and lived around Granite Creek for many years. He hired horses from Mrs. Hurst to snake in his wood until he got too old. He fussed about having someone else get his wood for him but she didn't want him to get hurt as her teams were quite skittish.

"Joe gave me my first bear meat. I liked it so much that he later gave me a young bear he had skinned out. He was a good Christian man.

"In the last few years we have some people who have moved here that are just too nosey. One fall I bought a big new tractor. One of my new neighbors said to me, 'Gracious sakes alive Rosie, you will never use that big tractor.' I said, I don't plan to but I'll hire someone who will use it for me.

"Anyhow, I think like this — God gave you a life to live, and that meant to the end and not until you get about 60 and then are put on the shelf to complain and make everybody else miserable too. I wouldn't trade my little head for some of the sheepheads that I know around here these days."

Long before the Priest Lake district got a first aid ambulance, Rose Hurst realized the need for an emergency system of some type. She reserved one acre of the plot along the Granite Creek road for a first aid station until the people in the area got "sympathetic enough to build a permanent facility."

She had seen two men die on the steps of the old post office while waiting for first aid. She saw many others suffer with mangled and broken legs, broken hands, and skin bruises, all waiting for a doctor or first aid.

Rose emphasized many times during the interview sessions that it was not easy to make a living in this end of Bonner County. In her judgment there were only three things; resorts, farming, or working for wages. She felt she was one of the lucky ones because she came when land was cheap. She made good money on the land she owned in addition to her main ranch. The land she cleared to raise hay and run cattle became very valuable. At one time she was running 150 to 160 head of beef cattle, primarily Aberdeen Angus.

Rose said, "I didn't get it sitting around waiting for prices to go up." The second year she was on the ranch she borrowed milk from several of her heifers that had come in to feed calves she had bought for $1.00 each from dairies around Spokane. At harvest time she sold the veal calves to pay her help.

"It took a lot of hard work to keep this place going. I had no difficulty carrying on the work when I could drive the old trucks and I could do anything there was to do.

"I'm not boasting, but I really don't know where I got the pep to do all the things I've done. Through the years I've sold hay in Spokane, to the Priest River Co-op, and one year I sold 100 tons to Diamond Match. Mr. Kerr handled the deal. He was an honest man and a good friend. He gave me a $4,000 check for the hay right out in the field. That was the best crop I ever raised."

In her collection Rose has a letter signed by U.S. Grant that had been given to her great-grandfather. She also has a sabre and a bayonet that were used in the Civil War. Also in her collection, is a picture of Father Cataldo that she got in connection with the erection of a monument in his honor. At that time she was President of the Morgan Acres Garden Club near Spokane. It had been her duty to deliver an address at the dedication ceremony. She wanted to make a good impression because the club had donated the structure. She also wanted to tell the truth about Father Cataldo's background and accomplishments because there had been a "lot of fanfare about his life, some of which did not happen." Among the audience were

Indians who had worshipped in Father Cataldo's church when it had a dirt floor. Some of the Indians who were attending had signed the peace treaty with the territorial governor, Isaac I. Stevens.

For information about Father Cataldo, she contacted a well-known Irishman who had lived around Spokane Falls for many years and had known Father Cataldo personally, and had attended his funeral. He took her to a cabin where Father Cataldo once lived. There they found a picture of him, as well as one of the "Treaty Tree" where Governor Stevens had met with the Indians. The cabin still had a deer skin door. It was occupied by a gracious old couple. When Mrs. Hurst asked to see the picture of Father Cataldo, the lady told her she could have it. Rose planned to make sure that the picture would go to Gonzaga University. From the information Mrs. Hurst got from her Irish friend, she was able to give a speech that she felt was "successful, short, to the point, and enlightening."

Cy Decker, who lived near Nordman was a special friend to Mrs. Hurst. He was an avid newspaper reader. She would go to visit with him to get caught up on the news. He was better company, according to Rose, than any woman who lived in the surrounding area. She was also fond of Mr. Hanna, whose name was given to Hanna Flats area just west of the airstrip across the highway from the Priest Lake Ranger Station. She would become concerned about him if he didn't show up for his mail at least once a week. She would go to his place with a cake or some cookies just to check up on him. "I've lived to see him sell out and move to Spokane. He had a wife there who apparently didn't like to live the rough life of northern Idaho.

"I went to Pullman to take a course in veterinary medicine. I used to keep up with them each year about the new antibiotics and that kind of thing. I had a clean herd and I kept it clean. I always believed that if you didn't know you had best find out! How could you tell somebody else what to do if you didn't understand it yourself?

"I never thought in my younger life there would be a time when I would go and sit on a seat and bid on the prize bull along side big men from Montana and other states. But the time came!

"In 1968, I went to Sandpoint for the yearly Bonner County Cattle Association's auction show for breeding stock. This was to encourage farmers to raise better stock. I bought a champion bull that year. He was a 'realer.' He was as good a bull as I'd ever seen sold in Spokane. He was from the Charlie Burdette herd. One of my neighbors bid against me. He hated to give in to a woman who was bidding against him. I sit back and take my whacks along side any of them and I don't expect men to do me favors just because I am a woman. It's really a hard road for a woman too; at least until you establish yourself.

"I sell beef and butcher one now and then and give quarters to my family. I've lived for my family all my life. They are wonderful to me. My great-grandson sent me a cablegram from Japan on my 89th birthday. He is an intelligence agent. I tell my family that if I make 90 I'm going to have a big party." She made it.

She died in Spokane, November 30, 1974, at the age of 91. She was buried December 3, in the Newport cemetery. She is survived by her four daughters, Laura Lee Hurst, Spokane; Freda Herr, Oakland, California; Fay Kalhar and Gladys Barr, both of Spokane; four grandchildren, 11 great-grandchildren, and one great-great-grandchild.

In 1977 the Rose Hurst Ranch was sold to Calvin A. Mosher of Palisade, Colorado.

6

MINES

In 1886, Jonathan Truesdale et al, filed claims on silver and lead deposits adjacent to Upper Priest Lake. The claims were called the Mountain Chief Mine. It has been reliably reported that in 1886-87, more than 2,000 prospectors were roaming what is now Bonner County.

According to C.N. Savage's report, *Geology and Mineral Resources of Bonner County*, gold, silver, lead, and copper were the first metals to attract attention . . . Some of the veins . . . in the district reportedly ran as high as 400 ounces of silver per ton of ore.

Due to the fact that very little has been recorded or published about the mineral potential of the area, Savage stated, "It would take money and courage to adequately explore the mineral potential of Bonner County . . . Silver may some day be economically produced."

Savage wrote in 1967 that the area had produced minerals worth more than $13,500,000. If unrecorded productions were included, he estimated that the total might be twice that amount. "The outlook for greater mineral production is good," he concluded.

An effort will be made to give a short history of a few mines and mention the names of several others that may be of interest to readers who might want to locate the sites.

Perhaps the best known and most productive mine in this area was the Continental Mine on Continental Mountain north of Upper Priest Lake. A.K. Klockman who developed the mine, gave a good account of the operation in his diary. He, along with Andy Coolin, could be called the chiefs of mining propaganda. Today they would be called public relations experts for Bonner County mines.

Newspaper stories in the 1880s and 90s carried many glowing reports of the marvelous future for mining in the Priest Lake district. The March 1, 1901 issue of the *Kootenai County Republican* gave the following description of Klockman's mine: "The mine shaft is down 140 feet and the ore is running 40 ounces of silver and 35% lead to the ton. Heitman and Wenz of Rathdrum own one fourth of the mine." In 1909, the Idaho Continental Mining Company was formed with offices in the Paulsen Building, Spokane.

Fig. 21 Andy Coolin's mine cabin, front view. Upper Priest Lake, 1978. (M. Rutherford)

Fig. 22 Rear view of Andy Coolin's mine cabin, Upper Priest Lake. (M. Rutherford)

By 1902, Klockman had done enough development work on the Continental Mine to "show its full merits." He induced some rich lumbermen from Duluth, Minnesota: Mr. Bailey, Henry Turrish, D.C. Clark, and a successful iron mine operator, Capt. Harry Roberts, to form the Minnesota Company to assist in the development work.

A wagon road was built for 26 miles along Boundary Creek to haul crude ore to the Pend Oreille River to be shipped to the smelter. The product averaged 25 ounces of silver and 65% in lead ore. The roads were impassable during the winter and the operation lost a lot of money and the Minnesota Company withdrew in 1909.

In 1903, Klockman began to apply for patents for other mining claims. At that time there were no survey records in the U.S. or Canada near Continental Mountain. An engineer and surveyor, Billy Ashley, took observations at night from the stars and established the first starting point for future surveys in the form of a large stone monument in which records were buried.

Prior to 1903, Klockman made canoe trips around both lakes inspecting work by men on some of his mining claims. He heard from Indians that they got lead for their bullets "from an immense outcrop of lead" on the summit of the hills back of Priest Lake. Actually he could have reached the "outcropping" of lead and silver in 1901. Billy Houston had located the outcropping from Cedar Creek.

After using the east shore trail along both lower and little Priest Lakes for several years, a better trail was located from the mine down Boundary Creek to the Kootenai River. The Boundary Creek trail was shorter and more suitable for pack trains.

Near the Porthill side in Canada, they ran across David McLoughlin, son of the Hudson's Bay trader chief, the "White Headed Eagle." McLoughlin had sent his son to France for an education, but young David forsook all offers of fine positions in the Hudson's Bay Company. He married an Indian girl, lived in a tent, and raised a family in the life style of the Indian. Some of his children still live near Porthill. David was probably one of the first social dropouts in the Kaniksu forest.

The March 1, 1901 issue of the *Kootenai County Republican* stated, "The Mountain Chief, situated at the head of the little lake, has a 180 foot tunnel. It has a ledge of three feet of solid galena ore carrying 60 ounces of silver and almost 46% lead ore per ton."

There was so much interest at the turn of the century in the mining in Bonner County and the Priest Lake area in particular, that the

Kootenai County Republican and several other county newspapers carried a weekly mining column.

Fig. 23 Left to right: Catherine Simpson, Mary Rutherford, and George King, standing on the corner stone foundation of the crusher building at the Nickleplate Mine.

The *North Idaho News*, June 22, 1906 dateline, Williams, Idaho, (Coolin) carried the following item: "It is the opinion of experts that the Woodrat is one of the best looking properties in the state . . . "

George Duffill said that when he was piloting Sam Byars' steamboat he used to pick up a lot of ore on his regular round trips to Coolin. There was a lot of galena taken out of the Woodrat. The Woodrat was a square hole in the ground with a rail fence around it.

By 1915, the Nickleplate Mine on the top of Nickleplate Mountain just north-northwest of Nordman was publicized as a "live-wire lead, copper, silver, and gold mine." As an interesting sidelight, James

Fordyce, the mine superintendent, and John Downing, the engineer, made the first automobile trip from Priest River to Nordman in July, 1916.

The December 6, 1917 issue of the *Priest River Times* stated, "Report is current about town, but the *Times* was unable to verify it as of this date, that a large body of platinum has been struck at the Nickleplate Mine. A chemist from Hillyard, who has been in the employ of the Great Northern for years, recently spent three weeks at the mine and on his return, it is stated, he reported platinum in the ore to the value of $820 per ton, and part of it also carried good values in copper, silver, and lead.

"If this report is true it will mean quick development of this property and consequently additional prosperity for all Priest River."

The following week another Nickleplate story was reported: *Priest River Times*, December 13, 1917, "S.T. Moore, president of the Nickleplate Mine was in Priest River last Friday and in a conversation with the *Times* he stated that the report in our last issue of the platinum being found at the Nickleplate was true. J.H. James of Hillyard, the assaying chemist, in the three tests he recently made found copper, cobalt, and palladium to the value of $215.80, $812.46, and $854.34 per ton.

"Mr. Moore states that with favorable conditions it is now only a matter of a few months until they will ship out their first car of ore and from its receipts contemplate the completion of their tramway and sawmill and then no more stock will be offered for sale, as he figures it will be on a paying basis.

"It has been a long hard pull for those interested in this property, handicapped as they have been by lack of capital, but since the reorganization of the company, it has been run on a business-like basis and the result has been that they have succeeded in placing thousands of dollars worth of machinery at the mine, drove five tunnels at different levels, and in each one have found large bodies of rich ore. The mine is so situated that with the completion of the tramway, all ore can be deposited on the flat at the base of the mountain by gravity, thereby eliminating a big cost in operation.

"All Priest River is glad to hear this late report concerning the value of the area at the Nickelplate and when this mine gets into full swing it will mean considerable to our little town and riches for those who have spent their time and money in the development of this property."

In January, 1918 the *Priest River Times* carried another

Nickleplate story. "F.S. Moore, the father of the Nickleplate Mine, and S.A. Wells, manager of the mine, were in Priest River last week on business for the company. They had with them some very interesting specimens of cobalt, also platinum and palladium sponge extracted from the ore of the Nickleplate. They also exhibited proofs by acid tests that the ore is carrying the platinum values as claimed.

"No reasonable man, after seeing these proofs and specimens, can help but believe that the Nickelplate Mine will, within a very few years, be near the top of the big dividend paying mines of the northwest."

Test holes, a tailing pile, and the remains of a steam engine may be found near the shoreline on Copper Bay of another mining dream that obviously did not pay. The 1974, Forest Visitor's Map does not name the bay. It is just north of Hagman's Resort along the east border of the SE corner of Sec. 8, T 61 N.

The tailing pile of a Milwaukee Mine is still visible on the south side of Upper Priest Lake about one-half mile from Plowboy Campground. Left on the trail to Navigation, above the tailing pile, the opening of the mine shaft is still visible. The cellar near the site of the mine cabin may also be located along the shoreline.

The strike at the Lucky Abe Mine in the Cabinet Range near the Continental Mine made a news item in the December 1, 1921 issue of the *Priest River Times*.

"Pete Chase, Andy Coolin, Abe Johnson, Spokane and Opportunity, with Mr. Nelson are interested in the Lucky Abe Mine. A two foot wide streak of sulphide was struck in a 70 to 80 foot vein that assays 7½% copper, besides carrying gold, silver, and lead. On the same property, a copper and galena vein 20 feet wide was uncovered that assays 26% copper ore.

"The mine also has a 150-foot tunnel with a vein 30 feet wide that assays 100 ounces of silver to the ton. The group is trying to interest more capital."

In September, 1927, mining stories were still being published. The following story is typical:

"Roy Rannels of this place, who has been doing assessment work this summer in the Upper Priest Lake country, says the following in regard to mining prospects: Mining in the Upper Priest Lake country looks better than ever before. Considerable prospecting was done this year. The Idaho Continental, being the only productive one at present, is one of Idaho's leading mines. She has produced four million pounds of lead yearly . . .

"Considerable work was done on the Gem this year. The Nell

Shipman is showing up some good zinc. The Woodrat reports a large body on the three-hundred-foot level."

When Rose Hurst bought the building that housed the compressor and other machinery that was used at the Nickleplate Mine, she got acquainted with Mrs. Gus Imans. Mrs. Imans' husband worked for the Nickleplate Mining Company and when the company went broke it owed Imans a lot of money for back wages. About all that Mrs. Imans got out of it was the money she got for the building and the sale of the compressor.

"Mrs. Imans was quite a woman," commented Mrs. Hurst. "She worked all summer cooking for a harvest crew at the age of 76 to get enough money to pay for the cremation of her husband's body as he wanted his ashes to be scattered over the site of the Nickleplate Mine.

"She came up here late one fall and asked me to go with her to scatter the ashes. I was glad to do it. She was so sincere and I knew it would be her last visit to the mine site. She could do no more!

"Mrs. Imans was a tall, Viking-looking Swedish woman who was getting along in years, but she walked ahead of me all the way up there. In those days I could hit the ball pretty well myself so I managed to keep up with her. She showed me everything on top of the hill while we were scattering the ashes.

"Before we left we sat down in front of the main cabin that had served as office, dining room, and bunkhouse for the mine. She said, 'I want to tell you this story about the mine. After Gus departed he came back to me during a seance in a spiritual setting and told me that he had worked the mine in the wrong direction. He told me the gold laid in the opposite direction in the tunnel.'

"It went in one of my ears and out the other. I think I have to make my living above the earth not inside it. I'm going to stay on top of the ground. There's plenty of room for me here. This country reeks of legend and lore!

"I shall never forget helping her spread the ashes of her husband. The sacredness of it and what was involved is a wonderful kind of a thing. She was a true and courageous woman. I tell you we had a lot of them up here."

Mrs. Hurst was convinced that if a railroad had been built to Nordman, the mine would still be operating. She also believed there was a lot of malachite, as well as gold, silver, and zinc in the mine. Before she went with Mrs. Imans, one of her hired men warned her not to let Mrs. Imans drag her into the dead mine as the tunnels were full of poisonous gases. Whether or not she believed it, will never be known.

It could be that Rose was right about the railroad to Nordman influencing the development of the mines in the area. It also could be possible that with the advanced technology and the scarcity of raw materials today, the mines may yet be reopened and developed.

Fig. 24 Old timers. Left to right: Pete Chase, Bob White, Frank Algren, Frank Brown, Cougar Gus Johnson, Maude Whittaker Collier, Dick Collier.

7

CHARLES W. BEARDMORE

No story about Priest Lakes would be complete without at least a brief reference to the Beardmore name. Charles W. Beardmore, businessman, logger, miner, sawmill owner, hotelman, stagecoach owner, and for a short time a Priest River town constable was, in Minnie M. Horsemann's (feature writer for the *Newport Miner*) words, "One of those sturdy pioneers who built the west out of the raw materials that came to hand — and the dreams in their heads."

Beardmore came west from Oshkosh, Wisconsin on a bicycle, stopping off at Yellowstone Park and the mines in Montana to earn money to finance his trip. In 1891, he arrived in Priest River and worked as a shingle weaver in a local mill. It wasn't long until he purchased the St. Elmo Hotel on the riverbank across the tracks at the end of main street.

At the turn of the century Priest River became the point of departure of Spokane business and professional men and their wives on the way to vacation land, Priest Lake. Passenger business became so good that he started a horse-drawn stage line to Coolin. At times it took six horses to pull the wagon and carriages because the mud was so deep. For many years the stage line had a government contract to haul mail from Priest River to Coolin.

His daughter, Vivienne Beardmore McAlexander, said as a child she could remember the wives as they were always so beautifully dressed in taffeta and velvet with lovely hats trimmed in plumes and feathers. She recalled an incident when one of the women was pitched out of the front seat of the carriage when the driver put on the brake too fast as they were coming down a steep grade. The lady wasn't hurt but she was mud, head to foot, in all her finery.

The first auto stage line to Coolin was formed by Beardmore. The stage was a White Motor Company chassis and motor with a canvas top and side curtains with five triple width seats. Round trip fare was $5.25.

His son George once remarked, "I'm absolutely amazed at the huge sum of money my dad spent on grubstaking miners and prospectors. At one time he had a small concentrator in Priest

Fig. 25 Beardmore Stage Line to Coolin, 1912.

BUY YOUR
ROUND TRIP TICKETS
HERE OVER

BEARDMORE'S

—FINE—
AUTO STAGE
—TO—

PRIEST LAKE
TO INSURE FIRST CLASS ACCOMMODATIONS

CHAS. W. BEARDMORE'S AUTO STAGE

ASK FOR TIME TABLE AND FURTHER
INFORMATION

ROUND TRIP RATE FROM PRIEST RIVER
AND RETURN $5.25

Fig. 26 A White truck.

River with a hired assayer to check on the diggings of the men he had grubstaked. He had a financial interest in the Mountain Chief and the Hawksnest on Upper Priest as well as several other mines."

The Beardmore logging operations on Caribou Creek produced millions of board feet of lumber when white pine was the king.

Fig. 27 Al Piper in front of the blacksmith shop, Beardmore logging camp on Caribou Creek. (Babe Piper)

The Gumaer name that is part of the story of Upper Priest Lake joined the Beardmore name with the marriage of Lucy E. Gumaer and Charles W. Beardmore, October 29, 1902. Lucy's father was Howard B. Gumaer who came to Priest River in 1898 as a timber cruiser for the Manasha Lumber Company based in Wisconsin. The Gumaers and Leonard Paul's mother lived next door to each other on what is now Wisconsin Street in Priest River. Lucy was the first woman to serve in the Idaho State Legislature, 1922-24.

8

AUNT BELLE ANGSTADT

Aunt Belle, Queen of the Hostesses on Priest Lake north of the narrows, was one of the most lovable, gracious, controversial, entertaining, and exciting women that ever graced the shores of Priest Lakes. She was born in 1867, the eldest daughter of Mr. and Mrs. R.A. Downey. She was named Annabelle but was often called Nell or Belle and then became known to hundreds of Priest Lakers as Aunt Belle, wife of Harry E. Angstadt. She had previously been married to a man named Hall. Several newspaper items referred to her as Mrs. Nell Williams. She was never, however, married to Walt Williams.

During her late teens, Aunt Belle became a professional dancer, singer, and entertainer. She was an accomplished piano player, but concentrated on dancing as a soloist or member of a chorus line. During an extended vaudeville performance in St. Louis, Missouri a young man from a very wealthy family by the name of Hall fell madly in love with Annabelle Downey. After a rapturous engagement, the young couple was married in spite of violent objections by the groom's parents. From the information available the marriage was a happy one for the young couple.

Young Hall's parents continually harrassed Annabelle because they felt their son had married beneath the family's name and position. In spite of this fact, the marriage was firmly based on love and respect. Hall's family continued to torment, abuse, and browbeat Annabelle until she agreed to accept a cash settlement and not contest a divorce suit. Years later Aunt Belle told Nell Shipman, "Wasn't I lucky to have accepted $100 a month for the rest of my life rather than my father-in-law's first offer of $10,000 in cash?"

The $100 a month, for almost 40 years that she lived, not only aided Aunt Belle to live a comfortable life, it was the financial base for the building and maintenance of Aunt Belle and Harry Angstadt's Lone Star Ranch located on the north side of Bear Creek across the narrows from Granite Creek.

The Downey family was a talented, hardworking, respectable group. Dee, one of Belle's brothers, was at one time a dancing teacher in Priest River, Idaho. He moved to Portland, Oregon, and had a very successful career in his profession. Brother Walt was with the Great Northern Railroad. Lee was on the police force in Spokane. A sister, Mrs. Hein, was married to a physician, Dr. Hein, and lived in Palouse, Washington. Their mother lived in Priest River for many years.

Hallie Griswold, a native of Priest River, knew Aunt Belle from the time she came to Priest River until she died in 1926. While he was going to school in Priest River, he was in and out of Belle Hall's home many times. His step-father, Charlie Jackson, operated a grocery store and Hallie would deliver milk and groceries to her home. He was also her paperboy for a long time.

During an interview, Hallie said, "I was in and out of Aunt Belle's home like it was my own. There was always cookies, cake, or candy around for me to eat whenever I took the notion. Aunt Belle loved children and showered affection on the neighborhood kids. I don't believe anyone ever disliked her. She would sing and play the piano for us. I'll never forget the beautiful 1890 songs she used to sing. The most distinct memory I have of her house is the large ship that was painted or etched on the long plate glass window in the front door of her house."

Aunt Belle, to say the least, was strong willed, bold to the point of muleishness, when things didn't go to suit her. Hallie told the story of Aunt Belle horsewhipping a girl who was working at a hotel, for messing around with her boyfriend, Walt Williams. The young woman did not heed Belle's warning and one day Belle drove down town in her horse and buggy, called the girl out on the street, and proceeded to use her buggy whip on her until she promised not to see Williams again.

This performance attracted a good audience along main street in front of Harvey Wright's saloon. (One newspaper referred to the saloon as belonging to Mike Prado). No one tried to stop the whipping as it was believed that the hotel girl had it coming. It was also well understood that nobody interferred with Belle.

MRS. NELL WILLIAMS SHOOTS AND KILLS JACK BURNETTE DURING A LOVER'S QUARREL was a *Spokesman-Review* headline, page 1, column 6, dated May 14, 1907. The subhead continued, "Rejected Lover Killed — Lumberjack at Priest River Shot by Woman — Was Kicking in the Door After His Trunk Had Been Put Out of the House."

The story is quoted, in part, as it appeared in the paper. "As the result of a lover's quarrel, Mrs. Nell Williams shot and killed Jack

Burnette, a lumberjack, here this (Tuesday) morning. The shot was fired through the door and took effect in the man's groin. Burnette lived about an hour.

" . . . The exact circumstances leading to the tragedy are not known. It was after a quarrel that Mrs. Williams put Burnette's belongings out in the street. He had been boarding there. He returned and when he found his property on the porch tried to effect an entrance. He was kicking the door when the shot was fired.

" . . . The couple had been on friendly terms, it is said, and had been in each other's society a great deal."

The exact details immediately before the shooting are sketchy. According to Hallie Griswold's account, who was 16 years old at the time, Aunt Belle had anticipated trouble with Jack Burnette, often called "Husky Jack," as she sent a note by messenger to Elmer Stone, stating that she had to talk to him immediately. Elmer got a substitute bartender and went at once to Belle's home. She was distraught and excited as she told Stone that she expected Burnette to kill her. Elmer talked to her until she finally calmed down and Stone thought she was all right.

A short time after Stone returned to the saloon, someone reported that Belle had shot Burnette. One newspaper reported that the shot was heard downtown. Hallie and his stepfather were the first men to reach Burnette after the fatal shot was fired. Burnette was still conscious and repeated over and over to Hallie and Charlie Jackson, "It was not Belle's fault! It was not Belle's fault! Don't blame her! I had no business trying to knock down the door. Don't blame her for any part of this!" Jackson later testified under oath at Aunt Belle's trial that as best he could remember those were the dying words of Jack Burnette.

Belle Hall was not arrested the day of the shooting as the local Justice of the Peace was not qualified to make an arrest or issue a citation. There was no one else in Priest River qualified to take action either. The coroner in Coeur d'Alene was notified because Priest River was in Kootenai County at that time.

The May 15, 1907 issue of the *Spokesman-Review* carried another front page story, quoted in part as follows: "HELD FOR KILLING BURNETTE, MRS. ANNABELLE HALL, SISTER OF A SPOKANE POLICEMAN.

"Mrs. Annabelle Hall, sometimes known as Mrs. Williams, who shot and killed Jack Burnette, a lumberjack here (Priest River) early this morning is under detention awaiting a preliminary hearing tomorrow morning. An inquest over the remains of the dead man will also be held tomorrow morning.

"Mrs. Hall is a sister of Lee Downey, a policeman on the Spokane police force. He is here at present; as are also two brothers who came today. Downey says the woman's right name is Annabelle Hall . . . " (This statement is proof that Annabelle was never married to Williams.)

BELLE HALL IS ACQUITTED BY JURY was a page 1 headline of the *North Idaho News* of June 27, 1907.

The trial was held in District Court, Sandpoint, Idaho. An all-male jury returned a verdict of "Not Guilty" after discussing the case for only a few minutes. The judge had instructed the jury to return such a verdict as the prosecution could not provide witnesses to prove her guilt.

For several years after the tragedy Aunt Belle lived a quiet life in Priest River. She was a good hostess and many local people, including children, were entertained in Belle's home.

The story is told that Belle was denied entrance to a local dance hall one night by the bouncer, Harry Angstadt. Not too long after the incident Aunt Belle turned on her charm and in due course she became the wife of Harry E. Angstadt. From all reports it was a good marriage. Harry was a devoted husband and treated Aunt Belle as his beloved idol.

After the marriage Aunt Belle and Harry built the main building of their dream place, The Lone Star Ranch, on Bear Creek. It became a haven for travelers between Coolin and Mosquito Bay, particularly during the winter months. Nell Shipman's article that appeared in the May, 1925 issue of *Atlantic Monthly*, p. 647, stated, "The ranch's main building is a low, long rambling affair of logs, built picturesquely upon a hill overlooking the lake and backed by an unconquered and unclimbed peak called 'The Chimney.' The *Priest River Times*, July 8, 1915 carried a one liner, "The Angstadts built several new cottages for rent at the Lone Star Ranch."

Sylvia Gumaer Burwell said during an interview, "Aunt Belle was a scream, the fun kind. She wrote some lovely poetry about her life and Priest Lake that she would read for company. For kicks, when she wasn't busy around the Lone Star, Belle, for her own amusement would put up her hair a different way each day. Harry would never notice that anything was different. She was a joy to be around.

"The success of the Lone Star Ranch was due to her many talents as an entertainer and hostess. Harry, too, was a good man and was very good to Belle.

Fig. 28 Mary Duffill, Lone Star Ranch rock, 1924. (G. Duffill)

"The ranch house was lovely inside. Aunt Belle had souvenirs from everywhere. She had lovely clothes, good furniture, and lived a wonderful life.

"When I was going to high school in Priest River we used to stop at Aunt Belle's home and have her tell stories to entertain us. She'd spin one yarn after another. A great entertainer.!"

Mary Duffill said that in the winter time after the tourists left, the highlights of the year were the dances that were held at the Lone Star Ranch. Young and old from one end of the lake to the other would

Fig. 29 Catherine Diener Yates, Lone Star Ranch rock, 1978.
(M. Rutherford)

come prepared to stay the night for dancing and partying. Aunt Belle
and Harry were always ready for all their guests and entertained
them royally. Aunt Belle was in her element as her professional
background enabled her to hold sway over her audience with grace
and aplomb.

Unfortunately, by this time Annabelle's family inherited affliction,
a goiter, was affecting her pretty facial features. The enlargement of
her thyroid glands caused a visible swelling at the front of her neck.
This also caused her eyes to protrude noticeably. Because of her
delightful personality, adults were unaffected by this irregularity, but
it was difficult for children to accept her unusual appearance. This
was a source of torment to her as she was so fond of children. She had
not been fortunate enough to have a child of her own.

Mary Duffill made the remark, "Belle never lost the shape of her
beautiful legs that she developed as a professional dancer.

"For two or three years before Aunt Belle died she was bothered by
recurrent heart attacks. From time to time I would stay with her and

Fig. 30 Mary Duffill and Aunt Belle Angstadt, 1924. (G. Duffill)

give her shots of digitalis. The heart condition she had was not too serious as she was able to be up and to take care of herself most of the time."

Sylvia Gumaer Burwell verified the story that Nell Shipman mentioned in her unpublished memoirs that Aunt Belle did receive $100 a month for life from the Hall family by stating, "I will always remember when Aunt Belle said to me, 'Wasn't I a lucky fool, when I didn't accept that $10,000 and took my $100 a month for the rest of my life?'"

Fig. 31 West view of the narrows between Bear and Granite Creeks. (M. Rutherford)

Fig. 32 Catherine Yates in front of the main cabin of the Gregory farm, 1978. (M. Rutherford)

Fig. 33 Stand pipe for the Lone Star Ranch water supply, 1978.
(M. Rutherford)

Annabelle died in Spokane in 1926. Her tombstone in the Priest
River Cemetery states simply:
AUNT BELLE ANGSTADT
WIFE OF
H.E. ANGSTADT
1867 - 1926

9

TALL BEAR TALES

Kaniksu bear stories have persisted down through the years. The majority of them have been handed down by word of mouth and any attempt to sort the fiction from the facts would be futile.

With minor exceptions the following bear incidents are first hand reports, written reports, or episodes that have been corroborated by two or more persons.

CONTINENTAL GRIZZLY

Albert J. Klockman's diary reports of his and Billy Houston's encounter with a female grizzly bear near their camp at the Continental Mine, north of Upper Priest Lake.

The men were climbing over a log and came face to face with a grizzly sow with three small cubs. The bear started toward the men to protect her cubs. Klockman emptied his 10-shot Mauser without stopping her.

Billy didn't raise his rifle, just stood quietly watching the oncoming bear. He let the bear come within 15 feet of him as Klockman stood beside him with his drawn hunting knife. Billy threw his hat at the bear, which enraged her and she stood up on her hind feet and marched toward them. Billy leveled his rifle and dropped the bear with one shot.

They raised the cubs at their camp. They finally gave them to the Spokane Twickenham Pleasure Park which was connected with the city street and railway system.

Billy told Klockman that the old Hudson's Bay trappers never wasted a single cartridge on an attacking bear. They had apparently developed the technique of throwing something at the bear to make it march erect up to them and then "with one well aimed blow of their axe simply split the bear's head open."

A HUGHES MEADOW GRIZZLY

In the early 1920s, Clarence Sutliff, Carl Clem, and Roger Billings, met a male grizzly coming toward them on an open trail in broad daylight. All three men shot but did not drop the bear. The bear reached Roger, knocked him face down, and was clawing his back before Sutliff and Clem shot and killed it while it was straddle of Roger's back.

George Duffill picked up the men at the mouth of Upper Priest River and took the mauled man to Coolin. The bear had bitten the man's hand as well as his arm, between his shoulder and elbow. Fortunately neither bite did serious injury to the bone and Roger recovered.

In the early 1920s all three men became career employees of the United States Forest Service. The story followed them for years.

COUGAR GUS AND A BEAR

The *Kootenai County Republican*, Sandpoint, Idaho, published an account, June 30, 1903, of Gust (later called "Cougar Gus") Johnson's hand-to-hand combat with a wounded bear. Gust was on a bear hunt with his friends, Crittendon and Wendt. Gust was apparently working his way up a steep hill when he shot a 300-pound bear twice with his 30-30. The bear charged. On the third pull of the trigger the gun only clicked. The bear attacked and bit Gust several times. Gust finally got his arms around his knees and pulled them up to his chin and when the bear attacked again, Gust planted his feet in the bear's belly and with all the force he had, kicked. The bear, being on the downhill side, went rolling down the hill. Gust played dead and the bear left.

Gust was able to get back to his cabin. At that time he had a timber claim he was working on in the Pack River district about 15 miles from Sandpoint.

On the same date, the *Republican* also carried a story stating that Oscar Derrick was exhibiting in Priest River a 550-pound grizzly he had killed on the Westbranch.

ANOTHER BEAR

Granddad Tonnett, a Priest Lake old-timer of Luby Bay, took a visiting Scotchman on a bear hunt on Hughes Meadow. The Scotchman was so eager on the hunt that he followed the dogs too closely. A grizzly waylaid him and mauled him badly. Tonnett finally got a shot and killed the bear. The Scotchman was thankful!

HANK'S HIATUS

During an interview session, Henry "Hank" Diener, related several bear stories. With minor deletions and changes the stories are printed in Hank's words.

"One year while I was running a snagging crew, we had about 100 men on a job of falling snags. Two of the men had fallen a very large butt of an old snag. I had just passed them when one of them yelled, 'Hey, Hank, there is something down in this hole.' It was during the month of March and the snow was still pretty deep and the men were working on top of the snow. When they chopped the snag, it was hollow in the center. I leaned over and saw fur down about 6 or 8 feet below the cut. I chopped off a dead limb from the snag and poked it down the hole. About that time I was looking at a bear, face to face!

"The bear jumped out of that stump and took off right down the middle of the crew. You should have seen those men take off! Axes, saws, and men flying in every direction! The bear was as glad to get away from them as they were to get away from the bear! It took us the rest of the afternoon to hunt up all the axes and saws that were buried in the snow.

"Another time I was blazing a trail and cutting a good-sized blaze on a tree about 18 inches in diameter. I was about finished when I looked up and here came a cub bear down the tree. About four feet above me he came to a screeching halt, took one leap, landed on the ground, and bounded off into the brush like a scared jack rabbit. I didn't have time to get scared as I was entranced with the act of the cub stopping on its way down, and leaping off the tree with such force."

THE BEAVER CREEK BEAR
Told by Hank Diener

"The only method we had of disposing garbage in my day at Beaver Creek Ranger Station was to dig a pit six or eight feet deep and build a wooden platform over the top with a hole about two and a half feet in diameter in the middle of it. One year, toward the last part of the season, we had a bear that would visit the pit every night and scatter paper and food all over the pit area.

"Les Eddy, as usual with his ingenuity, rigged up a contraption with a wire on the lid of the garbage pit that ran down to the main cabin where most of us slept. The wire was arranged in such a way that when the bear pawed the lid off the pit, it would trip a switch and turn on an electric light that was beamed toward Les's eyes so he would wake up. Elmer Berg heard about the deal and decided he would get in on the fun. He came over to sleep in the main cabin with us.

"In the middle of the first night the light came on and Les aroused Elmer and me. We got dressed and went up to the garbage pit, which was near the tree where we had the water tank. When we got there, the bear was down in the garbage pit.

"Elmer grabbed the lid, put it over the hole with the bear inside and sat on the lid. The bear, of course, tried to get out as soon as Elmer slammed the lid down over the hole. The bear was strong enough to bounce Elmer and the lid up and down, but couldn't get it high enough to dump him off. Elmer was swearing a blue streak in Swedish because Les and I were roaring with laughter. When Elmer got excited he would talk in Swedish so you couldn't understand anything but his swear words. He finally said in English, 'You so-and-sos, come and help me.' About that time the bear got a good foothold somehow and dumped Elmer and the lid off to one side and took off for the brush. In all the excitement we hadn't even taken a gun along. It would not have helped, because all we had were flashlights and we didn't want to kill the bear anyway. That was the last of the bear we saw that fall."

JANET BAILEY'S BEAR BOUT

During the summer of 1971, Jan Bailey had a terrifying experience with a brown bear. She first saw the bear across the Thorofare near the west end of the drift fence. She was on the dock in front of her house as the bear started swimming across the channel. She yelled at him and he went back to shore. About 45 minutes later she heard a commotion behind the tool shed about 40 feet from her front door. She stepped out on her porch and saw the bear up to his shoulders inside the burn barrel. He had tipped it over to get at some watermelon rinds that had been put in the barrel.

Jan clapped her hands and yelled at the bear, trying to frighten it away. Instead of leaving, the bear walked toward her. When he got within ten feet of her, he got up on his hind legs and kept approaching. "By this time," Jan said, "he was close enough to look down at me. I was paralyzed with fright. I knew I shouldn't turn away and let him follow me into the house. I just stood there and screamed, holding my hands in front of my face because I thought I might get swatted at any moment.

"Thank God, my neighbor, Snack Snackenberg, was in his cottage and heard me screaming. He came running and hollering. The bear got down on his four feet and ambled away. I knew the bear was a wild animal and he was annoyed that I got him out of the burn barrel where he had found food. I thought of a lot of things in those seconds. I was sure the bear was going to take a pass at me and rip my face and body with his huge claws."

ROXY'S ROMANCE WITH A GRIZZLY

Nora "Roxy" Grindle who was, for many years, one of the main contacts between the telephones in the outside world and the CBs north of Granite Creek, had a first hand experience with a grizzly bear that parallels a wild dream.

During one of the many years that Roxy worked at Glacier National Park in Montana, George Hanson, Elmer Olson, and Dave and Si Stevenson went to Goathaunt on Waterton Lake to get the resort ready for the tourist season. They arrived on a beautiful day, in time to store the supplies and have supper before dark.

After the dishes were done, Roxy put out the ham, eggs, and cereals for breakfast. Then she retired to her sleeping quarters, which was an attic loft that was reached by shinning up a ladder through a hole in the ceiling.

The men decided to play a round of cards before going to bed. They hadn't much more than started, when a grizzly bear came up to the big picture window in the front of the cabin and looked in at them. Within a matter of seconds, the bear stood on his hind legs and walked right through that plate glass window as if it were thin air. As he reared up, all four men made a beeline for the ladder and scrambled into the attic.

Fortunately, Roxy had the habit of keeping her 30-30 loaded and with her all the time. In their haste, not one of the men took time to grab a gun. Roxy handed Elmer her gun and he fired a warning shot. Instead of being afraid, the grizzly stuck his head through the opening in the ceiling and put his front paws on the floor of the attic.

Elmer fired two quick shots at point blank range into the bear's head. The grizzly dropped to the floor and Elmer fired one more insurance shot before the men ventured down the ladder.

With a block and tackle the men dragged the carcass through the window frame. When they reported the incident, a taxidermist from Browning, Montana, came and got the bear. The grizzly weighed 900 pounds and was 9'9" from tip to tail.

THE RUTHERFORD-SIMPSON
FOURTH OF JULY BEAR HUNT

During the summer of 1959, the Forest Service had a large blister rust crew camped on the site of the old Beaver Creek Ranger Station. That year bears were causing a lot of trouble around the camps in Glacier National Park. To get rid of some of them, a truck load was dumped near the Canadian border in the Idaho Panhandle.

Being experienced camp robbers, several of the bears took one sniff of the wind from the southwest and made a beeline for the garbage dump behind the blister rust camp. Along the way they passed thousands of pounds of beautiful huckleberries and other native food for bears, but they couldn't be bothered with "food in the rough."

Within a few days the garbage supply got pretty well picked over and one of the battle-scarred brown bears began making the rounds of the cabins at Beaver Creek Camp. After the bear had wrecked the back porches of several cabins and smashed open the war surplus coolerators, members of the association complained to the local game warden of the damage. The warden gave his consent to have the bear shot with the understanding that the hide and meat could not be sold or consumed.

For some reason, lost to history, Gordon Rutherford and Claude Simpson were appointed, or self-appointed, to shoot the bear.

A collection of large beef bones were donated to the cause by Clark's Grocery in Pullman, Washington. The purpose, of course, was to attract the bear to a spot where he could be shot.

Before daybreak, July 4, 1959, the hunters stationed themselves for the big kill near the bones that were hung in a tree along the path usually taken by the bear. By 4:30 AM it was obvious that the bear was smarter than the hunters. They decided to give up and go back to bed. As they were leaving the hunters saw bear tracks in the dew-covered grass. They followed the tracks across several lots. From the back of the Hilty lot the rear end of the bear was spotted in the doorway of what was left of the Bundy back porch.

After a brief consultation, it was decided that Simpson would sneak around the front side of the McCall and Bundy cabins, scare the bear, and Rutherford was to shoot him on his way out.

Simpson very carefully picked his way along the beach and stealthily crept up along the north side of the Bundy cabin. He could hear snoring and snuffing and was sure the bear was in the bag. He looked up over the half-wall of the porch, but no bear! The sounds were emanating from the back porch bedroom where another would-be hunter was snoring, with his 30-30 by his side.

Simpson motioned to Rutherford to come on up the trail. While they were debating what to do next, they simultaneously spotted the bear standing across Beaver Creek, facing them. Rutherford calmly leaned his 30-06 against the trunk of a tree, sighted, and pulled the trigger. The bear dropped out of sight in the tall grass and brush. Almost instantly he jumped up and took off toward the Thorofare. Rutherford cried, "I couldn't have missed him. I had him dead to right!"

They crossed Beaver Creek on the old log footbridge and cautiously worked their way along the north bank until they found the spot where the bear had crushed the grass and brush when he dropped. But there was no bear! The hunters followed on up the trail and about 20 feet from where the bear had originally dropped they found a splotch of blood. About every 15 or 18 feet for 101 steps, approximately 300 feet, they found splotches of blood. At that point there lay a huge, scarfaced brown bear. Dead! Estimates were made of his weight that varied from 450 to 600 pounds. The story doesn't end here, however.

The shot had awakened about everyone in camp, except the mighty hunter who was snoring on Bundy's back porch. He slept through the entire episode.

Simpson and Rutherford were treated to a royal breakfast. Other members of the Beaver Creek Camp Association volunteered to dig a hole and bury the bear. And still the story didn't end!

The next morning some of the kids went to see the grave site and rushed back with the news that the bear was lying on top of the ground. It was unbelievable! Several adults visited the site and to the consternation of those who assembled, the bear was indeed on top of the ground. He was reburied and the following day the carcass was again on top of the ground.

The mystery was not solved until old-timer, Seeley Smith, came by and explained that it was not uncommon for bear to dig up a carcass of their fellow creatures and not consume the meat. And the story didn't end here!

Within a few days it was impossible to walk along the trail because the disintegrating carcass had such a vile, powerful, repulsive odor that the trail had to be abandoned until after it froze up that fall.

Some second generation BCCA'ers still treasure a bear claw or two as a memento of the "hunt." End of story!

HANK'S HORROR

"One fall we had a pretty good-sized crew building an air landing strip on Hughes Meadow. We got a call one day that a bear was regularly breaking into the cookhouse. The cookhouse was only a tent with a fly stretched over it, that served as an eating space. The bears were getting pretty brave and destroying food as well as battering up the cooking utensils.

"It was during hunting season so I decided I would go up and kill the bear for the hide and what meat the men would eat. When the bear came in the first night I was there, the cook called me. The bear ran away a short distance, probably 50 or 60 feet, and stood up facing me. It was early morning with plenty of light to shoot. It was an easy shot and I got him in the exact spot on his chest.

"As soon as the shot hit him, he crossed his front paws over his chest, dropped his head forward, began to cry, and crumpled to the ground. That was bad enough!

"I skinned him out and strung him up on a big tree branch. His carcass hanging there by his hind legs looked like the body of a naked man! Never again, I said, will I ever shoot a bear. And I never have.

"I have had several opportunities since, but I could never pull the trigger on my gun. It was almost human, the way he acted when I shot him. I fired one shot. Got one bear. Never again!"

Fig. 34 George Duffill, 1920.

10

THE DUFFILL DUO AND DADDY

Fig. 35 Daddy Duffill, 1927.

Fig. 36 Mary Duffill with her foot on Byars' "Papoose."

Fig. 37 Mary Duffill driving one of Nell Shipman's dog teams, 1923.

William "Daddy" or "Billy" Duffill was born in Whitby by the Sea, Yorkshire, England, in 1858. He came to Cherry Creek, New York, as a young man where he married Charlotte Hadley. Four children were born to the union: Elizabeth (Betty), Grace, George, and Mary Jane. The duo in the story is Mary and George.

George was born in Cherry Creek, May 6, 1897. Mary Jane was also born in Cherry Creek, January 27, 1904. With a straight face and a smile in her eyes that signalled a humorous remark, without trying to be funny or clever, "I'll bet I was welcomed, coming seven years later!"

The Duffills had two small farms near Cherry Creek. By 1914, Billy Duffill was tired of farming and working for the neighbors. He was always fond of a nip or two and in 1914, Mamma Duffill, in desperation, told Daddy he had to choose either his bottle or his family. Daddy put his bottle under his arm and headed west. He never returned.

When he arrived in the Idaho Panhandle he worked around Pend Oreille Lake for about two years and came to Priest Lake in 1916. He came to the lake with a man by the name of Shilling. For the next 16 years he trapped, worked for Sam Byars, Nell Shipman, and the Forest Service. His home was a houseboat tied up most of the time across the Thorofare from Forest Lodge Hotel. While he was working for Shipman Productions his houseboat was docked just south of Shipman Point.

George Duffill, Daddy's only son, was discharged from the Marines in Washington, D.C. at the end of WW I. He lived there a short time with his mother and two younger sisters who had moved to D.C. from Cherry Creek.

In 1919, he went to Richmond, Indiana where he met and married Beulah Hanley. He brought his wife and infant daughter, Mildred to Priest Lake. They lived in the red cabin, now owned by Al Piper, a short distance up the Thorofare from the site of Forest Lodge. For the next five years, he piloted Sam Byars' steamboat in the summer and trapped and hunted in the winter. Before he and his family returned east in 1925, another daughter, Mary Francis, was born in Newport, Washington.

In February, 1922, while the entire family was fishing through the ice at the mouth of the Thorofare, Daddy's houseboat burned and they lost everything except their fish poles and the clothes on their backs. The fire started from an overheated can of neats foot oil. During the rest of the winter, they all lived in George and Beulah's one-room cabin.

After graduation from high school, Mary came west at the age of 17 to visit her father at Priest Lake. From all reports, Mary was a very attractive young woman. She was one of the first women on Priest Lake to regularly wear slacks. Most of the time she dressed in Malone wool pants, heavy wool socks, boots, and a mackinaw. She could wear clothes and looked good in anything.

Mary said during the interview, "I don't know how I had the nerve to go out west and live with Dad at Priest Lake. You know how it is though — 17 years old, you are not afraid of doing anything!" Mary was not only unafraid, she was a pioneer outdoors woman and enjoyed and loved every minute of it. It can also truthfully be written that she was loved by all those who knew her during her 25 years in the Idaho Panhandle.

Mary had a great deal of respect and admiration for her mother. When Billy left the family, two of the older girls, Betty and Grace, were married and Mrs. Duffill kept the family together by working in the local cannery. George trapped for fur-bearing animals during the winters while attending school. Mary also worked part-time in the community.

Both Mary and George indicated that they didn't live in luxury but managed to get by. Mother Duffill was a meticulous housekeeper and she taught order and love of a home to all her children. One of the Duffill farms was rented for $65 a year. From the other one they got five cords of wood or 25 bushels of potatoes or both, depending on the luck or ambition of the renter.

The Duffill interview was centered or maneuvered to get an insight into the social and economic aspects of life on Priest Lake, north of the narrows in the 1920s, and to encourage George and Mary to recall incidents of their years at the lake.

Many of their experiences were routine life in the early days. Some were comical, others serious, and a few tragic. The trio, to say the least, was courageous, physically strong, cheerful, witty, lovers of life, and capable of coping with the elements — pioneers at heart. Today they would probably be referred to as dropouts or copouts from the mainstream of society.

George and Mary told several of their favorite stories about their dad. One day "Daddy" was on a trail that had a very sharp switchback where he met a bear, face to face. Neither saw the other because of the dense brush. When Billy turned to retreat the bear snapped at him and caught his back pocket. George remarked, "Dad never got a scratch out of it. The bear got Dad's plug of tobacco. It pays to chew when you are in the woods!"

Mary nicknamed Daddy's boathouse "The Palace of Steam." "Boy, the amount of moonshine that went through that place would have floated a battleship," said Mary. "Everybody that went by stopped for a while. Nobody ever went on by. They all stopped!

"Dad got up one morning after he and Pete Chase had spent most of the night getting themselves well oiled and, like all old-timers, they went to bed with their socks on. The socks were always gray wool Malones. Dad woke up the next morning with about one eye open and it was redder than a blanket. He looked down at the end of the bed and said to me while I was getting breakfast, 'Mary Jane, if I knew which one of those sets of feet were mine, I'd get up.'"

Daddy Duffill was in at least one of Nell Shipman's two-reel thrillers. Mary and George remembered a still shot of Daddy with his hand in a bear trap. Dad's favorite silent film was Nell's two-reeler, "Trail of the Northwind."

Dad, his dog Jiggs, and his pipe were constant companions. Mary told the story of Jiggs and the bear. "One day we went up Lion Creek to check on Daddy's bear traps. Jiggs followed us beautifully until he caught scent of the bear, long before we knew there was a bear in the trap. Jiggs rushed ahead of us, every hair on his body stiff and pointed forward. His ears were forward, stiff as a board. He planted each foot down firmly and courageously as he marched toward the bear. We stood and watched him. Pretty soon there was a yip, yip, yip, and here came Jiggs, tail between his legs, his back feet were hitting the ground far out in front of his front legs. He couldn't stop when he got to us and went on down the trail. What a contrast to the way he had approached the bear, but one look at the bear had changed his attitude. You would have had to see it to appreciate how funny it was; a yip every jump, and now a completely docile dog following behind us at a respectable distance."

Daddy placed his bear traps in an unsophisticated but effective setting. He had a reputation of being able to catch bear. Along a trail or bear run, Dad would erect a chute-like contraption using branches leaned up against trees or piled on the ground against stakes. At the end of the chute he would place a gallon jar of well-rotted fish. Along the run he set his traps intermittently and covered them lightly with dead cedar, pine, or fir boughs. The dead fish scent and the lightly-covered traps apparently were the key to Dad's success. He had taken the trouble to have hidden himself for many hours where he could see how a bear approached the jar of dead fish. The old bears, in particular, would approach the scent very slowly. When they reached the area covered with boughs, they would stop and with their paws cover the area inch by inch, lightly putting their paws on the boughs as they worked their way toward the jar of fish. The traps were set at different pressure levels and Dad was a master at outguessing the bears.

Mary told about many trips she made from the head of Priest Lake to Coolin by snowshoes, dogsled, boat, or skates. On one of the trips she and her husband, Bill Donaldson, went to Coolin on snowshoes for mail and supplies pulling a sled. On the way back, they went through the ice at Granite Creek. Joe Cyr, who lived nearby, came out on the ice and pulled them out. They were able to salvage the mail and food. They later retrieved, by canoe, three oak kegs that floated into open water when the sled went under. Mary said that Pete really needed the kegs for moonshine storage as he was having a productive winter.

One winter Mary and Bill made a trip on snowshoes to the top of Lookout Mountain. Another winter they had a trapline to the top of Squawman.

The first winter Shipman Productions was on location at Priest Lake, they leased Sam Byars' hotel and out buildings. George, Daddy, and Mary helped take care of the animals that were housed in the barn and other outbuildings. One day George had three of Nell's Alaskan dogs on chains and was leading them to the sled area when he tripped and fell. All three dogs jumped on him, but somehow he got back on his feet and as he stood up, the dogs backed away. George said, "That taught me a real lesson about Alaskan sled dogs. Never, never leave your feet when you are around them if they are out of their harness."

George also gave his opinion of the use of the word "mush" while driving a dog team. "The word is a lot of horse manure. You can holler anything you want to. They know when you are ready. Words like, let's go, giddap, it's time, or okay, we're off, are used most often. "Mush," that's what you put milk on!"

George was the main pilot of Sam Byars' steamer. He said that the 26-foot boat was small enough to get up the Thorofare except in very low water in the late fall. George continued, "The boiler for the launch looked like a steel drum with a firebox not much larger than a 5 gallon milk can. It had a bunch of ½ inch pipes running through it. Normally, we carried 125 pounds of steam pressure. The wood Daddy cut for the steamer was 18 inches long and not much larger than wood for a cook stove. The exhaust went through the smokestack and made a slow poom, poom, poom, sound.

"I towed Nell Shipman's animals and supplies from Coolin to the sandspit on a barge that Sam had made from 2x8's and logs, well caulked.

"I'll never forget the uproar when we landed the barge. There was yipping, howling, growling, barking, cackling — you name it! Everybody on the lake knew we had arrived. It continued until the animals were fed because they had not eaten since we had left Coolin. It was a long trip."

George also drove one of Nell's dog teams from Canoe Point to Mosquito Bay when Bert Winslow could not get the "W.W. Slee" any farther than Canoe Point, even though he had an ice breaker in front of the steamer.

"When Sam sent me to Coolin with the barge to bring a load of Nell Shipman's zoo animals to Forest Lodge, Nell's veterinarian, called the "Mad Russian" got mad at me. He got real upset when I made him shift some of his animal cages to one side or the other to keep the barge on an even keel. I'll have to give the bird his dues, as he really knew his animals. He would talk to them in a way that I'm sure they knew what he was telling them, as he put their cages in a different place than where they were used to."

The summer after the Duffill houseboat burned, Mary and Bill built a floathouse. Bill did the outside and Mary the inside. It was sided and panelled with shakes split from cedars cut near the log footbridge across the trail on Lion Creek. Their dinette set was made from solid pieces of cedar. Mary remarked, "Our boathouse was pretty on the outside and inside too." After they sold the floathouse, they built a house in Coolin on the hill back of Leonard Paul's store. Marj and Jim Roberts bought that house and Mary and Bill moved to a house near the road going toward Highway #57.

Food, particularly in the winter time, was a major problem. Huckleberries, meat, and fish were almost a steady diet. Each fall, near the end of hunting season, everyone participated in a deer drive for a meat supply. The venison supply was supplemented now and then because as George said, "Occasionally someone would be out in the woods and there lay a dead deer. You couldn't go away and let the coyotes have it, so you dragged the carcass in, skinned it out, and took good care of the meat."

One fall a short drive netted five deer. George said, "There were too many to pack out so I went up and got Earl Geisinger and his horses to help pack out the deer. This was living high on the hog in those days."

George had a favorite recipe for cooking oil that was on the shelf the year around. It was made with half deer tallow fried out and half

Fig. 38 Bill Donaldson driving a piling for Mary and Bill's houseboat.

Fig. 39 Mary Duffill Donaldson, Forest Lodge, 1933.

bear fat from a young black bear. "The bear fat had to be from a black bear," said George. "The oil from a brown or a grizzly bear was too strong.

"Butter was a rarity in those days. We did have fresh ice cream all winter long — with no freezer to crank. We took the usual mixture of eggs and milk, put it out in the snowbank and took turns going out to stir the mixture until it got so stiff that you couldn't stir it any longer and it was finished. It didn't take too long on lots of those cold days. Carnation milk was a great help to us.

"I remember the time Earl Geisinger and I skated all the way to Coolin to get mail and a case of Eagle Brand milk for the baby. Coming back we ran into a patch of ice that had piled up and was covered with snow. I came down on my face and the half case of milk on my back was so heavy I got skinned up a little. In fact, my face was sore for days.

"We had some dandy happenings up there. We were on the lake when radio was first brought out to the public. We would go down to Mike Moore's restaurant in Coolin to listen. He had the first radio on the lake. We would go down there to dance to radio music from Chicago and New York. About half the time all you could hear was a s-q-u-a-w-k!"

In George's book, according to Mary, beaver tail soup was a rare treat. "In fact he liked all kinds of wild game: bear, deer, porcupine, muskrat, skunk, beaver, otter, grouse, geese, rabbit, you name it. I don't share his enthusiam for all those 'gamey' dishes but I've tried, cooked them all, and ate them all. I still like venison the best.

"Once I tried cooking a loon. I boiled the blasted thing for two days, took one taste, dumped it in the brush and, this is the truth, even Jiggs wouldn't eat it!"

George chimed in, "We ate a lot of beaver meat. There's fine food! If you ever get a chance to get a fresh carcass be sure to do it. The tail is the 'pork loin' of a beaver. The biggest beaver we ever caught up there weighed 61 pounds. You will find them very fine eating. We never threw a carcass away. We would dry the hides and bootleg them. One of our neighbors on the little lake usually took care of the hides and got them to Spokane. He knew how to get rid of the hides for money. We got between $20 and $30 per hide and the cash always went for food. We also caught a few otter while we were up there.

"This is going to sound kinda funny, and I probably shouldn't tell you, but it was part of living on Priest in the 1920s. There was a well-worn path between the hotel and the ice house that passed in front of the two cabins on the Thorofare. It was right along the top of the bank. The trail was so well travelled in those days that it must still be there. I made hundreds of trips from the lodge to my cabin and to the ice house. We always put up ice in those days. One year the ice on the Thorofare was so thick that we cut the ice in 24″ square blocks.

"If you could get a metal rod with a point on it and walk up the path and pound it down in the ground about three feet, you might find the remains of a five gallon oil can turned bottomside up that is full of beaver hides. I can't tell you on which side of the path it was, but it may still be there. I wouldn't know who put them there — no never!

"Another boner I pulled would probably land me in jail today. I went up the Thorofare one day to look at a trapline I had on Caribou Creek. I tied my boat at the mouth and took my boat hook with me as a cane as the snow was a mile deep anywhere you looked.

"Coming back, about 50 feet from my boat, I saw a bald eagle sitting on top of an old snag. While looking at him he dove off the snag and landed 'kerplunk.' He didn't fly off so I decided to wallow through the snow to see what was going on. When I got there all I could see was six or eight inches of his tail feathers sticking up in the middle of the hole in the snow. I reached over and got under him with my boat hook and gave a tug. The funny part was, he didn't come up tail first. He came up head first, fighting mad! My dog, Spot, tore into him. The eagle reached out with his claws and gripped my dog. Spot wouldn't let go and I guess the eagle couldn't get loose, and there was squealing, hollering, growling, and snow flying in every direction. Pretty soon I got a chance and I broke my boat hook over his head. That whack took care of it.

"I brought him into camp and told Sam Byars I was going to have him stuffed. Good old Sam told me I had better dump him in the brush and let the coyotes have a feed or Uncle Sam would be feeding me at the county courthouse in Sandpoint.

"If you want to print it, I'll swear it is a true story and Mary Jane was there to see it."

"A lot of times during the year," Mary said, "there was nothing much to do so we would get together to eat, play cards, and have a few rounds with a jug of moonshine. One night a bunch of us got together at our house and someone got the idea of going up to Pete's (Chase) place and have a party. Later in the evening, everyone was pretty well-oiled and we were really roaring. Everyone, except Pete, finally got bedded down. Pete had to check his sourdough pot for a breakfast of hotcakes for the bunch. He dragged a two-gallon crock from under the bed where Dad was sleeping, added a few ingredients and slid it back under the bed.

"When Dad started to get up the next morning he was still as loaded as an owl. He stuck one foot over the edge of the bed and it went down into the crock of sourdough. He lifted his foot out of the crock and here was all that sourdough streaming down from his sock. He looked at the mess and grumbled, 'What the *hell* is that! I don't want that on my foot.' So he just pulled off his sock and dropped the whole mess, sock and all back into the crock, pushed it farther under the bed and laid back down again.

"After awhile Pete came in and said, 'I don't know about the rest of you, but I think I can eat a hotcake!' He picked up his crock and started stirring the dough. After a stir or two he growled, 'My God, that's a bit stiff isn't it?' Yup, it was a mite thick. I don't know what would have happened if my husband, Bill, hadn't stopped him, that's as far as he could let it go. Everytime Bill and I got together over the years, we would have a good laugh over the incident. There were so many funny things that happened, it made life worth living in those days."

"Billy Duffill was a small man who didn't talk very much to adults," said the only man who was interviewed who knew Daddy personally. "He was what I would call a typical hillbilly, with whiskers and a pipe in his mouth. I had only a few short conversations with him. I was in Mary and Bill Donaldson's home many times when Daddy was there, but he never talked much.

"The only story I remember about him was his habit of putting frozen maggots in his mouth while baiting his fishhooks when he was fishing for whitefish."

Mary remarked on several occasions that, "Daddy was a kind, quiet, funny little old man. He was a good hunter, a real fisherman, a better than average trapper, and I might add a real lover of the free life in the Kaniksu.

"For many years Dad cut and split wood for Sam Byars' steamer. This he loved to do and spent most of each summer, when he wasn't gardening or picking huckleberries, on his woodpile on the sandspit. Sam paid him $75 for his summer's woodcutting.

"Dad remained very loyal to Nell Shipman. He loved to take care of the animals and spent many hours rustling food for them after Nell had to throw in the sponge."

Madlyn Byars Gillis said during an interview, "Daddy Duffill, bless his heart, was a dear old man. He helped us around the place. He raised an excellent garden for us each summer. In fact, just before

Fig. 40 Daddy Duffill's woodpile for Byars' steamer.

Fig. 41 Left to right: "Huck Finn" (Madlyn Byars) and
"Tom Sawyer" (Mary Duffill). (Duffill Collection)

Fig. 42 "The Gladiators." Left to right: Mary
Duffill and Madlyn Byars, 1921.
(Duffill Collection)

he came to Forest Lodge he worked for a Mrs. McFarland in
Sandpoint as a gardener. The McFarlands had a big house on the
corner below the courthouse. It was still there in 1978.

"The first summer Daddy came to Priest he and his sidekick,
Shilling, picked huckleberries for the market. Their headquarters
was a tent below the lodge.

"I don't know what I would have done while living at Priest Lake if
Mary Duffill hadn't been there," continued Madlyn. "She was a little
older than I was, but what fun we had! We hit it off right from the
start. The four years difference in our ages didn't seem to matter a
great deal. She was young enough that she still liked to play. I
remember very well the time we made swords and with wash boiler
lids we squared off for a battle royal. We used to entertain the guests
at Forest Lodge by dumping each other out of my canoe while

playing in the Thorofare. We also spent a lot of time playing Tom Sawyer and Huckleberry Finn.

"Mary could always supply the humor to any situation. She was always unruffled about everything. She was as strong as any man on the lake and always carried her share of the load.

"I used to go over to Daddy's boathouse and listen to the stories he would tell Mary and me about England.

"When he was a young man he had a very good singing voice. He told us many times about his father taking him to the pub, when he was four or five years old, set him on the bar, where he would sing for the men. He probably got a few sixpence for his talents.

"Once in awhile he would come to our campfires and tell stories and sing. The one song I've never forgotten was 'Over Went the Captain.'

Over went the captain
Over went the crew
Over went the first mate
And the little middies too.
And over went the boatswain
Who swore his love was true
She couldn't have them all
So what was this poor girl to do?"

Mary and Madlyn remained lifelong friends. In 1977, Mary drove to Spokane from her home in Sebastian, Florida to visit Madlyn. They attended the Shipman Point dedication together, which led to the interviews that provided first hand information for this and the Byars' chapters of this book.

While living in Coolin, after Bill quit the Forest Service, Leonard Paul asked Mary if she would keep books for him. Toward the end of the month she gathered up all the billing pads that carried the customer charges for the month and took them to the office. She asked Mr. Paul where he kept his adding machine. "In typical Leonard Paul style, he exploded, 'Adding machine?' He pointed to my head," Mary said, "and roared as he left the office, 'You got one right up there. What do you want another one for?' That settled that, quick!"

Bill Donaldson and a partner built houses and fireplaces around the lake for the next several years. Later the family moved to Priest River and then Newport. After Mary retired she moved to Sebastian, Florida where she lives now with her sister, Betty. When George retired he and his wife also moved to Sebastian.

George paid his Dad a backhanded compliment when he told

about going with him up near the snowline on Lookout Mountain to hunt deer. "When I first got to Priest Lake, Dad wanted me to kill a deer so I'd know how to do it. I was young, eager to hunt, and full of spring water. We started up the trail which seemed to me to be a snail's pace. I thought at this rate we'd never get there. We got about halfway up that mountain and I thought the old man was primed! He was running, according to my speed, by that time. I was doing my level best to keep up with him. Daddy was still doing the same thing he did when we started — plodding right along. Boy, I'm tellin you, by that time I was all in. It takes a little while to get used to that stuff."

Mary mentioned in a letter that she was taking a copy of the *Priest River Times'* article about the Shipman dedication to her son Bill, as he was too young to remember Priest Lake. William Donaldson, Jr. is a lieutenant commander, U.S.N. and will soon complete his tour of duty at the Pentagon in Washington, D.C.

Mary also mentioned in the letter that "Bill is very interested in 'Mama's life in the rough.' I think it all sounds like a James Oliver Curwood or Jack London story to him. It all happened so long ago, even I sometimes wonder if I really lived that kind of a life — a far cry from '78."

When Mary was asked if she was with Aunt Belle in the picture, she replied in a letter, January 3, 1979, "Yep, that's me with Aunt Belle. Gad, was I really that young once upon a time? The days of the Charleston, knickers, middy blouses, and pageboy bobs, 1924. I was 20 years old. I'll be 75 this month.

"It's a long trail from 20 to 75, but in my case, nothing spectacular, just the usual assortment of happiness, tragedy, disappointments, blissful interludes, and lots of change. I never seem to sit and rock much, always on the go. Right here in Sebastian has been the most monotonous time of my life."

11

PETE CHASE

Lewis "Pete" Chase, also known as Panhandle Pete, was as colorful and as well-known as any Chicago dropout that ever hit Priest Lake.

He was a gentleman, a first-rate host, and one of the most sophisticated inhabitants on Upper Priest Lake. He had a cabin and mine claim in Section 19, a short distance northwest of the mouth of Trapper Creek. His name does not appear on any of the legal records of Sec. 19 so it can be assumed that he never homesteaded or purchased land in that area.

It is documented by legal records and by several first hand reports that Pete was engaged, from time to time, in the business of moonshining. His reputation as the maker of the best moonshine in the Idaho Panhandle was indisputable. His product was sold under the label, *Uncle Pete's Monogram*. It has been reported from reliable sources that Pete's chief outlet for his product was the world famous Davenport Hotel in Spokane. It is a known fact that Pete got very perturbed when a fellow moonshiner tried to pass off his moonshine as *Uncle Pete's Monogram*.

Pete had a lot of friends in the Panhandle and knew most of the leg-men bootleggers in Spokane. He quite frequently had any number of good looking girls from Spokane up to his Trapper Creek cabin for rest and recuperation. One early day Forest Service employee said he had been to several of Pete's Saturday night parties. Those invited would take food and Pete would furnish a plentiful supply of *UPM* and occasionally a house full of girls.

From various stories that were printed in the *Priest River Times* it can be deduced that Pete was good newspaper copy, and a man with an excellent sense of humor.

PRT, 7/23/1914 — "Pete Chase phoned down the other day and said the huckleberries were so large that it took only two to make a pie. Now, Pete, is that true?"

PRT, 9/10/1914 — "We understand that Pete Chase ... was heard to remark that he had just 'daffidilled' around long enough and now he intended to get right to business.

"Asked what doing? 'Grafting pineapple shoots onto pine trees,' says Pete. We wonder why we never thought about that ourselves."

PRT, 6/10/1915 — "Pete Chase is a man who has had much experience with bear and now one more is reported to add to his best. He set a trap back on Old Snowy near the summit, and caught a cub. An immense grizzly bear ate the young one. Pete reset the trap and later caught the grizzly and now has two bears in one, but would get only one bounty and that's what bothered him."

PRT, 7/1/1915 — "Pete Chase sold his grizzly bear hide to Hill's Brothers of Portland. Pete said he and the Hills were satisfied with the sale. As for the bear, Pete didn't care a tap whether he was satisfied or not as it was the same one (bear) that ate the cub bear out of the trap that Pete set."

Catherine Diener Simpson and her sister, Charlotte, can confirm, by personal experience, Pete's reputation as a good host. The sisters were spending a summer vacation at Elmer Berg's Shady Rest Resort in 1931. Elmer invited them to ride to Upper Priest Lake where he was delivering supplies for the Forest Service. They docked at Trapper Creek and were met by Pete Chase. He helped unload the boat and invited them to his cabin.

After the usual amenities Pete disappeared and soon returned with a gallon jug. He poured liquid from the jug into four tin cups and passed them to his guests with the elegance of a hostess at a sophisticated tea party. Catherine had never seen whiskey before, let alone taste it. She gamely took a swallow and still vividly remembers how the moonshine seemed to burn all the way down and back. Charlotte, who had had previous experience with liquor knew enough to barely sip the drink. Needless to say, Elmer, who had for years been one of Pete's drinking friends, drained his cup and Catherine's too.

Vivienne Beardmore McAlexander called Pete a good old sourdough. Everyone liked him because he was such a happy-go-lucky type. He trapped, made a little moonshine, picked huckleberries, and somehow made a living. When the mood struck him he would dig a little in his mine.

Vivienne said, "Pete was always willing to share what little bit he had. Anyone who came along cold, hungry, or just to visit found a haven at Pete's. He always had plenty of sourdough on hand. I remember when he would bring his furs and a bottle or two to Priest River. He always stayed at my Dad's St. Elmo Hotel."

Pete was a frequent visitor at the Geisingers. He, like Ike Daugherty, always called Fern, Vern. Fern remarked during an interview, "I have often wondered as I grow older if Pete Chase had a story behind him. His name wasn't Chase. He came from Chicago to Priest Lake.

"Pete was always a perfect gentleman to me. I never tasted his whiskey but from what I have heard it was pretty good moonshine. He would often stop by, come into the house and have coffee, a piece of pie, cake, or bread and was so refined and nice to have around."

Rose Hurst got very well acquainted with Pete when she was the Nordman postmaster. Her commentary on Pete was inimitable, to say the least.

"I welcomed conversation with Pete Chase. He had something to say that was worth listening to. He was just as sweet and tender as if he had been raised in a boy's college. His language, his appearance, his everything was just perfection. I was much attracted to him.

"I went up to vist him one time and when he met us at the dock he had on a new pair of pants, red socks, and house slippers. With white string he had taken from a flour sack he had put patches on the knees of his new overalls. The patches were more like a quilt. I said, 'Mr. Pete, you have intrigued me, why the patches on your new pants?' He said, 'Why that's where they wear out.' And how royally he entertained us! I wouldn't take a monkey-lot for the experiences I have had with these people.

"I really think that Pete made a little moonshine on the side. I never imbibe in the stuff. I don't like it and I don't like the results of it. I feel that if he wished to do it that was his own business and his privilege. I know he passed around a bottle very generously the night we were up there.

"I was very much saddened when I learned that Pete had drowned in the Thorofare. I felt that I had lost a good friend."

Pete always had the toe as well as the inside of his left shoe cut away to ease his painful ingrown toenail and bunion, observed an acquaintance of Pete's.

Pete was picked up from time to time by authorities for making moonshine. His friend, Elmer Berg, repeatedly told the story of one of his visits to the Sandpoint jail to see Pete. When he inquired at the desk about Pete, one of the deputies hollered at the jailer that a friend had come to see Pete. The jailer yelled back, "He's not in right now, he went downtown to get his breakfast."

Elmer also reported that Pete made a good thing out of his confinement. The jail was warm and confortable in the winter and he didn't have to cut the wood to keep it that way, as he would have had to do at his cabin on the lake. Besides the comforts, he practically had free run of the place.

Richard "Dick" Stejer, a vacationer and summer resident of Priest Lake for many years, said that while tramping the Upper Priest Lake trails late one fall he stopped by Pete's cabin and discovered a sign on the door. It read, "In jail in Sandpoint. Come in, I'll be back next spring."

Pete was very tight-lipped about his life prior to coming to Priest

Fig. 43 Pete Chase and Frank Algren in front of Pete's cabin. (H. Branyan Collection)

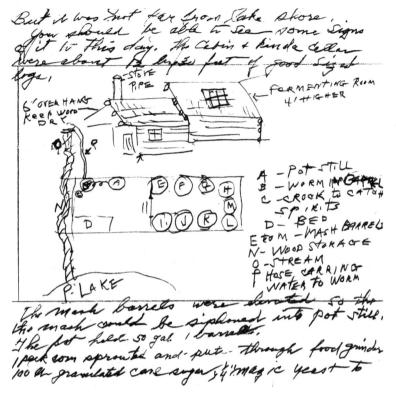

But it was not far from lake shore. You should be able to see some signs of it to this day. The cabin + kinda cellar were about 16 lyper feet of good sized logs.

STORE PIPE

FERMENTING ROOM 4' HIGHER

6' OVER HANG keep wood DRY

A — POT STILL
B — WORM IN BARREL
C — CROCK to CATCH SPIRITS
D — BED
E to M — MASH BARRELS
N — WOOD STORAGE
O — STREAM
P — HOSE CARRING WATER TO WORM

P. LAKE

The mash barrels were elevated so the the mash could be siphoned into pot still. The pot held 50 gal 1 barrel. 1 peck corn sprouted and put through food grinder 100 th granulated cane sugar, 4" magic yeast to

Fig. 44 Floor plan of Pete Chase's still. (Drawn by Harold Branyan in 1979)

Lake. Rumors abound about his past but no plausible story could be documented. Elmer knew that Pete was born and raised around Chicago.

Harold Branyan mentioned in a personal letter written in February, 1979, that Pete was like most of the other old-timers, very quiet, sincere, and honest.

"He was one of my favorite characters. I was 19 and he really tried to teach me the ways of life. He was a good trapper, conservative hunter, and did not kill for the sake of killing. We never caught more fish than we could eat.

"One time I trapped a skunk and Pete was going to show me how to skin him without the scent tainting the pelt. I had tied the trap to a small sapling as per instructions, as a skunk will not throw scent when in a trap. Pete cut the sapling and, holding it like a fish pole, drowned the skunk. He skinned it in the usual way and started to remove the scent glands, but there were no glands. The skunk was one of the Geisinger's descented escapees or it could have been one of Nell Shipman's descented skunks.

"Most of my stories came about at a fall bender held after the lake was closed and one in the spring after the tonic was out, rectified, and turning red in charred oak kegs. They were sampling parties and a good time was had by all.

According to Harold Branyan, Pete's still house was in a small bay between Granite Point (the rock bluff on the north side of Upper Priest Lake) and Trapper Creek. A small stream empties into the lake in shallow water. A dense undergrowth made the house hard to see from the lake. The cabin, with a cellar-like room, was about 12 x 30 feet and made of good-sized logs.

The mash barrels were elevated so the mash could be siphoned into the still pot. The still pot held 50 gallons. The recipe for the "product" included: one peck of corn sprouts, run through a food grinder, 100 pounds of granulated cane sugar, one-fourth pound of Magic yeast to each barrel. Fermenting time varied from 10 to 14 days.

Fig. 45 Harold Branyan's hunting dog, "Stub." (H. Branyan)

"Pete's spirits were double distilled and washed in about half sour mash. The liquor was 140% proof. It was cut to 100% proof with boiling hot spring water, filtered through charcoal and pure sand, and aged in new charred white oak kegs. It was a high quality pure product.

"During at least two or three tasting parties, Pete, with tears in his eyes, told about his old dog, Snyder. Pete made a pack saddle for Snyder as he always wanted to carry something. When Pete and Frank Brown were rum-running from Canada, Snyder carried four bottles in his pack saddle. After Snyder got old, Pete just put on the empty saddle.

"At one of the tasting parties, Pete's spirits loosened Cougar Gus' usually quiet tongue. He told about the time Hugh and he were running booze from Canada down the Kootenai. The water was swift and white, and when the Border Patrol yelled, Cougar rolled the canoe over and dumped the whiskey. 'Well, I lost the load, but by *Got* they didn't catch us anyhow.'

"One winter Pete Chase accidentally drove a pick through his left foot. Like anyone else that got hurt, Pete headed for Geisingers. Earl (Geisinger) was a druggist and had medicines and also a lot of nerve. He scrubbed Pete's foot, no simple job because Pete ran around barefooted most of the time. Earl took strips of gauze, poked them into the hole on top of Pete's foot and out the bottom. He put the foot in a basin of bichloride solution and drew the strips back and forth through the wound.

"Pete didn't move or say anything until the foot was bandaged. Then he said, 'Earl, that was pretty *salty*.' Earl gave Pete a bottle of the solution to keep the bandage wet. Pete got in his boat and went back to his cabin on Trapper Creek."

On his way home from visiting Elmer one evening, Pete drowned in the Thorofare at the S curve. It was never verified as to whether or not Pete suffered a severe heart attack or fell out of his boat while trying to start his outboard motor with the rope starter. Many people believe that he had imbibed too much at Elmer's and was a victim of his own well-known product.

Evidence of Pete's meticulous habits may be observed around the log building that now houses the Priest Lake Library. The building was constructed in 1934, during the WPA era, with Pete Chase serving as the log craftsman. Pete taught the seven-man crew how to peel, cut, and scribe the logs.

The crew was paid $35 a month for an 8 to 10 hour day, five days a week. The construction budget started at $60 to buy the logs.

Fig. 46 Pete Chase loading ore on his dock, Trapper Creek, Upper Priest Lake, 1924. (H. Branyan)

The building was the last log school house that was built in the State of Idaho. It housed the Priest Lake Elementary School until the present school house was built at Lamb Creek.

Friends of Pete took up a collection and gave Pete his last wish, by paying a pilot to scatter his ashes over the Thorofare and Upper Priest Lake.

Pete's name lives on, as Chase Lake, in Sec. 14, about three miles southwest of Coolin, bears his name. No date could be established as to the year the lake was given Pete's name. The name, Chase, was given to the lake sometime between 1894 and 1911. No record could be found as to when Pete arrived in the Priest Lake area, but the U.S. Geological Survey map of 1911, labels the body of water, Chase Lake.

For years it has been assumed that the lake was so named because Pete had a homestead on the lake. Neither the tract sheets in the Safeco Abstract Office or the deed books in the County Auditor's Office, Sandpoint, record a homestead for any person in Sec. 14. The

112

Fig. 47 Elmer Stone setting a trap on Chase Lake. (H. Branyan)

section was deeded to the State of Idaho by the U.S. Government on May 30, 1920. The State of Idaho declared it school property on December 5, 1921.

12

THE GEISINGER STORY
AN INCREDIBLE EPIC

The Geisinger story, rivaled only by the Shipman saga, spanned three decades shortly after the turn of the 20th century. In 1919, Earl Geisinger, in search of a place to realize his dream of outdoor living and wealth, landed on the upper end of the famous Priest Lake Thorofare.

Earl was born in Waterloo, Indiana, April 1, 1896, the only son of Lavina and Alfred Geisinger. He was destined, according to his family background, to be a medical doctor. At the time of his birth there had been 20 doctors before him in the Geisinger family. When he was discharged from the army after WW I he did study medicine for a year but his yen to live outdoors was stronger.

In 1916, prior to enlisting in the Armed Services during WW I, Earl received a degree in Pharmacy from the University of Indiana. The inside work was too confining for his peace of mind. It could be said that he was a restless young man who was blessed, or cursed, with a streak of wanderlust in his heart.

During the year Earl was studying medicine he wrote to a government bureau in Washington, D.C. and inquired about a place to raise silver fox. He was informed that the northern part of the State of Idaho was the best place in the United States to raise fur producing animals. He was also told that there was a place on Upper Priest Lake that was open for homesteading.

With this information and a dwindling desire to be a medical doctor, Earl and his partner, Carl Ritenour, left Indiana by car and headed west. When they got to Upper Priest Lake, the first of a series of adversities or events occurred that would try the patience of Job.

The tract of land that was available for homesteading when Earl wrote the government office, had been filed on by Alva Allen, a mail carrier from Spokane.

Earl's love of the outdoors and his undaunted desire to gamble with nature compelled him to investigate other sites for his dream spot to make a living raising silver foxes. Earl's partner, Ritenour,

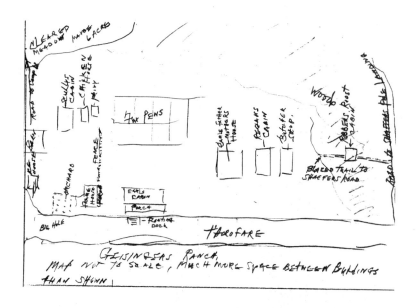

Fig. 48 The Geisinger Ranch. (Drawn by Harold Branyan, 1980)

was equally enthusiastic about the fur enterprise. They talked to Sam Byars who was an early homesteader near the mouth of the Thorofare. Byars told the men that J.F. "Johnnie" Malcolm had homesteaded a quarter section of land at the head of the Thorofare and wanted to sell. Malcolm still had several months to live on his homestead before he could prove up on the property. Earl made a deal that allowed him and Ritenour to live with Malcolm until the final papers were signed for ownership of the homesteaded acreage.

On the homestead Malcolm had built a good three-room frame house with an attic. It remained in good repair until after WW II. When the deal for purchase was made, Earl and Carl helped with some of the finish work and other improvements on the property.

Malcolm was a well-known Priest Laker and as early as May, 1914, the *Priest River Times* newspaper carried a personal item that, "J.F. Malcolm is spending a few days in our midst and reported that fishing was fine in the little lake."

As irony would have it for Earl, when Malcolm went to Coeur d'Alene, Idaho, to prove up on his homestead, he was notified that the land did not belong to the United States Government. The land

115

was railroad property from the original railroad right-of-way land grant. As a sidelight the *Priest River Times* reported, in part, that, "It is hoped that the railroad company would have a heart and relinquish its right and, in lieu of script." According to the tract sheets on file in the Safeco Abstract Office in Sandpoint, Idaho, the railroad did have a heart and deeded the property to John F. Malcolm, October 30, 1919. At the time the mistake was discovered, Malcolm had lived on the homestead for five years.

Fig. 49 Lavina Geisinger and her pet silver fox, "Gretta," 1925.
(Geisinger Collection)

After the property issue was settled and the Geisingers became the legal owners, Earl engaged the services of a Canadian fur expert to teach him the details of raising foxes. Together they built the pens and shelters to produce the best type of silver fox pelts. The original foxes that were obtained by Earl came from the fur expert's Canadian farm. The largest number of foxes that the Geisingers had at one time was six pairs.

During this era the pelt of silver foxes was highly prized as material for women's coats and neckpieces. The silver fox is a color phase of the North American red fox. The color of the fur is black and the individual hairs tipped with white. Foxes of this type are bred for their beautiful pelts.

In due course, fox farming became routine and Earl's thoughts dwelt more frequently on Fern Merritt, the girl he had left in Indiana, who was by that time teaching school. Fern was born August 7, 1895 in Seymour, Iowa. She was the daughter of William and Josephine Merritt. She was graduated in teacher-training from Valparaiso University in Indiana. For several years Fern taught school in Greybull, Wyoming and Ottumwa, Iowa. During the summer of 1920, she came west and on July 26, she and Earl were married in the Sandpoint Methodist Church parsonage at eight o'clock in the evening.

The day after Fern and Earl were married, they went to Priest River where they met Earl's grandparents, an aunt, and a young cousin who had just arrived from Indiana. They all went together to the Geisinger home at the mouth of Upper Priest Lake. A few days later the entire family went to the Schurr farm to pick strawberries, gooseberries, and blueberries. Fern had not been out in the sun for any length of time that summer and she commented, "I got sunburned to beat the band. I didn't eat much breakfast and we didn't take much lunch. With my sunburn and hunger I hated the country and everybody in it."

Later in the same year Fern had another experience that didn't endear the country to her either. She, Earl, an aunt, Earl's father, and grandfather went on a deer hunting trip between Trapper Creek and the head of Upper Priest River. The party took along dried venison and munched away on it during the day. Fern was carrying the guns on the return trip because Earl and his father were each carrying a deer that they had bagged. She was struggling along the side of the mountain where there was no trail. Earl finally said to her, "I'll carry the guns from here. You will do well if you get yourself down out of here." Fern replied, "I'll make it somehow, even though I'm going to die right on the spot if I don't get a drink." About that time she tried to crawl over a deadfall with a gun in each hand, and caught the seat of her pants on a broken limb. She exclaimed, "Oh my! There I was trying to hang onto some bushes and the guns and trying to get myself unhooked! I dropped both guns and started fighting the air with both my hands and feet. I wish I had a picture of the men laughing at me while I was trying to get off that snag.

"We finally got down to the lake and Grandfather Geisinger was sitting on a rock waiting for us. I was so thirsty I laid down on my

117

stomach in front of him, which was the first spot I hit near the water, and started to drink, even though the seat of my pants was still hanging on the limb that I got caught on. Grandfather was a good sport because all he said was, the lake went down two inches while I was getting a drink. Water never tasted so good! We had a lot of experiences at Priest Lake."

One fall a young Forest Service employee and his wife were staying at the Beaver Creek Ranger Station. They came frequently to the Geisinger home to play pinochle during the long evenings. The two couples got along very well even though the young wife was an eastern girl and the west was nothing but bad news for her.

One evening the young man asked the Geisingers what they were going to do all winter. He was told that they had their foxes, chickens, and cows to tend, which took a lot of time. Earl also had the job of keeping the snow shoveled off the roofs of the Beardmore logging camp buildings on Caribou Creek.

They generally read until three or four o'clock in the morning. The source of the reading material came from the Schurrs who had a niece in Newport, Washington who had a newspaper and magazine shop. She would tear off the front cover of the magazines that did not sell and send them back to get a refund. She would put the magazines, minus covers, in a box for the Schurrs who would share them with the Geisingers. Both families had ample reading material for the long winter nights. When the Geisinger cabin was torn down for the timber, there were hundreds of magazines stored everywhere in the house.

Another story that had a sad ending for the Geisingers involved the young Forest Service employee. He misread his map and told Earl and Fern they owned some well-timbered land across the Thorofare. He told them the land was part of the original Malcolm property. Within a day or two he came up with his map and with Earl ran a boundary line according to the map. It was about a quarter of a mile down the Thorofare and almost an equal distance along the south shoreline of Upper Priest Lake. He suggested that Earl log the land as the timber was mature and ready to cut.

Mrs. Geisinger remarked, "We did it as innocently as my cat! On the basis of our good log crop we decided to buy a new car and take a trip back east to visit my folks in Iowa and Earl's folks in Indiana. While we were visiting we got word from the Forest Service that we owed them for the timber that we had cut. On our way back we stopped in Missoula, Montana, and Earl talked to a good friend of his who was in the main office of the Kaniksu National Forest. He was not able to help us.

"The young man that told us the property was ours had left the country. He turned out to be a fickle individual. Had he been around, he might have stood up for us, but I doubt it. We surely got in bad with that deal. We thought we had some money and we really didn't make a dime."

At one time or another the Geisingers befriended practically every old-timer who lived on Upper Priest Lake. One winter Tommy Warden, a trapper, had a serious stroke. Earl and his partner, Ritenour, pulled him on a sled over ice, snow, and slush from the mouth of Upper Priest River to Coolin, a distance of approximately 26 miles. Many times they had to put in to shore as the ice was not safe to travel on.

They did get Tommy to Coolin and put him on the stage for Priest River. They arranged with friends in Priest River to put the old gentleman on the train and send him to the Old Soldier's Home in Boise, Idaho. For several years Tommy had told Fern that he would give her his cabin because she had been so good to him. He never got around to it. Ike Daugherty eventually moved into the cabin.

"In one way," Mrs. Geisinger said, "I'm glad Ike Daugherty got Tommy's cabin as he really was a good neighbor. He would tow things in our rowboat down the lake for us and bring back anything we needed. I really don't know how he did it. He always called me 'Vern' for he could never say 'Fern.' He talked a lot but after an evening of talking he would say, 'Now Vern and Earl, don't believe all the things I tell you.!'

"Ike was Molly Moyer's father. Molly and I spent a lot of time together canning and drying foodstuffs. One year Molly put up 80 pints of wild asparagus and shared them with us. I used to fish a lot with Molly's husband, Dewey. He was like Earl. Everyone used to say that Earl Geisinger could put a bucket in the backyard and catch fish from it.

"Ike Daugherty would come to our house quite often in the winter time just to argue with Earl. I didn't mind that so much but he would spit tobacco juice on our living room stove. I crabbed so much about it that Earl got a coffee can and filled it half full of sawdust. Earl said, 'Now when he comes tell him to spit in the can.' The next time he came he got ready to spit on the stove and I yelled at him, 'Wait a minute.' I ran out and got the coffee can, gave it to him and said, 'Here spit in this when you are in my house.' From that time on when he came he would bring the coffee can in from the porch where I kept it.

"He would tell the wildest tales. After dinner one day Earl finally said, 'I've got to go to work.' Ike said, 'Anybody who works is a damn fool!' Earl said, 'I like to eat and I have to work to eat.' It didn't bother Ike in the least. Most of the time he lived on practically nothing except what he could shoot on land or catch out of the lake."

Fig. 50 Ike Daugherty with his hand-made boat, "The Snail." (H. Branyan)

Another old-timer, Frank "The Finn" Algren, told Fern that he wasn't going to live very long and he wanted to give her his houseboat. By that time she was getting a bit gun-shy of such offers and told Frank, in plain English, that if he really wanted to give her anything to put it in black and white and then she would have claim to it. He told her he would do it. He died before he got around to writing a will or giving Fern a written statement that she was to have his houseboat.

Late in the fall one year, two young men showed up at the Geisingers and asked if they could build a small cabin back of their place. They claimed to be writers. They had plenty of money to pay for a huge grubstake they brought up for the winter and the lumber and supplies they hauled from Leonard Paul's store to build their cabin. The men had their mail go to a girl in Ohio who sent it out west to them. While building their cabin they lived in one of the Geisinger's small cabins.

The boys took turns doing the cooking and seemed to get along very well. Earl was at their cabin one day and he picked up a book and was thumbing through it when he noticed the two looking at each other. Whatever it was that Earl saw, the boys knew that he had found out something about them. Mrs. Geisinger had forgotten the details but the information gave the boys away. They gave Earl a Colt-45 which was later stolen. It was one of the two items in all the years they lived on Upper Priest Lake that was stolen from their cabin. Earl always thought the '45 was given to him as a bribe, but he never had any notion of turning the boys in. The other item was her sewing machine.

Before the end of the first year one of the boys, known as Bob, got cold feet and left the country. The other, known as Don McRae lived with the Gumaers at the head of the little lake after Bob left. Don gave Sylvia Gumaer a good violin that he had. Fern said of the young men, "I have always thought they were guilty of deserting the army as they claimed they had retired from the service."

Life in the early days on Priest Lake was an individual affair. No one took any time to pry into a neighbor's background. All the old-timers respected the rights of his fellow man and went about his own business and kept his mouth shut.

One winter Earl was criticized by local people and members of the Humane Society because he fed old horses to the foxes. In answer to the criticism Pop Geisinger always said, "Is it better to let old horses without teeth slowly starve to death around a straw stack or put them out of their misery and utilize the body for animal food? Who is to say which is right and which is wrong."

One spring Earl was getting ready to take the winter's pelts to market. Prior to setting a day to go to Nordman with the load, he checked with Mary and Bill Donaldson who had just returned from a trip to Granite Creek. The Donaldsons reported that the ice was crusted on top and held up by blue ice underneath, which indicated it was safe to travel on.

The next day, Fern, Earl, and their friend, Harold Branyan, loaded seven pelts and four live foxes on a big sled and started from the head of the big lake, pulling and pushing the sled. By the time they got halfway to Granite Creek the ice got bad. They were in the middle of the wide part of the lake between Tripod Point and East Twin Island. They had to keep going for it was as bad to turn back as it was to go on and each hour the weather was getting warmer.

In anticipation of having to cope with bad ice, Earl had loaded a long pole and a 10 foot one inch x 12 inch board on the sled. He would test the ice with the pole and if it seemed critical he would get to the back of the sled and place the 10 foot board under the sled between the runners and push the sled to the end of it by walking on the board. He repeated the process over and over to get across the air holes and the dangerous spots. Harold would push or pull the sled when the ice was safe and change jobs with Earl from time to time. Fern said she screamed each time the sled broke through. Her screaming finally got to Earl and he calmly sat down on the board and said, "Everytime you scream I get paralyzed. If I don't stay relaxed we'll never make it."

Earl was a good man on the ice. He had respect for it but at the same time had a lot of confidence in his ability to cope with the various ice conditions on the lake. One time the ice was so clear and smooth he skated from Forest Lodge to Coolin in one hour and 15 minutes with a strong north wind at his back. He made the return trip the same day in two hours and 45 minutes. Fern said that Earl taught her how to travel on ice. When she first started she got so tired she couldn't keep up to Earl and he was pulling a sled. Under Earl's tutelage she learned to relax by changing pace and occasionally trotting a little to keep all leg and arm muscles loose and relaxed. A relaxed condition of the body is absolutely necessary when traveling over thin or rotten ice.

Fern relived the experience as she told the story. Her voice, on tape, responded to the gravity of the situation, by stating, "I steeled myself against screaming. I died a thousand deaths during the next seven or eight hours of trying to get off the ice. We kept going and I'll admit the Lord was looking after us. I really don't know how we made it. We finally got down to a spot between East Twin Island and where Two Mouth Creek enters the lake." At this point Earl decided to send Fern and Harold ahead in an attempt to reach the shore. He would take the sled and the load across the ice, such as it was. The little fox terrier dog was put on the sled as he was played out fighting the slush. Fern and Harold carefully inched their way across the rotten ice. They finally reached a tree that had fallen into the lake and dragged themselves to the bank. Fern said she sat half dazed, on the log, watching Earl out there on the slush, creeping along as lightly as possible, wondering how he would ever get out of it. What seemed to her an eternity, Earl gamely got the sled with its precious load safely to the shore.

After a hurried conference it was decided to send Fern along the trail to Roy Gregory's ranch across the narrows from the W.E. Stevens' Granite Creek Resort. Earl made it very clear to his wife that he didn't want her back on the ice regardless of what happened. She replied, just as emphatically, that she had no intention of ever taking one step on bad ice for as long as she lived!

Fig. 51 Earl Geisinger and pet horse, "Charlie," 1925.
(Geisinger Collection)

When Fern reached the Gregorys she reported that Earl and Harold would spend the night at one of the Angstadt cabins. She said that she had not been afraid of walking the last two miles at night because she had her fox terrier with her. He was little but brave and could bark loud and clear when necessary.

As soon as Fern arrived, Mrs. Gregory immediately packed food for the men and foxes and Roy took it to the cabin where Earl and Harold were holed up for the night. By the time Gregory got there they had a good fire going and were drying their clothes. The cabin was warm and comfortable for the men and the live foxes.

Fig. 52 Alfred Geisinger, 1925. (Geisinger Collection)

The next morning Joe Cyr, who lived near the mouth of Granite Creek across the lake, saw smoke coming from the Angstadt cabin. He went over in his boat and invited Earl and Harold for breakfast. The foxes, pelts, and the sled were put into Joe's boat and rowed across the narrows to Joe's place. He cooked them a first class breakfast of meat, pancakes, and coffee. Mrs. Geisinger slept the clock around in Gregory's bunkhouse and after a famous Mrs. Gregory breakfast Fern was taken by boat to Granite Creek. The sled with the year's work aboard was pulled to Nordman and sent by stage to market via Priest River.

One of the first stories that Elmer Berg would tell his guests was about the time two foolhardy young men drove a Model T Ford up the lake on the ice from Granite Creek to the Thorofare. Some guests doubted the story. In January, 1980 the author got a letter from Harold Branyan that gives credence to Elmer's story.

"In the middle of January, 1930 I walked out on the ice to get the mail. The ice looked good but it had a few cracks here and there. As a precaution I carried an eight foot, eight inch cedar board instead of a thumping pole and had no trouble. I stayed with a smoke chaser friend, Earl Colburn, who lived with his parents at Reeder Creek.

"The next morning was cold, windstill, and bright sunshine. Earl suggested that he take me back to Geisingers in his Model T. I wasn't too keen on it, because I had a lot of respect for the lake. I got foolish and said, 'OK.'

"Dalkena had a logging operation on Granite Creek and the road was open to the mouth of the creek. We got on the ice and headed north. The ice was just rough enough to give fair traction with no snow to slow us down. Earl pulled the Ford's ears down and she ran smooth and probably got up to 40 or 50 miles per hour. I was scared of the cracks, but she skipped over them with just a slight hushed thump. In minutes we were on the beach a little north of Daddy Duffill's boat house. Dad had us in for a drink which settled my nerves.

"Earl left for the return trip and I took what mail I had left and walked up the Thorofare trail. I know I would have backed out of a return trip by car. Earl made it back without any trouble."

In 1923, Earl's parents sold their farm in Indiana and moved west to join Earl and Fern at the fox farm on Upper Priest Lake. Earl's father rode west in a box car that held farm horses, one cow, 17 chickens, three dogs, a piano, and enough furniture and other furnishing to equip a four-room house. Sam Byars met Pop Geisinger at Coolin when he arrived by wagon freight with his load from Priest River. Sam towed his barge loaded with all the freight to Forest Lodge on the north side of the mouth of the Thorofare. It was dark when they arrived, which was par for the trip, as Fern remarked from time to time, "For a dozen reasons, if a trip was completed in the daylight hours it was a miracle."

The next morning when they went down to the dock the barge was lopsided, the cow was standing in three feet of water, the bedding and most of the household goods were soaking wet, but the chickens were high and dry. Sam had the foresight to put the chicken crate in the launch the night before.

When Earl's mother saw the mess she put her hands on her hips and said, "I think I'll go right back to Indiana!" Everything but the cow and the piano was hauled up the Thorofare to the farm by rowboat. The cow was led up the trail. The water was too low in the Thorofare to haul the piano in a rowboat. Sam Byars bought it and it graced the living room of his Forest Lodge Hotel until the building and all its contents burned during the fire in November, 1940.

The wet bedding, boxes, and everything else that got soaked were put on the porch of the Geisinger house. It took the rest of the winter to dry it out over the cook stove and wood heater.

THE DUCOMMUN DRAMA

A well-known story and one of the most dramatic events to come out of the Priest Lake country was the attempted rescue and the drowning of trapper George Ducommun.

Fern Geisinger and her daughter Ann, were the heroines of the ill-fated struggle. The Sandpoint, Idaho newspaper, *The Daily Bulletin*, dated Monday, January 24, 1938, carried the story as told by the men who recovered and brought the body out to civilization from the roadless area of Upper Priest Lake. The dramatic account as it appeared in the newspaper is included in its entirety and it will be followed by the story as told by Fern and her daughter, Ann, during a personal interview, April 9 and 10, 1978.

WOMAN IS HEROINE OF LAKE TRAGEDY

"The story of the heroic struggle of a woman to rescue a trapper from drowning and the struggle of two men to bring the body out to civilization, was unfolded to Sheriff Warren Rapp and Highway Patrolman Robert C. Thomas Sunday morning when they received a call from Elkins Resort at Reeder Bay on Priest Lake.

The two men who brought the body, Dewey Moyer and Elmer Berg, told the two officers the following story.

On Wednesday, January 19, about 12:30 or 1:00 PM George Ducommun, who had been trapping in the region for the past three years, attempted to cross the ice near the head of the Thorofare between lower and upper Priest lakes. The thin ice gave way and he fell into about 15 feet of water.

He wore snowshoes and carried a loaded packsack. The place where the accident occurred was about a half mile north of the home of Mr. and Mrs. Earl Geisinger.

Fig. 53 George Ducommun, 1886-1938
(June Wells Collection)

WENT TO AID

Mrs. Geisinger and her daughter, Josephine (Ann) heard Ducommun's cries for help and she went immediately to his rescue. She attempted to go to his aid by using a boat, but found it impossible to reach Ducommun because of the intervening ice, so she jumped into the water and swam out to the edge of the ice and attempted to break away the ice with an axe and an oar but still could not reach the trapper. Mrs. Geisinger then swam back to shore, got a long pole and again swam to the edge of the ice near the trapper, but still was unable to reach the man.

Ducommun spoke a few words to her and then seemed to lose consciousness and turned upside down with his head under water and his feet upright. Mrs. Geisinger then swam back to shore, warmed herself at her cabin, secured an old boat, and rowed two miles to Forest Lodge down the Thorofare to the place of Mr. and Mrs. Dewey Moyer, arriving there about 4:00 PM. Moyer went across the Thorofare and notified Mr. Berg, who returned with him. Mr. and Mrs. Moyer, Mr. Berg, and Mrs. Geisinger all rowed back to the Geisinger place arriving about 8:00 PM.

BODY RECOVERED

Berg and Moyer dragged a boat along the shore ice and launched it near where the trapper disappeared. They found his body, floating upside down, in the cold water about 10:30 PM.

Berg and Moyer lashed the body to the boat and went ashore to the Geisinger cabin for the night. At daylight on Thursday, Berg and Moyer dragged the laden boat near shore, secured a motor belonging to Ducommun from the latter's cabin, and went down the Thorofare, which was open water as far as Forest Lodge.

There the men took the boat to Berg's place, loaded the boat with the body on two hand sleds, and pulled the boat on the sleds about one and one half miles to Tripod Point.

It took all day to make the complete trip from the Geisinger house to Tripod Point and when the men got to the open water and started to launch the boat it immediately sank with the body in 20 feet of water because it had become water-logged. The two men fished the boat and body out of the lake again and put the body underneath the overturned boat for the night.

Friday at daylight the ice was mushy on the lake and a heavy wind was blowing from the southwest. To add to their disagreeable task, it was snowing heavily. So the men decided to stay at Tripod Point all day and rest.

LAKE TOO ROUGH

Saturday it had cleared and they dragged the laden boat over the snow to open water and mushy ice to Bottle Bay. The lake was so rough that they could not launch the boat so the men had to stay there all night. Early Sunday morning, before daylight, they got the boat into the water and rowed to Elkins Resort on Reeder Bay, arriving there about 8:00 AM.

Sheriff Rapp was called and he and Thomas drove the 60 miles to the resort and brought the body to the Moon Mortuary here.

Ducommun had a sign on his cabin door stating that in case of death or illness, one should notify Mrs. Mary Messerly, Route 1, Florence, Kansas.

He had no known relatives here and came to the Priest Lake area from Wyoming about three years before.

Recalling the story as she remembered it and supplemented and verified by daughter Ann, Mrs. Geisinger related the following sequence of events on the fateful day, January 19, 1938.

The day was sunny and warm. George just happened to drop by while Ann and her mother were having a late breakfast. He was invited to join them. During the meal, Ducommun said that he was on his way to Upper Priest River country to check his trap line. Fern said, "I warned him to be sure to stay on safe ice by going to his left away from the shoreline over toward the 'big rock.'"

After breakfast George waved a cheery goodbye. Mrs. Geisinger again warned him to stay clear of the bad ice along the shore where a small creek runs into the lake. Ann went upstairs to her playhouse. Mrs. Geisinger closed the door because she had to keep the family's pet deer, Mary Lou, inside until George got out of sight because she would follow along behind him wherever he went.

Fern got busy baking bread as she had told George to stop by for dinner and she would have light bread biscuits, one of George's favorite foods.

A short time after Ducommun left, Ann called to her mother that she could hear George calling. Mrs. Geisinger could not hear a voice but she could hear the chickens around the steps. She made light of Ann's comment and told her that it was only the chickens outside. Ann insisted that it was George calling. When Fern opened the door she heard the words, "Help! Help!" Looking north she immediately realized that George had not heeded her warning and had struck out directly across the ice where the creek water had softened it. The voice continued to call so Ann and her mother ran to the Thorofare where they kept their rowboat and rowed to the ice on the lake. They couldn't break the slush ice on the lake from where they were in the open water of the Thorofare.

Fern said to her daughter, "I'll go on as I have my rubber boots on." Ann said, "I don't want to go over there!" Fern said, "You don't have to go!" Fern went over to where George was and he said, "Oh, I knew you would come! But you're too late, I'm gone now!" She said, "No, you're not, you just hang on. I'm going to get you out!" She said to herself, "Oh, what will I do? What will I do? How can I help him?"

Fern continued, "I went up the creek a little way and found a long pole. I had brought along one oar from the boat so I pushed the pole and the oar out as far as I could. From there I hollered to Ann to go to George's porch and get a rope that he always kept there. But George was funny. He always locked his door but never the screen door on the porch. That morning he had locked his screen door too, so Ann couldn't get the rope. I said to George, 'Just hang on, I'll be back.' We kept yelling back and forth. Then George said, 'I'm gone.' He let his elbows slide off the ice and down he went. I just walked back to the house carrying my boots as I had gotten them full of water."

After changing to dry clothing Ann and her mother rowed their boat to Forest Lodge at the mouth of the Thorofare. They reported George's drowning to Dewey and Molly Moyer who were staying at the lodge that winter. Dewey went over to Elmer Berg's place and the two of them started to gather the gear necessary for an attempt to locate the body. By the time the party got back to the Geisinger home it was almost dark.

Dewey and Elmer, even though it was late, immediately took their pike poles, grappling hooks, and ropes, loaded them into a boat and dragged it across the ice to the open water where George went down. It didn't take too long to locate the body and get it to shore.

When the men returned, Molly and Fern had dinner waiting and since it was so late the Moyers and Elmer stayed the night.

Early the next morning Dewey and Elmer walked along the shore and got George's body, which was frozen stiff, and carried it to the open water at the head of the Thorofare in front of the Geisinger house. After breakfast the Moyers and Elmer took the body to Elmer's cabin. Elmer and Dewey told Fern and Ann essentially the same story about the trip down the big lake as was reported in the *Sandpoint Daily Bulletin*.

The Ducommun file at the Moon Mortuary in Sandpoint contained the following highlights to complete the story.

George Ducommun was born in Switzerland about 1886 as his age at death was determined at "about 52." He served an apprenticeship as a Swiss watchmaker and as a young man migrated to the United States. He worked at his trade until he enlisted in WW I, October 4, 1917. Prior to coming to Upper Priest Lake in 1931, he had been employed as a cook at Washington State College.

Ducommun's aunt, Mary Messerly, requested that George's body be buried in a good cemetery. He was buried in the Sandpoint Pinecrest Cemetery, the American Legion plot, January 28, 1938.

The story was picked up by Associated Press and published in many newspapers throughout the country. Later in 1938, the story was dramatized over a Chicago radio station.

Several tales of a legendary nature have developed over the drowning of George Ducommun. One well-known version relates the story of how Mrs. Geisinger walked to Elmer Berg's on a beautiful moonlight night when the forests and the Thorofare were covered by a mantle of new snow. Emphasis is given in the tale to how Mrs. Geisinger had such a guilty feeling before God for thinking how beautiful the night was when she was going forth on such a tragic errand. Fern remarked that it was a lovely setting but a long way from the truth.

The dramatics of the story inspired Pam Hilty of BCCA to write the words for a folk song telling the story, to the tune of "Go Tell Aunt Rhoda." It has not been possible to trace the story as to where Pam got the name 'Flo.' The song is sung around the campfires of Beaver Creek Camp so often that many old-timers have been surprised to learn that the heroine's name was 'Fern' and not 'Flo.' It was not necessary to "go tell" the person that attempted the rescue, nor did he drown in the Thorofare!

> Go tell Flo Geisinger
> Go tell Flo Geisinger
> Go tell Flo Geisinger
> That George Ducommun is dead.
>
> He died in the Thorofare
> He died in the Thorofare
> He died in the Thorofare
> Standing on his head.
>
> The pack he was carrying
> The pack he was carrying
> The pack he was carrying
> Was heavier than lead.

The biscuits she was making
The biscuits she was making
The biscuits she was making
She need not have made.

It was true, however, that George's pack was "heavier than lead." He was trapping bear as well as smaller animals. He carried a bear trap vise in his pack as it was impossible to set the bear traps without a vise to hold the steel springs when the jaws were set. The vise and the traps probably weighed 75 or 80 pounds.

Mrs. Geisinger mentioned several times during the interview that in spite of the fact that Priest Lake was a long way from civilization she never had a dull moment. She was a good cook and loved to do it. She was a warm-hearted person and loved to read or visit.

Fig. 54 The Geisinger home, 1928. (H. Branyan)

Care of the livestock they kept on the farm occupied a lot of time. Fern always had chickens around. She said, "If I knew then what I know now I would have had a lot more chickens when I was at Priest Lake. I could really talk them into laying, even in the winter time. I needed a lot of eggs to cook with and the loggers, trappers, and campers were all willing to pay good money for fresh eggs."

In addition to the daily routine of caring for the animals, gathering and storing of food was almost a continuous task. In late

Fig. 55 The Geisinger chicken house, 1956. (H. Branyan)

summer wild hay had to be cut and stacked on Armstrong Meadow and the meadow behind Sam Byars' resort. It was not possible to raise tame hay or feed grains in the area. In addition to the wild hay, they would spend many days each fall pulling tule stalks from the bay on the south side of the upper lake just across the Thorofare. The stalks were dried for cow and horse feed. The cows liked the stalks and did very well on the diet of wild hay and dried tules. The tules had a bitter taste to a human but when they were properly dried no taste could be detected in the milk.

One year when a good crop of hay was cut on the meadow back of the Byars' resort, the Thorofare froze over with ice thick enough to hold a team of horses and a sleigh full of hay. Some days when Earl would have to haul hay, the day would warm up enough to make the ice unsafe to return. When this happened he would take the team and sleigh to Byars in the evening, load the hay, and the next morning at daybreak would pull the load up the Thorofare.

One night the temperature dropped to 35° below at the Geisingers and 17° below at Byars. Earl got worried about Fern keeping warm so he started from Byars at 4:00 AM and arrived home a little after 5:00 AM only to find that Fern had everything under control.

133

Throughout the night she got up every two hours, stoked the heater and the cook stove, the heater in the cellar, and a little wood stove they had in the chicken house.

Later Fern wrote to the family back in Indiana and told them that they had been pretty busy. One day they put up hay in the barn and the next day they put up ice.

Cabin fires during the cold winter months were a continuous threat to the peace of mind for people in the north woods. The types of stoves, chimneys, and roof jacks left a lot to be desired for safety features. Over the years Frank Brown, Pete Chase, Ike Daugherty, Daddy Duffill, and the Forest Lodge all burned out.

Harold Branyan related a fire story of the Geisinger house when he and his dad stayed in during the winter of 1928-29.

"I was getting ready to retire and had just finished stoking the stove when a burning ember dropped from the ceiling along the stove pipe.

"Dad went up the ladder to the attic and I handed him the bucket of drinking water. I grabbed an empty and ran to the spring barefooted and in my long-johns. It was -30° with a wind blowing. I chopped the ice over the water hole at the spring, filled the bucket, scaled the ladder that always stood leaning on the porch, just in case, poured the water over a 2 foot square of burning shakes. The water froze on the shakes as soon as it hit the roof.

"I don't know how many times I repeated the process. Dad was doing the same thing inside the attic. When we got the fire out my feet were frozen, but after rubbing them with bear gall and getting them warmed up by the stove, they were OK. From that time on we checked the stove pipe every day during the cold snap.

"Cougar Gus was the one person on the lake that never burned out. He was very, very careful about fire. He had only one stove in his float house. It was a small airtight sheet metal heater half full of clay and ashes. It sat in the center of a framework filled with five or six inches of sand. He cooked on it as well as used it to heat the room. Before he left his cabin he always stirred the live embers into the ashes, set the airtight lid, and then rechecked it."

One of Fern's favorite foods and one which she enjoyed making was Hawaiian Belle pie. It was a light cream pie made with whipped egg whites. One day she felt like being creative and started to make her Hawaiian Belle pie. Many of her eggs had been in salt storage for some time so she had trouble making them whip properly. After several attempts she did get a batch to stand up and she made a lovely pie. Earl had always said that he didn't care for soft pies but preferred apple pie. So to please Earl she also made an apple pie.

At lunch she coaxed her husband to eat a very small sliver of her Hawaiian Belle pie. About the time he had finished the sliver of pie the dogs began to bark and Fern, with hands folded said, "Dear Lord, please send men that will eat my Hawaiian Belle pie." Earl opened the door to see what the commotion was about and there stood Elmer Berg, his friend Jack Rule, and Daddy Duffill. Earl said, "Come in, men, come in. You are the answer to a woman's prayer!" They consumed the Hawaiian Belle pie as well as the apple pie and Earl had to be content with his sliver of soft pie.

Each year Molly Moyer and Fern would get together to can jars and jars of mushrooms. Fern said that she was afraid of mushrooms until George Ducommun told her to watch the squirrels and eat only those that the squirrels gathered. He also told her that, if she ever suspected that a jar of mushrooms were bad, to put a penny in the jar and if the penny turned green she should bury them because they were poisonous.

One year Fern went back east to visit her parents and when she got back to Coolin she was to go up the lake with Sam Byars. He invited her to have some lunch before they left. She told him that she was not hungry but she really didn't want to take the time to eat as she was so anxious to get home. Sam didn't say anything but went in to Mrs. Handy's and ate.

On the way up the lake Sam pulled in at every bay and resort to deliver mail, supplies, and passengers and it was dark by the time the launch docked at Forest Lodge. "By that time, "Fern said, "I was so starved, I could have eaten the boards off the side of the boat." Earl was at the dock and Sam remarked, "I guess your wife is almost starved to death. I told her we were going to eat before we left but she wasn't hungry then!"

"It was just another Priest Lake lesson to be learned. You eat when there is food," was Fern's concluding remark.

In 1926, Earl's father and mother decided to go back to Indiana and start a fox farm there. Earl and Fern raised foxes for three more years.

THE STAR SKUNKS

The winter after the elder Geisingers went back to Indiana, Fern's parents sent her $135 to go into the skunk raising business. The $100 was to buy four skunks, one male and three females. The $35 was for material to build the pens.

The day was set for the arrival of the skunks and Earl and Fern went to Granite Creek in their wooden boat, powered by a small putt-

putt motor. They went on to Priest River and brought the descented skunks back in a crate on the stage. When they got back to Granite Creek the ice was so thick that they did not attempt to go back up the lake that night. They stayed the night in an old deserted cabin. They built a fire in an oil can, but the can got so hot it burned the floor so they had to toss it outside. It had provided enough heat to warm the cabin for the night. The next day the ice was still in. They were befriended by a young couple who had a nice cabin near the mouth of Granite Creek.

Fig. 56 "Old Jerry," a deer, "Stubby," and H. Branyan's father, October, 1929. (H. Branyan)

The following day the ice had shifted enough for them to return home with the skunks. They put them in their pens, and with the Geisinger luck running true to form, the skunks were gone the next morning. Without rancor or emotion Mrs. Geisinger said, "We didn't know anything about skunks and when we built the pens we didn't bury the wire or put in heavy planks for a floor and they proceeded to dig under the logs that were just setting on top of the ground.

"If you ever see any skunks running around Priest Lake with a star on their forehead, they are the grandchildren, several times over, of the star skunks we imported from Denver, Colorado. There must be at least 35 or 40 generations of fine fur-bearing star skunks in the Kaniksu National Forest."

Just before the arrival of daughter, Josephine Ann, they decided to move to Spokane where medical services were available. After Ann was born, November, 1929, Earl got an offer to operate a fox fur farm in Tacoma. He accepted the offer as it seemed in the best interests for infant Ann as well as financially for the entire family.

During those depression years the fox farm in Tacoma went out of business and Earl, along with millions of others, lost everything they had and were in the unemployment lines.

Earl, with his ability to promote various ventures, promoted and operated a rabbit business for two years in Tacoma. "It went kaput," in Fern's words. "We lost our shirts and Earl almost lost his mind worrying about it."

Then they decided to buy a tie mill in Tacoma and ship it to Twin Lakes and go into the railroad tie business. The venture was not a success. Earl then decided he would go logging. Earl's mother was with the family at the time and it seemed best for the women to go back to Priest Lake as they didn't have money to rent a house. When he finished logging, he searched for another job to earn money for food. He had let his pharmacy license lapse so that possibility was out. He did settle for a job with the Employment Office of the State of Idaho. After a training period he was sent to Sandpoint.

During the late summer of 1938, Fern, Ann, and Grandma Geisinger moved to Sandpoint where Earl had rented a house that had reverted to the Household Owner's Loan Corporation. They took an option to buy it. They put a lot of hard work in on the place only to have it sold out from under them, through no fault of their own.

They purchased a 14-acre tract out of Sandpoint on Sandcreek, toward Bonners Ferry. They lived there for almost five years before Earl was transferred to the Boise office. In Boise, Fern worked as a bank messenger until she got a contract to teach in the Boise Public Schools.

The Employment Service put Earl on what he called the "milk run" and he spent most of his working days travelling to towns in southern Idaho. This he did not enjoy, so he quit his job, got a partner and started an auction commission house in Boise. He later sold out to his partner and started an auction commission house in Mountain Home, Idaho. It didn't pay its way so he rented the old Masonic Temple building in Mountain Home and started a secondhand store.

Fern continued her teaching in Boise. Earl's health was failing. He went to the Veteran's Hospital in Boise. After a month of examinations, an inoperable tumor was found on his lungs. Earl died September 19, 1959. He was buried in the Cloverdale Cemetery, Boise, Idaho.

The major catastrophe that occurred in the lives of the Geisinger family was undoubtedly the loss of their farm on Upper Priest Lake. It started in 1931 when the Geisinger property was deeded to Bonner County for unpaid taxes. After Earl and Fern left Upper Priest Lake they assumed that his mother was paying the taxes and she assumed that Earl was paying them.

In 1934, Earl wrote to the Bonner County Tax Collector to notify him as soon as the State of Indiana paid a WW I veteran's bonus he would pay up the back taxes on the property on Upper Priest Lake. His mother, Lavina Geisinger, was half owner of the property.

Shortly after Earl and Fern moved to Twin Lakes, a Priest Lake friend, Mary Duffill Donaldson, wrote that their Priest Lake property was about to be sold for taxes. Earl again wrote the tax collector that as soon as he received his veteran's bonus he would pay all back taxes. He swore at a hearing that he never received a reply and assumed the agreement was satisfactory.

The next news they heard about their property was that it had been sold, July 2, 1936, to Pete Jacobs of Kellogg, Idaho, for delinquent taxes for a sum of $159.95 on 142.21 acres of land. Earl also swore on the stand that he had not received a notice of any kind that the property was to be sold for taxes.

When they heard the property had been sold, they drove to Sandpoint and asked the tax collector why they had not been notified by registered mail. The law required that of an impending tax sale. They were told that the notice had been sent by registered mail and returned marked, "Can not be located." They asked to see the letter and envelope but the tax collector could not produce it.

The Geisingers then contacted attorneys O.J. and Glenn Bandelin, explained the case, paid a $50 retainer fee, and asked that their case be presented in court. The attorney for Pete Jacobs intimated on several occasions that he would pay a reasonable sum for the property if the Geisingers would drop the case and sign a deed transferring the property to him. Due to the lack of funds to pay attorney fees and the serious illness of Earl's mother, who was half owner of the property, the action started by the Bandelins was never pressed.

In 1940, Mrs. Lavina Geisinger died, which further complicated the problem financially and otherwise. Earl and Fern reconciled themselves to the fact that to fight it further was futile.

Fig. 57 The Geisinger home, 1956. Left to right: Josie and Clara Branyan. (H. Branyan)

"We kept going back to the place for years after we lost it," said Mrs. Geisinger. "Pete Jacobs had told me when I was weeping and pleading with him to accept our money for the $159.95 he paid, that we could use that cabin as long as we wanted to. He didn't ever plan to go there to live. When Pete died, two of his sisters inherited the property. They soon sold it to two doctors from Spokane. They came into the grapes with it."

Fern never really felt reconciled until the property was taken over in 1966, by the Federal Government under the Public Domain Act. She said during the interview that, "I know it was carelessness on our part, but I was convinced there was a crooked deal going on."

As late as September, 1957, Pete Jacobs told two local summer residents who were interested in helping the Geisingers regain their property that the case was still not settled and there might be an outside chance for them to regain ownership. The period of grace apparently came to an end when the Forest Service annexed the property as part of the Kaniksu National Forest.

In a letter, dated April 14, 1958 from Vivian E. Shoemaker, a former owner of a Sandpoint title office, stated the following facts about the Geisinger property. The property was deeded to the county on April 1, 1936 for unpaid taxes. The county deeded the property to P.E. Jacobs July 2, 1936. A suit to quit title, Geisinger vs. Jacobs was dismissed for want of prosecution October 6, 1947. A summons was duly advertised in June, 1958, by the Clerk of the District Court in and for Bonner County to P.E. Jacobs, Plaintiff vs. Chester Earl Geisinger *et al.* defendants. The action was brougat by the plaintiff to obtain a decree quitting title for the Geisinger property.

To complete the legal history of the property, Robert E. Brown, executor of Pete Jacob's estate, gave a WD to Kermit Peterson, June 28, 1962. Peterson platted the property as a subdivision August 2, 1965. Peterson granted Nature Conservancy a mortgage June 26, 1964.

On November 7, 1966, Peterson *et al.* granted a deed to the Department of Agriculture. This action placed the Geisinger property in the Scenic Area under the control and supervision of the US Department of Agriculture.

Fern Geisinger retired from the Boise Public Schools in 1961. For several years she travelled but made her home in Boise, Idaho. On July 4, 1973, Fern moved to Billings, Montana, where she has lived with her daughter, Ann Emmons, 1820 Westwood Drive.

In the spring of 1978, Fern had the misfortune to fall on the ice and break her hip. She was hospitalized for several weeks. On July 8, her doctor told her she could go home in six weeks, if she regained the strength in her legs. She wrote in a letter, "God willing and my hard work with my walker, I'll go home before that." She made it on August 4. By mid summer, 1979, she was making plans to make another visit to Priest Lake.

This indomitable spirit that is evident throughout Fern Merritt Geisinger's life as portrayed in this epic must be admired by all who have known or read about this remarkable, courageous, self-reliant, sunny-dispositioned lady. Our hearts go out to you, Fern, for the inspiration you have given to all those who have known and loved you. As the now generation say, "She really had her act together."

13

BEAVER CREEK RANGER STATION

The Romantic Period When the Men of the United States Forest Service Matched the Mountains of the Kaniksu National Forest

The following story of Beaver Creek Ranger Station is based primarily on interviews with Henry "Hank" Diener. Hank started out in the Forest Service in 1930 as a smokechaser on Lookout Mountain almost directly east of the north end of Priest Lake. In those days the lookout station on Lookout Mountain was a two-man post, the lookout and a smokechaser.

The district had 22 fires that year that had to be manned and Hank was on 11 of them. The following year he was dispatcher at the Beaver Creek Ranger Station.

Prior to the end of World War II there were no roads in the area served by BCRS and all material, food, supplies, men, and pack string animals had to be transported by boat, barge, or trail. The pack train played an important as well as very romantic, if not a sentimental, phase of the development of forest service in the Kaniksu National Forest.

A launch, named "The Kaniksu," was a real workhorse for the Forest Service, practically from the time the service was created until the BCRS was abandoned as a distribution point in the early 1950s. When the mouth of the Thorofare and the channel from the mouth of Caribou Creek down stream to the S curve were dredged, a launch could tow a barge with a pack string of mules, supplies, and men to Upper Priest Lake. The areas now used for the Trapper Creek and Navigation Camp Grounds served as distribution points for supplies to the various lookout stations and for the fire crews in the Upper Priest Lake region.

The Packers

Anyone who had the good fortune to watch an experienced packer

141

saddle and load a seven or eight mule pack string couldn't help being impressed with his ingenuity, courage, stamina, and determination. Some mules were docile and content with the ordeal of having 160 to 175 pound packs tied on their backs. Others refused to cooperate and did everything from holding their breath when the packer started to tighten the cinch to bucking off a half-tied pack. Generally, a well placed belly kick by the packer's pointed cowboy boot took the wind out of a mule's belly. A mule's head snubbed to a tree or a stout hitching rack took care of a mean, ornery mule who didn't like the feel of a cold pack on his back at 4:30 AM. As a rule, a mule knew in the long run who was boss of the pack string and would cooperate accordingly.

Most of the mules used for a forest service pack string were big, well disciplined, well fed, and in good physical condition. Some mules were so well trained that a case of eggs could be packed up and down rugged trails without a thought given to broken eggs.

It was a common occurrence for pack strings to transport the lumber, supplies, and equipment for a complete lookout. One of the most spectacular loads carried by a mule train was a 2200-foot continuous cable carried by a 20-mule pack string. The picture from Barney Stone's collection shows, in part, how the cable was carried, by each mule. It was transported from St. Maries, Idaho, to a steam donkey operation in the back country east of the town.

Not all pack trips were a routine operation. Hank commented on one bad accident when a pack train had to travel at night to a fire about halfway between Navigation station and Snowy Top Mountain. The packer with his string of mules started up a brushy stretch of the trail and on a sharp switchback, one of the mules in the center of the string was dragged off the trail by a stalled mule in front of him. That caused a chain reaction and there were mules scattered all over the side of the mountain. Only one mule was killed in the accident. Normally a pack train would never be sent out at night, but on a bad fire it had to be attempted. It was a tough time for man and beast. Manpower, mules, and a few saddle horses were all that were available and the men made the best of it. Occasionally, while carrying a heavy pack, a mule would misjudge a rock or tree and lose his balance. From time to time a mule would be lost due to a broken leg.

During a moderate fire season a packer carried supplies to each lookout station about once a month. In a heavy fire season the packers were on the trails constantly. A summer pack train to an

Fig. 58 USFS launch, "Papoose," barge, and packstring.

Fig. 59 Stan Spurgeon's pack string loaded with material for Blacktail, etc. 1932. (H. Diener)

Fig. 60 Mules waiting to be loaded. (Barney Stone)

Fig. 61 Gas lanterns and equipment for air strip runway,
Hughes Meadow, 1939. (Barney Stone)

144

individual lookout would be a saddle horse and two mules. When the lookouts were moved in at the beginning of each season the string would be one saddle horse and six to eight mules.

In 1932, three pack strings were packing out of BCRS the entire summer. Supplies were brought in by boat from Reeder Creek, Coolin, and the Forest Service warehouse at Kalispel Bay.

Packers, like modern-day truck drivers, varied considerably. Stan Spurgeon was packing for the Forest Service when he was 16 years old. His rating as a packer was excellent. He was a husky young man born and raised around pack stock. Two other packers that Hank Diener remembered were Murdock and George. Murdock was from the Columbia River country near Coulee Dam and Okanogan. He had a good rating as a packer but was hard on the stock. George was a first-class cowboy from Montana who could handle stock with the best of them. He was the only man who could single-handedly pack the orneriest mule that ever hit Beaver Creek, Old Dynamite. Before the summer was over packer George had Old Dynamite carrying the eggs.

Mules, like people, come in all stripes. Some would dodge every tree and rock bluff on the trail. Some would on their own volition back off the trail at a switch back in order to make a turn if a tree or rock was apt to interfere with their pack. A few of the ornery mules would deliberately scrape their packs against a tree or rock trying to knock it off.

I discussed some of the mule problems with retired Forest Ranger Leslie Eddy. Les was with the Forest Service from the mid-20s until he resigned to enlist in the Armed Forces at the start of WW II.

Les made the comment that one summer after a mule train disaster a ranking officer at headquarters decided that the Forest Service needed donkeys to use as pack animals. Several were sent to Beaver Creek. In Les's words, "They were a damn nuisance. They couldn't be kept anywhere. They just disappeared when they were needed. We finally got a string of them packed with waterbags at Navigation to take water to Plowboy Lookout. The donkeys got so dry on the way up they drank all the water they were carrying before they got to the top of the mountain. After trying to use them one summer we took them to the Columbia River near Vantage for winter pasture, and they just disappeared! We were relieved!"

The real experience to test a packer's skill was to pack 10- and 12-foot lumber from 1"x4" to 4"x4" on a mule. The lumber would have to cross the pack saddle and be fastened in front with nails and tied to the saddle so it would balance over the mule's neck and not touch the ground on either side. It would be lashed down with a diamond hitch. Some mules would go wild when they saw the lumber sticking above their necks. The stock had to be tested and picked according to temperament, strength, and willingness to put up with various types of loads.

The lookout cabins were built with precut lumber tied in bundles for packing. The average per pack was about 160 pounds. If a packer had two bundles of 60 pounds each, one would be tied to each side of the mule and another pack of 20 to 60 pounds would be lashed on top of the saddle. Windows, doors, nails, and everything else had to be packed in by mules.

The Lookouts

For summer visitors to Priest Lake who ventured north of Granite Creek, Lookout and Plowboy mountains are the most attractive peaks for hikers. Lookout Mountain was the best-known peak in the Kaniksu for hiking as it was topped by a well-equipped two-man lookout station. It was the first station to be manned each summer and the last to come out in the fall.

The original trail followed the south slope of the mountain and the snow melted early. It was also the most accessible peak to BCRS. When a man was in good physical shape he could hike from Mosquito Bay to the top in two hours and come down in an hour and 15 minutes. Prior to the late 1930s, the old five-mile lookout trail went up Lion Creek to Lucky Creek and up this creek to the spring and then followed the steep rock slope from the tree line to the top. In the middle 1930s, Hank Diener located and built the trail that went around the west base of the mountain about a quarter of a mile from what is now Lionhead Campground and turned right up the north slope to the ridge. The trail followed the ridge until it intersected the old trail at the spring on Lucky Creek. It was 7½ miles long but a much easier grade for pack trains and hikers.

The normal procedure to install a lookout in a station was for a member of the administrative staff to accompany the pack train and the lookout on the first trip. The administrator would assist in storing and arranging of the gear and supplies according to the needs of the site. He usually stayed two or more days, depending on the background and previous training of the man. As early as the 1930s the Forest Service was appointing women as lookouts, especially if the woman was accompanied by her husband who was to be the smokechaser.

146

By the beginning of WW II, the use of women as lookouts was occasionally cause for embarrassment when an administrator had to spend two or three days at the site instructing the new lookout for "manning" her station.

Such principal stations as Blacktail, Goblin Knob, Gold Peak, Hughes Ridge, Lookout, Phoebe Tip, Plowboy, and Trapper Creek were continually manned and it was a rare occasion if a lookout was pulled off such stations. The district had the advantage of the stations on Snowy Top, in the Sullivan Lake district, and Boundary, next to the Canadian border, to aid during bad storms.

A number of the lookout points in the back country were tent observation posts and were manned only a few weeks each summer.

Plowboy lookout was a one-man station. The trail, while steep in places, was only three miles long. Navigation station at the base of the mountain was used as a distribution and smokechaser point. Water for Plowboy was about half way down the trail at Navigation Creek. Water for several of the lookout points was a problem. Water on Lookout Mountain was about as close as any lookout in the Kaniksu but it was a four-mile round trip with water bags strapped on the employee's back. Two trips a day would furnish all the water needed for a two-man crew if water conservation was rigidly practiced.

Conservation usually meant, start out with water to cook with, save what you could to wash the dishes, and then store the dishwater to daily wash your socks and shorts. There was no rain gutter on the cabin to catch rain water since the roof area was so small it didn't provide enough space to make a runoff worthwhile.

Hank Diener solved the eight-mile daily backpack trip for water by rigging up a high line device from the top of the 400-foot cliff to the spring below. The spring, as it was called, was really runoff from the snowfield at the bottom of the cliff. In early summer the runoff was near the base of the cliff. By late August the water bags had to be filled near Lookout Lake, which is also fed from the snowfield.

As Hank recalled, the tripod for the high line was built about 75 feet northwest of the cabin, along the brow of the cliff. The main pole held one end of the #9 telephone wire which was anchored to a "dead man" behind the tripod frame. The other end was extended to the spring below the cliff and secured to a big rock. The wire was strung over the point of the tripod to hold the water bags away from the face of the cliff. Seven hundred feet of wire was used for the highline. A pulley was placed on the high wire. The 5 gallon water bags were hung on the pulley and with a ¼" manilla rope tied to the pulley, it

147

would let the weight of the water bags pull the rope down the wire to the runoff spring below.

The smokechaser would hike down the ridge, over and around rocks to where the bottom end of the wire was anchored. The bags would be filled and fastened to the pulley. The return trip to the top was over a rugged trail but easily traversed without a backpack.

With the use of a handmade windlass, built of alpine poles and set back of the tripod frame, the water bags would be pulled up the high wire by the rope wrapping around the hand windlass. The mechanism was crude but serviceable and saved a lot of time and energy.

The cabin on Lookout Mountain had a cupola on top of it where the alidade and fire map were located. The lookout had to shinny up a ladder into the cupola. He came down as if he were coming down a fireman's pole.

It is quite an experience on a lookout during an electrical storm. All lookout stations have a lightning protective device. A lot of people have a misconception of how lightning protection works. They think that the device takes the electricity out of the air and grounds it. The process is in exact reverse. The device actually neutralizes the current and dispenses it into the air. There is nothing in the ground surrounding the lookout cabin and area protected to attract the lightning bolt. As a consequence when an electrical storm is going overhead there will be what apparently is a blue flame that is not a flame at all, because you can stick your finger right into it and it won't burn or shock you. It is static electricity that is coming off the end of the lightning rods. The flames will vary from a slight glow to some that will be 5" to 7" high, according to the nearness and intensity of the storm. There is no heat in it. The first few experiences seeing the blue flame is a scary thing, but a lookout gets used to it. When the storm goes over, many times the blue flames will jump from the telephone to the stove and from the stove to the map base. When a lightning bolt hits a dead snag or a green tree the wood bursts into flame as if it had been saturated with gasoline. Sometimes as the lightning hits the ground it will follow the tree's root system and make a trench in the soil.

During the early years of WW II, when a lot of young people were appointed as lookouts, a dispatcher spent many hours talking to the kids in order to keep up their courage and convince them to stay on the lookout. Once in awhile a dispatcher lost ground and the young lookout would leave his post and hike to the nearest ranger station.

Fig. 62 Original cabin, Lookout Mountain, 1977.
Left to right: Betty Nyman, Catherine Simpson,
Mary Rutherford. (C. Simpson)

Fig. 63 Hand-powered windlass, Lookout Mountain,
1930. (H. Diener)

Fig. 64 Mountain goats in doorway of
cabin on Lookout Mountain,
August, 1930. (Ryder Chronic)

Fig. 65 State of Idaho's Lookout Mountain cabin, 1977.

Fig. 66 Julie Turnbull, station's first operator for the modern tower on Lookout Mountain.

Fig. 67 Plowboy Mountain lookout
cabin, 1929. (Les Eddy Collection)

Fig. 68 Tent camp lookout station,
Phoebe Tip. Neil Fullerton
operator, 1932.
(Les Eddy Collection)

Fig. 69 Green Bonnet Lookout, a high-rise type.

Diener said, "I remember one young man I installed on Black Mountain Lookout near Bonners Ferry. During a bad storm the evening I left him, he beat me back to the ranger station, and I was riding a horse! I spent the next day with him at the dispatcher's desk and persuaded him to go back on duty. Before the summer was over he was a first rate lookout."

Fig. 70 Smokechaser Hank Diener.

A Lookout's Daily Routine

In 1931, a new system of reporting was begun at BCRS. Prior to that time, each lookout would call in on a set schedule beginning at 7:00 AM, again at 10:00 AM, 2:00 PM, and 5:00 PM. Each call period would take the dispatcher at least an hour to talk to all points. Under the new system four different telephone lines were run into BCRS and the dispatcher would call all lookouts on each line. The lookouts would report in, each listening to the other, and the time was reduced to 12 minutes for each call period. The system got to be forest-wide with telephones and extended to radio when they replaced the telephone. The new system got everyone on the same schedule and the office was reasonably sure that all lookouts were out of the sack by 7:00 AM for a look around their territory. An experienced dispatcher knew, of course, that a few of them reported in from the sack, but at least they were awake enough to answer for their post.

153

The next task was breakfast, followed by wood and water detail which was reported at 10:00 AM. From that time on the lookout was expected to spend at least 15 minutes every hour looking for smoke in his area. It was difficult to compel a lookout to do this, but a dispatcher had to rely on the integrity of the lookout. From time to time spot fires would be purposely set to keep the lookouts continually on the job.

A good lookout is one who loves to look at the forests. After the first few days as a lookout, some would get too busy cutting wood, clearing trails, checking telephone lines, or getting water, that they forgot to look. Most lookouts when they first get on a post are impressed with the beauty of the sight. All are enthralled with the tremendous expanse of country that can be seen.

Hank remarked, "After you look at it for a period of time you have done it all. When I was a lookout I would often get to cooking, particularly cakes, and I would forget to look. One time I read the cake directions that said, fold in the whites of 3 eggs'. I immediately called the dispatcher to send up an egg folder with the next pack train. It took me a long time to live that one down!"

"A good lookout is a person who is inclined to be a little bit lazy, a person who would rather look than to do anything else. The best lookouts were usually the ones who didn't have their dishes washed when they were visited, the woodpile had only a stick or two of split wood on it, and their water supply down to a few drops."

As the heat of the day approached and particularly where logging was going on or where there were campers, the areas got continuous inspection. Areas where a storm had passed within a 10-day period also received intense inspection.

From 5:00 or 6:00 PM to 8:30 or 9:00 PM, with permission from the dispatcher, a lookout could leave his post to go down to a pickup point for mail or fresh supplies. Occasionally a lookout was permitted to stay overnight at a lower station if conditions permitted. Once in awhile a lookout would report in for his station, but he would actually be in the sack at a smokechaser's post or at another lookout point.

The Dispatcher

The Forest Service dispatcher's office was a central office or place for recording events. His prime function during fires was to get enough men on a fire soon enough to control it before it got too big. The skill of dispatching lies in knowing how many men to send on a particular fire and what kind of backup coverage is needed. The value of an experienced lookout, such as Bill Blake, came into many decisions. If the glow of a fire began to spread, the dispatcher was notified by the lookout and additional men were sent in. The backup crews generally came from blister rust, CCC, telephone, and road crews, or any number of men who could be hired from anywhere.

If a fire was over-manned a Forest Service fire supervisor would figuratively chop the dispatcher's ears off. The skill of a dispatcher was measured when he could man a fire so it could be controlled at a small stage with no possibility for the fire to get away. Depending on his ears and the eyes of the lookout a dispatcher made his decisions. Such facts as: where the fire is, on a north, east, west, or south exposure, on a mountain or on the east or west side of a creek, how far up the mountain the fire is spotted, what the ground cover is, what the timber cover is, a dispatcher makes up his mind on his knowledge of the district and the report from the lookout.

Diener said, "As an example, we had a fire on Hughes Ridge. I called Clarence Sutliff who had a road crew of 20 men not too far from the fire. Jim Ryan called and wanted to know what I wanted the road crew for. It turned out to my credit that we needed them and two more crews before we got the spread under control. Dispatchers were canned with some regularity because of inept decisions. I enjoyed being a dispatcher in spite of the tensions of split-second decisions that had to be made from time to time."

In 1977, the State of Idaho Forestry Division installed a 40-foot steel supported tower on Lookout Mountain. It could be classed as an ultramodern facility when compared to the original cabin that still stands at the foot of the new tower, or to the 70-foot wooden pole supported tower that replaced the original cabin as the observation post.

No mule trains were used to transport the equipment and supplies for the new structure. A road was bulldozed along the base of the Lion Heads from the well-travelled logging road that follows Lion Creek from Priest Lake. The road spur is steep and treacherous and is closed to the public.

The cabin at the top of the tower is modern in almost every respect, wall to wall carpeting, gas heat, a gas cooking range, water under pressure hauled up by a 4 x 4 Jeep, gas and electric lights, and a vacuum cleaner for the carpet. Miss Judy Turnbull had the privilege of being the lookout for the first year the new facility was operated. Judy was an experienced observer from the Horton Ridge Lookout which was abandoned when the Lookout Mountain post was opened.

155

At this point during the interview Diener was asked to reminisce on the highlights of his more than 10-year career with the Forest Service. "Thinking back on my experiences of 48 years ago brings me back to that wild country that it was. In fact, a lot of it is still wild country. I was completely enthralled with it and still love that God's country.

"Warren 'Uppie' Upham came into my life in 1932," Diener reported. "He came to Priest Lake from Maine where he had been a timber cruiser. He came west on his doctor's orders in an attempt to cure a lung ailment. Uppie worked for the Forest Service that summer on a project to study fuel hazards that were visible from present and potential lookout observation points in the districts."

Upham became an ardent outdoorsman. He spent his spare time paddling around the lake in his canoe, fishing, and sunbathing. He wore shorts and no shirt during most of the summer. He rigged up his canoe for a set of oars and could row it exceptionally fast. Occasionally, for exercise and sunshine, he would paddle or row his canoe to Coolin. His canoe was the only form of transportation he ever had during the years he lived on the lake.

Hank said, "Uppie turned out to be a very rugged individual. He completely rebuilt his body through his outdoor living. He was still cruising timber for the Forest Service from his home base in Coolin during the middle 1940s. I lost track of him after I got out of the Navy at the end of WW II.

"I suppose I was at a young and impressionable age, but I worked my heart out for that country. We worked on trail maintenance during the spring of the year. As an example, we'd start out from BCRS to go to, say, Boulder Lookout, an even 10 miles up there and back, working all the way. You might get to within a mile of the top and you still had deadfalls to cut with an axe or crosscut saw and you'd decide it was better to work another two hours to clear the trail than to walk back again the next day. We usually would make the decision to clear it and hike back to BCRS in the dark, arriving at 8:30 or 9:00 PM. A lot of times we would put in an 18-hour day and we didn't get or expect overtime pay. We did it because we loved the job and everything that went with it.

"Sometimes in the spring when we were on telephone maintenance it would take us three or four days or more to clear blowdowns and repair the lines. We always worked from home base and hiked to and from as part of the job. In many ways the Forest Service men in those days were a bunch of innovative, self-sufficient, hardworking men.

They were for the most part lumberjacks. A typical example was Ranger Jim Lord who used to row a boat from Coolin to Upper Priest when the old Coolin Forest Service district and the Beaver Creek Station were combined. This was in the days before outboard motors appeared on Priest Lake.

"The major piece of machinery we had was the Pacific Marine water pump built by the Johnson Outboard Motor Company. The engine was the same one that was on the 32-horse Johnson outboard motor. It was a four-cylinder engine that laid horizontally instead of standing up as on the outboard motor. On one end of the main drive shaft was a very compact centrifugal pump. It would charge a 1½" fire hose and lift water 300 feet. As I remember, the first high-speed motors were developed by the outboard motor companies and this unit was one of the first on the market. These motors would turn up to 4500 rpm's compared to automobiles in those days of about 2500 rpm's.

"This pump was a terrific thing to fight fires in those days. They wouldn't last too long, but they could sure throw the water. If we needed to lift water more than 300 feet from a creek or a lake, we would dig a sump every 300 feet and set up another pump and go on up the hill for as far as 1500 feet if necessary. The Johnson Marine pump was first used by the Forest Service. It was later used by the Navy in WW II.

"The Forest Service pioneered several other things. The pulaski* is a forest service invention. The bulldozer was definitely pioneered by the Forest Service. They didn't build it but they were the first to use it to prove the tremendous versatility of the dozer. The old Cletrac 55 was the first bulldozer in the woods, building roads, surrounding fires, and piling brush.

"The normal season at BCRS started in the middle of April by taking off shutters, shovelling snow, unpacking gear, and cleaning up the camp for the crew that would move in by early May. We would close BCRS in the fall, depending on how tough a fire season we'd had, the number of axes to be sharpened, the number of saws to be filed, tents to dry, and usual maintenance of equipment, all of which had to be completed before we could leave. We usually tried to get out by Thanksgiving. In the winter time Elmer Berg was hired to shovel snow off the roofs and do the necessary checking for man and animal mischief.

"I don't remember the year we built the fireplace at the west end of the main cabin. It was a year when we had extra heavy fall rains and we brought the lookouts and smokechasers down early. Those that

Fig. 71 Wash house and shower room, BCRS, 1914. Still in use at BCCA.

Fig. 72 Senior Forest Ranger Les
Eddy and a friend, BCRS,
1931. (Les Eddy Collection)

Fig. 73 1930 BCRS crew. Left to right: Ernest Grambo, Stan
Spurgeon. Back row: Kenneth Nelson, Graydon
Winslow, Mark Hurd, Ora Ludeman, Herman
Walker, William Blake. The bunkhouse in the
background is still in use at BCCA.

were not college students we put to work building the fireplace. We were usually able to keep the non-college part of the crew busy until early October. We tried to keep them working as long as it was practical to do so.

"The fireplace, which is still standing on the BCRS site, was promoted from one of Les Eddy's intense hobbies. Whatever he studied he became proficient at it. For several years when he was locating trails or telephone lines, just after WW I, he couldn't cross a rock slide without picking up and examining the rocks. He eventually gathered a sizeable collection of north Idaho gems. He studied and identified them with marvelous accuracy. All of them were found within a 25-mile radius of BCRS.

"With the idea of using the gems in a fireplace front arrangement we got a $250 appropriation to build a fireplace in the main cabin. We hauled most of the fireplace rock from the Granite Creek area. We took a selection of Les's gems and arranged them in a design in a cake tin full of soft concrete. This unit was placed in center front of the fire box. The Idaho gems were surrounded by narrow stones in circular arrangement making a central focal point. Ernie Grambo, Bill Donaldson, Kenny Nelson, and I all had a hand in designing the fireplace. We all worked at laying the rock.

"I didn't ever know the real value of the collection that Les Eddy had accumulated. Whoever took it when the cabin was torn down knew what they got.

"I remember one fall we slashed brush just north of the station and cleared up 15 or 20 acres that we fenced for a mule pasture. We even seeded grass that became good feed for the pack mules. One fall we built a big barn that would hold 35 or 40 mules. It had a big hay mow down the middle of it.

"Another year we built a couple of bunk houses. Another fall we brought an old cabin up the lake on a barge. With block and tackle and a hand winch we snaked it from the lake up the hill and located it opposite the barn. Another fall we built a boathouse to house our launch, the motor powered Kaniksu. It was a two day job for three or four men to winch that boat to the boathouse.

"The ram at BCRS was operating when I was there. It was the only pump that the station had. The tank held 250 gallons of water and at times when a bad fire season came along the ram couldn't pump enough water for showers but was ample for the kitchen and drinking water.

"To give you some idea of how a wild bunch of young smoke-chasers would dream up things to do I will tell you a story of a shared

Fig. 74 Ranger's cabin, BCRS, 1930. (Les Eddy Collection)

Fig. 75 A boathouse towed up the lake, winched up the hill, and served
as a bunkhouse at BCRS, 1930. (Les Eddy Collection)

161

cat at BCRS. The cat was really owned by Elmer Berg, but we kept her during the summer because we had a lot of mice around the warehouse where we stored food for the fire fighters. She was really worth her weight in gold. During Elmer's long winter months he taught his dogs and cat a lot of tricks. He had taught this particular cat to jump through his arms when he held them together a foot or so off the floor. She would do it repeatedly.

"One weekend we had a party and wound up with about a half inch of *Uncle Pete's Monogram* in a quart bottle. During the next week we were all sitting around in the cook house one evening and someone suggested we give the cat a shot of booze. We poured a dish half full of canned milk and added some *Monogram*. She drank all she would, but it wasn't enough to get her tipsy. So we decided to spoon it into her. We got a spoon and started to pour it into the cat. She didn't like it but we held her and stayed with it until we got the rest of the booze down her.

"Within a few minutes we started to put her through her trick. Someone would hold his hands in a circle in front of her and she would jump straight up and would fall back on her butt instead of jumping through the hoop made for her. We would crumble up a newspaper into a ball, throw it across the floor and she would make a jump for it and swat at it with her paw with such force she would go rolling over and over sidewise.

"She finally went over next to a leg on one of the tables, sat down, wrapped her front paws around it and began rotating her head round and round. With each revolution she would let out the loudest M-E-O-W I ever heard. Finally she gave up, curled up, and went to sleep.

"Several times in my life I've seen drunk animals, but that's the best show I ever saw.

"As a courtesy to the squatters, trappers, boathousemen, and settlers on the upper lake, the Byars, and Elmer Berg, the Forest Service would throw the switches at the BCRS to the Coolin line and connect it with the Navigation line. Jim Ward at the Coolin station had the switchboard in his house. He could take calls all winter if the lines were not knocked down by snow or falling trees. This permitted calls from Navigation to Coolin from the wall phones that were on the porch of both Navigation and Beaver Creek stations.

"In those days most of the people on the upper lake were clustered around the mouth of Upper Priest River and Trapper Creek. This gave them access to the outside world if they had problems of any kind. They had at least a 50-50 chance to get in contact with a doctor, coroner, or the sheriff. This was standard practice during all the years that there was a Forest Service station at Beaver Creek.

"It wasn't until 1934, that I approached the status of a full year's work as an alternate ranger with the Forest Service. The ranger was the only full-time employee at the station until the middle of the 1930s.

"I could have gone back into the Forest Service after WW II, but my wife, Ruth, just wasn't the type of girl to enjoy forest service life in the 1940s. It was a hard and rugged life for a woman in those days. Wives of foresters had to be willing to enjoy living under difficult circumstances. They couldn't be afraid of the dark, being alone, storms, animals, bugs, rough roads, living in tents, and for the most part exist without electricity and refrigeration.

"In spite of the fact that the Forest Service now has 60 or 70 full time employees at the Priest Lake Ranger Station, I don't believe they take any better care of the forests today than we did back in the 1930s."

A policy of the Forest Service, that started many years ago, of hiring young men for summer work has paid big dividends. The program started primarily because forestry in the early days was a seasonal operation. For hundreds of young men who were employed during the summer, it not only provided a training ground for young foresters but enabled many to earn money for a college education in other fields.

One case in point is the career of G.K. "Yak" Yacorzynski. Yak was a student at Washington State College in 1927-28, and got a job at the BCRS on the recommendation of President E.O. Holland. Yak lived in the president's garage apartment and drove the president's Cadillac to pay for his room. He was hired as a smokechaser and lookout for the first three years. In 1931 and 1932, he carried the title of Assistant Ranger.

Yacorzynski transferred to the University of Washington after one year at WSC and received a Ph.D. degree in Psychology. He retired in 1977, after serving many years as Professor and Head, Division of Psychology, Northwestern University Medical School, Chicago.

In 1975, Yak and his wife Linda visited Beaver Creek for the first time since 1932. He had fond memories of Leonard Paul, Les Eddy, Elmer Berg, Lee Tracy, and Andy Coolin. He facetiously remarked, "My only claim to fame was having the 'Yak Fire' named in my honor and building two bunkhouse cabins at BCRS.

"I was in charge of a fire crew and the boss told me to keep them busy. The crew was sleeping in tents so I supervised the cutting of the logs and the construction of the cabins. The boss looked them over and commented, 'They're strong, but it's a pretty rough job.'"

One cabin in its original state, with names of former occupants written on the walls is still in use at Beaver Creek Camp. Another one was razed by a BCCA lot owner, the logs labeled and numbered, skidded to the lake, towed to the lot site, and reconstructed in its original state. It serves as a bedroom to a new section of the owner's cabin. A third cabin that served as a boiler room and wash house stands in its original state on a BCCA lot.

About all that remains on the BCRS site that is reminiscent of the once large and busy ranger station is the fireplace of the main cabin, a few cement blocks that were part of the boathouse, a clearing where the mule barn stood, a few fence posts and wire that once encircled the mule pasture, a platform on a tamarack tree that held the water tank, the stone housing of the ram pump house, and the foundation logs of Heberling's squatter cabin.

Heberling built the cabin a short distance from the stream that runs from the spring that furnished water for BCRS. The story that Heberling homesteaded the site and later deeded it back to the Forest Service is not true. The tract sheets in the Safeco Abstract Office in Sandpoint has no record of the land ever being homesteaded, proved up, or deeded.

Appendix BCRS
*The pulaski, a single axe with an adz-shaped hoe extending from the back, was invented by Edward C. Pulaski. It is one of the most useful tools in today's Forest Service work. It is a required tool in several states in a set of firefighting equipment for logging operations and firefighting crews.

According to Webster's New Collegiate Dictionary, 1975 Edition, p. 933, Pulaski was a 20th century American Forest Ranger.

14

HUNGATE RELATES FIREFIGHTING EXPERIENCES DURING HUGE FIRE OF 1926

Robert E. Hungate, who spent his first summer at Priest Lake in 1913, had the exciting experience of being a member of the large fire-fighting crew that battled the 1926 fires in the Kaniksu National Forest. Bob and hundreds of other men fought fires for 34 consecutive days.

Bob was a member of a blister rust crew stationed at Lamb Creek. One night early in July, the crew was called out at 1:00 AM and marched down to Kalispel Bay on Priest Lake. The entire forest was continually lit up as thunder and lightning rolled and flashed over miles and miles of the Selkirk Range from Washington and British Columbia, to the Rockies in Montana.

The crew was picked up by Bert Winslow in his steamboat, the "W.W. Slee," and transported to the Beaver Creek Ranger Station at the head of Priest Lake. Bob had been a vacationer at Priest Lake for 14 consecutive years and knew the current and shallows of the Thorofare between upper and lower Priest lakes so was chosen as navigator for the boat load of hay for the pack mules that was to be taken to Navigation Ranger Station on Upper Priest Lake. The rest of the crew had to hike the six miles up the Navigation Trail. From Navigation the crew hiked to the Big Creek fire, a distance of about three miles.

"Shortly after daylight," said Bob, "the first day of the fire, as we passed an open area you could see a huge mushroom cloud that seemed to cover all the north country. It was beautiful, but tragic! The many, many fires that were started less than nine or ten hours earlier by lightning was just one big boom and the whole country was afire. The updraft at Beaver Creek, pulling the ground air upward could be felt distinctly by the firefighters. It was frightening, as well as awe inspiring.

"The fire boss, Bill Guernsey, and I circled the the Big Creek fire to see what the job was. When we got back the decision was to work on the windward side in an attempt to trench the fire. One of the crew members, I think his name was Kelvie, ran behind a tree as someone yelled, 'timber' and almost instantaneously, the burning tree fell within three feet of him. The incident frightened him so that he became violently ill and had to leave the job.

"About 6:00 o'clock that night, we were pulled off the Big Creek fire and had to hike to the Canadian border where another fire was burning out of control. I vividly remember as we were hiking up the hill, some of the crew were so hot and so exhausted that they were crying. In fact, I didn't feel too happy myself! We had had only one meal and no sleep for more than 36 hours. The foreman was a good guy! He knew how to handle men, kids. He kidded the boys, told stories, and got them to sing occasionally and to march in cadence to their singing. He would say, 'OK boys, a five minute stop and in exactly five minutes he would say, OK men, let's get going.'

"Late in the afternoon, one of the boys began to cry between stops because his pack was so heavy and his feet were so badly blistered that he couldn't help it.

"At each stop the boy would say, 'I'll get her stopped in five minutes,' and to his credit, most times he did, only to break down again before the next five minute break. At the succeeding stop he would say, 'OK boss, I got her stopped.' After the five minutes, the boss would say, 'OK, on your feet.'

"After dozens of such stops the crew got to Cedar Creek, and camp was made, such as it was. Cold canned food, cookies, and hot water was the meal, and we slept on the softest ground I ever remember lying on.

"The next morning, after a hot breakfast, cooked by a regular Forest Service cook, and one of the most sumptuous meals I ever had, the pack train from Navigation with the food had caught up with us. The crew hiked to the Continental Mountain fire and worked there until it was brought under control by trenching. While there, another fire was located up over the Canadian border. We were sent there and spent another two days trenching that one.

"Early in the morning the following day we left four members of our crew to patrol the area and the rest of us hiked back to Beaver Creek. After one night's sleep we were sent up Lion Creek where we finally corralled a fire on the west slope of Kent Peak. While the fire was being trenched, another fire was discovered on the east side of Kent Lake. Roscoe Bell and I were sent across the peak to control that one. It took us one day to bring the blaze under control. That night, with palousers, we hiked the seven miles back to Beaver Creek.

"I was given time to take a cold bath, the first in two weeks, and eat a good hot meal in the ranger station cookhouse, before I was sent, without sleep, to Gold Creek, via Boulder Mountain lookout to deliver a message. The lookout was manned by two men from the Bronx, New York. The young men had come west for the first time to work for the Forest Service. They both admitted they were having a real forest experience. They put a tent up for me to sleep in. During the night, a high wind blew it down."

The next day as Bob hiked toward Gold Creek, he walked through the 1910 burn, and thought he was hearing the sounds of a distant cheering section at a football game when the high wind created a tremendous noise as it blew through the old black snags left by the worst fire ever to hit the Selkirks.

When Bob neared Gold Creek, he caught up with a pack train going in. The packer said, "Son, if you can ride a pack saddle on a mule, I'll give you a lift."

"Now if you have ever ridden two six-inch boards, on edge," said Bob, "you have some vague idea of what it is like to ride a pack saddle astride a mule. I climbed aboard the lead mule and made the best of it to get a needed rest for my feet. Fortunately, I had bought a pair of White loggers in Spokane, which incidentally, I still wear after 49 years of summer hiking. My feet were in good shape, but tired and somewhat bruised, and it was a relief in spite of the pack saddle boards, to be sitting instead of walking.

"When I had delivered my message to the boss on the Gold Creek fire, he thanked me and assigned me to the job of water boy on the fire. I was incensed, deflated, if not downright angry at the demotion. I was 20 years old, had fought fire for almost four weeks, and I didn't appreciate being a mere water boy; but I didn't argue my stand."

The fire had been cornered in a gulch, but was still pretty hot. The boss decided to clean out the corner by letting the entire fire burn itself out. This was more than Bob could stand and he told the boss in front of the men that the blister rust crew had recently been instructed to fight fire by felling everything toward the fire. He ignored Bob's advice and started firing the entire gulch. It was not more than an hour later that the fire was so hot it began to crown on three sides.

The boss got so excited at the turn of events that all he could do was to yell, 'Water boy, water boy, bring some water.' Bob dropped his water bags and went to the axe foreman. The foreman took stock and gave the crew all available axes and instructed them to begin felling all trees toward the fire in an attempt to stop the crowning. It took the rest of the day to check it.

Shortly after this fire, the rains started and the blister rust crew was called off the fire lines and returned to their jobs at Lamb Creek.

Bob's reply to the question about his most memorable experience as a fire fighter in the days when men matched their wits, brawn, and determination against the elements was, "I'll never forget the sight from the top of Boulder Mountain. I could look in any direction and see raging fires. It was an awe-inspiring sight, in spite of the tragedy."

The fire hit Nordman on July 18 and wiped out the Post Office, the Pleasant Inn, the buildings on the Kenyon property, Ole Hager's ranch buildings, and the Meyer's ranch near the Nordman school. By a strange coincidence, the Nordman school did not burn.

The 1926 fire season was later classed as the worst fire in the Kaniksu since the disastrous 1910 holocaust.

15

FISH, FOLLY, FACTS, AND MAN'S FOOLISHNESS

If a Priest Lake fish history were written today, the demise and extinction of the dodo bird or the pre-historic reptiles would be a good outline to follow.

The many fish stories related by old-timers, even if half true, or less, gives credence to the fact that Priest Lakes and feeder creeks were at one time a fisherman's paradise.

In the teen years and the 1920s, a summer vacationer from Pullman, Washington, got free room and board at Mrs. Handy's hotel in Coolin for his fly fishing prowess. For years he caught the native jewels in sufficient numbers to feed Mrs. Handy's hotel guests a daily trout dinner.

A well-known Spokane doctor who had one of the first Chris Crafts on the lake made daily trips during his vacation to Upper Priest and many times in one or two hours would catch a limit of cutthroats.

Another Spokane man, a well-known automobile dealer, started fly fishing at Priest Lake in 1920. He was, without question, one of the best fly fishermen on the lake. He caught most of his fish with a barbless hook and never kept a cutthroat below 12 inches. He lived long enough, unfortunately, to witness the near eradication of the world famous native cutthroats of Priest Lakes.

A resort owner, and undoubtedly one of the top half dozen real fly fishermen on Priest Lakes, relates from time to time stories of unbelievable catches of redbellies that his guests used to get in a couple of hours in the late afternoon on Upper Priest Lake. He said, "Many times I have taken several fly fishermen to the little lake in my launch for evening fishing. The launch had a long deck and three or four good flycasters could fish at the same time. What a thrill it was to have three or four 16" cutthroats on lines at the same time. Many times I have seen cutthroats take a fly, when on a poor backcast, the fly would hit the water. That day is probably gone forever on Priest Lake."

Fig. 76 1933 cutthroats. (Duffill Collection)

Fig. 77 Cutthroats caught on a dry fly, 1950.

Karl C. Paulson, Route 2, Spokane, an excellent sports fisherman, is of the opinion that the planting of mackinaw trout was the least harmful of the various interferences of nature's plan of survival, but stupid nonetheless.

"No place in the world had as fine wild trout as the Priest Lake area," stated Paulson. "If the Game Department had not planted eastern brooks in the streams and had used reasonable judgment when taking cutthroat spawn to plant elsewhere, there would still be good fishing in Priest Lakes. Trapped cutthroat spawners were so carelessly stripped that the majority of the spawners died. The hatchery built on Gold Creek was an excellent idea but by sending the fingerlings elsewhere, Gold Creek was lost as a natural spawning area to replenish cutts for sport fishing in Priest Lakes."

The whitefish and the cutthroats are the two native fish of Priest Lakes. There is some evidence that the dolly vardens may also be included in this category.

The whitefish are gone. The famous whitefish runs, in the first half of the 20th century, reported and witnessed by many present day Priest Lakers, are a thing of the past.

The demise of the whitefish that supplied winter food for local inhabitants as well as Indians from Montana, Washington, and Idaho, is a direct result of the white man's desire to interfere with nature's plan of survival.

The first mistake that interrupted the cycle was planting mackinaw trout in 1925. This was followed by the planting of kokanee, also called bluebacks or silvers. An ecologist or an ichthyologist with a minimum of training should have known that the kokanee's diet was plankton, the same diet of the whitefish. In addition, he would know that a silver is a very aggressive forager and that a whitefish could not compete for food with the silvers. The silvers multiplied very rapidly and each year supplied the fat, oily mack with thousands of fish for his survival.

As is the case in America, big must be better, and when the first 42-pound mack was caught in 1952, the news media spread the story worldwide. In 1953, a record 51-pound mack was caught and lunkers are still being caught each year.

The next major blow for the native fish came when many lakeshore property owners became irritated when the lake level began to drop in July and continued until it hit its natural low pool. Pressure was put on the state government to build a dam at Outlet to hold the water level at constant pool from July 1 through Labor Day, the end of the tourist season.

An agreement was made with the Department of Fish and Game to permit the Washington Water Power Company of Spokane to erect a makeshift dam a few yards downstream from the lake outlet. The company was to work with the Department of Fish and Game of the State of Idaho and let the water down gradually from Labor Day until November 1, to reach the normal low level flow. This agreement was partially honored for the first few years.

Soon pressure from lakeshore property owners began to hold the lake level high enough so that boats could be used until the lake froze. One early survey showed that out of 147 questionnaires returned, by September 90 residents remained on the lake; 69 in October and 44 on November 1. In spite of this fact and the agreement beween WWP and the Fish and Game Department, the lake level was well above low pool on November 1. In some years the proper spawning level was not reached until December or early January.

In 1957, biologist Bjorn wrote a special unpublished report for the Department of Fish and Game stating that he found that "kokanee is part of the diet of lake mackinaw and dolly varden trout." In 1956, he published another report that noted, "cutthroat spawners going downriver in the spring were trapped in the river when the dam boards were installed." He also warned in the report that "trout and whitefish are not suited to the present drawdown operation, while rough fish are."

172

November 1974, Paul Frederick Doyle published his MA thesis, *Analysis of Alternative Water Release Operations for Priest Lake, Idaho.* His findings and recommendations are very critical of the water release operation of Priest Lake. His major recommendations are as follows:

"More data must be gathered on present and future uses of the river at various flow regimes, river water quality at high and low flows, kokanee losses due to drawdown and overall effect of these losses on lake fisheries; more detailed assessment of lake levels on lakeshore residents and resorts should be obtained through questionnaires; hydraulic and water quality, testing, site visits, interviews, etc. should be studied."

Two of his conclusions are quoted below:

1. "... some minimum flow greater than the present summer flows and some maximum flow less than the present maximum must be established. This range of flows needs to be selected in light of the recreation interests on the lake and the timing of the drawdown."

2. "The present system of releasing all stored water in a great surge in the fall is unacceptable even if the present system of operation is kept. Much more refinement in removing the stop-logs is needed so that water is released gradually with less damaging effects. Alternate operations will require some removal and installation of a few stop-logs during the summer as well."

A new dam was constructed in 1978-79 with an acceptable mechanical system designed to release stored water gradually throughout the Labor Day to November 1 required drawdown period.

Doyle stated in his thesis that biologist Irizarry reported his 1973-74 studies (Project F-53, Job No. VIII for the Idaho Fish and Game Department) found, "Dewatering of kokanee eggs on drawdown is a major problem, for kokanee survival." Another department biologist, Levsink, found egg losses due to dewatering on drawdown during the years 1966 to 1968. Levsink (1966) and Irizarry (1974) both found the peak of spawning to be late November with the start of spawning for silvers around the first of November.

A well-known resort owner mentioned during an interview that he could remember the days in the 1950s and early 1960s when the silver spawners came in November, the bottom of the lake in front of his docks would be solid red and purple up to the shore line where they were preparing spawning beds. He further reported that when the Fish and Game Department representatives came in 1978, to check the early spawners that always show up the first week of November, they counted seven (7) spawners. He also commented on the fact that the months of May and October were, for years, their best months for cottage rentals. "Now, nobody comes for early and late fishing."

It is an ironic fact, as reported by Doyle, that the near eradication of game fish in Priest Lakes can be balanced against a mere $78,000 worth of electricity generated from the late drawdown of stored water. It is difficult to measure the loss to the economy of Priest Lake due to the poor early and late fishing.

The January 24, 1980 issue of the *Priest River Times,* carried a mysis shrimp article by Jerry Van Slyke. His conclusion was that by the planting of mysis shrimp in Priest Lake, man may be learning "through the school of hard knocks, not to upset the delicate balance of nature."

There is not a fisherman on Priest Lake who will quarrel with the fact that silver (kokanee) fishing is about gone. Van Slyke reported that federal and state biologists are planning to change the seeding pattern for the kokanee fry and perhaps introduce ling cod to the fish population in Priest Lake in an attempt to revive sport fishing. The introduction of ling cod could well be another disaster.

One well-known Priest Lake fisherman has dedicated himself to the eradication of mackinaws. He catches his legal limit each day during fishing season. In fact, he has privately encouraged the dynamiting of feeding holes of the macks in an attempt to reduce the mack populations.

At least one Priest Lake dry fly fisherman would publicly support a project of this type. He is sure the 2, 4, 6, and 8 pound mackinaws that are roaming the entire area of the big lake are rapidly reducing the cutthroat population.

The many pictures of cutthroats that were caught in the lakes prior to 1950, attest to the fact that the lake at one time was an elysian body of water for a dry fly fisherman.

Van Slyke's article stated, "Many fishermen . . . have reported finding up to 30 fry at a time in one mackinaw's stomach." 'A mackinaw trout will eat up to five small silvers a day,' said John Grant recently, a knowledgeable Priest Lake fisherman."

The tallest fish tale in the Kaniksu that was uncovered during research for this chapter is taken from A.K. Klockman's diary, pp. 33-34. Bill Stoner and Klockmann took a "white fly," (a stick of dynamite) with them on a trip up to American Falls on Upper Priest River to get a big char that they had previously seen in the pool at the foot of the falls.

According to a quote from the diary, "Bill carefully lowered the

Fig. 78 Winter catch of fish, Upper Priest Lake, 1925. Left to right:
Lavina and Fern Geisinger.

dynamite just under the large shelf of rock, lit the fuse, and told me to
run down into the middle of the river, where it was shallow and watch
for the stunned whale. I did, the explosion came, and soon after there
came the fish on his back, his mouth open and closing showing large
teeth, so that I actually hesitated to grab him behind his gills. I called
for Bill, who came running and grabbed the fish with both hands
behind the gills and dragged him out to the shore.

″ . . . Stoner, fully six feet two inches tall, put a heavy stick through
his gills and carried him over his shoulder. To give you an idea of the
size of the fish, his tail was dragging on the ground behind Stoner.

″We butchered him like an animal . . . and he had several large
trout in his stomach.

175

"It was a huge char, a species of trout. I have regretted ever since that we didn't take the time to skin him and have him stuffed, as I think he would have been the largest and the oldest specimen of his kind known to be in existence . . . What a pity that we carried no kodak with us in those days."

Fig. 79 Char and cuts in the 1920s. (Duffill Collection)

16

THE ELKINS

Elkins' Resort, like its predecessors, Bert Winslow's landing and the Jarrett Brother's fishing camp, was the takeoff point for trips north on Priest Lake in the 1930s. Ike and Sue built 32 log cabins and the main lodge at their resort during the winter months of 1931-32. By 1936, it had become a favorite spot for early and late fishermen, vacationers, a place to rent boats, or hire launch transport to points north.

Isaac Albert "Ike" Elkins was born near Rogersville, Tennessee, ran away from home when he was 16 years old, and landed in Newport on July 5, 1910. On his way out he got a job in Illinois tamping ties on a railroad track to earn enough money to travel to Newport where he had two cousins. He regretted that he didn't have enough money to stop in Montana to see the Jeffries-Johnson fight on July 4th.

Ed Dowd was Ike's first boss when he started to work in the lumber yard for the Fidelity Lumber Company. When the 1910 fire jumped the Pend Oreille River and started to burn on the hill back of where the Diamond mill now stands, all the men were put on fire lines. There was a logging operation on the hill and the horses had to be led through the fire down into the river to save them. Ike spent 42 days as a water boy on the fire in and around Usk.

Ike said, "It was so smoky that you couldn't see more than 100 feet in any direction." The fire went halfway through Montana before it burned itself out. It has been estimated that the fire burned more timber than has been logged since. It was the worst forest fire that ever hit the North American continent.

Ike was also on the 1931 Freeman Lake fire. He said, "When it came over the hill, boy was it a traveler! Forest Service supervisor Jim Ryan called me at my garage and asked me if I would take four or five of my men and go up and take a look at it.

"By the time we got there it was crowning and going up the next hill. When I got back I told Jim it was going to be a bad one and he had better get 400 or 500 men and get them out there, quick. Jim said,

'Don't you think you are a little excited, Ike?' I said, "no, she's going to go in this wind.

"A few minutes later the lookout on Stone Johnny Mountain called in and said to Jim, 'The fire is getting awfully close, in fact it hit the tent right now, goodbye!' He made it out with only three or four slight burns. The fire cost more than $90,000. More than 1,000 men were needed on the fire line to corral it."

Shortly after the 1910 fire, Ike started working for the J.C. Lilly logging outfit. Most of the time he waited on tables and helped in the kitchen. From time to time he worked in the woods if the boss was shorthanded. He loved the outdoors and his interest in and aptitude for logging stayed with him throughout his life.

He learned to know the lumber end of logging when he worked as a lumber grader for Fidelity. A few months before he enlisted in the army for WW I, he had a few small logging contracts near Newport.

When Ike came to Newport, Oldtown, Idaho, was a wide open town. In his words, "I don't know how many saloons there were there, but there were a lot of them. It was wide open for everything. There were at least 75 girls most of the time in those places. In those days I had a Cadillac, one of the two cars in Newport. A doctor had the other one. The girls would come from Spokane on the 'Dinky' train. I hired a young fellow to drive my car and he would pick up the girls and take them to Oldtown. We would also take them shopping and back to the railroad station when they were ready to return to Spokane. I had a pretty good thing going there for awhile."

Just before Ike went into the Armed Forces, he had logged the Hanson homestead near the corner where the Priest Lake Library now stands. He gained confidence as a young man through his logging experience as a lumber grader and logging contractor. This was to his advantage when he went into the army.

Ike was sent to boot camp at Fort Lewis, Washington. Before he finished basic training, word came down from the C.O. that he wanted to talk to anyone who had had experience as a logger. Ike was the only man in the company who admitted he had worked in the woods. The C.O. believed his story and he was transferred to Fort Vancouver, Washington. From there he was sent to Bridal Veil Falls, Oregon, on the Columbia River to cut spruce for airplane construction.

The soldier-loggers were paid regular logger wages, ate with the officers, and were treated royally. Portland and Vancouver were ruled off limits for the soldiers. They had too much money to spend and it would not look good to throw money around during war time.

There wasn't much to do around the logging camp for recreation so the loggers and officers made their own recreation, playing poker.

Ike put his former training from the bunk houses of logging camps to work. He said, "I had to work two shifts to put all my training into gear, one in the woods and the other around the poker table. When I was discharged at the end of two years I had $20,000 in the bank. That money set me up in business. I had one of the first garages in Newport as well as a logging operation in Pend Oreille and Bonner counties."

Ike didn't like the indoor work connected with his Buick-Chevrolet garage so he got the Shackleton brothers to go into partnership with him. The partnership lasted for many years and expanded to include garages in Ione and Metaline Falls.

Ike's brother, John, came west to help him with the contract logging. They set up the base of their operation on the Tom Strayer place about a mile downriver from the east end of the Oldtown bridge. In the beginning, Ike had one team of horses, an old Republic truck with hard rubber tires, and a minimum of other logging tools. They logged throughout the country, as far north as Nordman and downriver to Ione.

Shortly after the 1931 Freeman Lake fire, Ike got a contract to log out 7,000,000 board feet of white pine from the Pine Creek area. The smallest top to take out was ten inches and no log was taken unless it had 50% gradeable lumber. He laid out the logging roads for transporting the logs to the log dump on Priest River.

At the height of the operation 18 to 20 teams of horses were skidding and hauling logs, sometimes in six feet of snow. Twenty-five trucks were hauling the logs to the river. "It was a good operation," Ike commented. "The trucks hauled the seven million feet out in 42 days."

Through the years, Ike worked on six different Priest River log drives. The big boss on the river drives was Joe Williams. Ike entered into several other ventures as a silent partner or a financial backer.

In the late 1920s Ike loaned $3,000 to Tom and Bud Jarrett to purchase the property, that is now Elkins' Resort, from Bert "Scotty" Winslow, for a fishing camp. Bert was an old-timer on Priest Lake who had a good reputation as pilot and owner of the steamer, "W.W. Slee."

By 1931, near the bottom of the Great Depression, the Jarretts decided they could not make a go of the fishing camp and told Ike he could have the property for their $3,000 loan. It occurred at the right time as Ike still had his crew from the Pine Creek job. He made a deal

179

with them that if they would stay with him, he could pay $1.50 a day and board and room. Jobs were few and far between, so the crew gladly accepted his offer. They cut enough cedar and tamarack from where they had logged the white pine to build 32 cabins and a lodge for a resort on the Winslow property.

There was no sale for cedar, red fir, or tamarack at that time so the cedar mills were glad to cut shakes and shingles on a share arrangement. Ike had his own sawmill to cut the tamarack and red fir needed for the resort job. While the crew cut the logs and dumped them into the lake, Ike laid out the roads, cabin spaces, and the lodge area. The original cabins for the resort were all constructed with logs and poles from the Pine Creek burn. It was virgin timber and the fire burned mostly the needles and left a lot of perfect trees for logs. The beautifully matched logs of the original 32 cabins at Elkins' Resort attest to this fact.

Sue Fischer met Ike Elkins while she was teaching in Newport. Sue was born in Duran, Wisconsin, a small town east of Minneapolis, Minnesota, and came to Newport with her parents, Thomas and Cara Phelps Fischer. Sue and Ike were married June 27, 1920.

Sue's first trip to Priest Lake was July 4, 1921. She remembers well the wagon road from Priest River to Coolin. She also vividly remembers the beautiful tall trees that were so thick that the sky could be seen only here and there.

She remarked, "I was so impressed with the beauty of the lake. In spite of the fact that Ike was working elsewhere until the last few years, we have had the good fortune to share the beauty and serenity of Priest Lake. Each summer for many years we made several trips to the little lake. I don't think there ever has been a trip up the channel that one or the other of us has not remarked, it is unbelievable how beautiful it is."

During the early years of the Elkins' Resort operation, Sue came up only for the summer months. She stayed at their home in Newport so their three children, Al, Janet, and Joan, could attend school. When the children were older, Sue shared the work with Ike. "It was hard work and long hours," said Sue. "Fishermen would begin arriving April 15, and we had lots of them, until the end of fishing season in October or November. Everything had to be reserved: cabins, boats, and motors. We had to have a cabin, a boat to go with the cabin, and motor to go with the boat. Nobody ever brought up a boat in those days, let alone keep one at the lake. I had charge of all this.

"We didn't hire a cook until the first of July, so I told the fishermen that if they wanted to come out to the kitchen to eat their meals family style, I would cook for them. For breakfast, as an example, I would prepare big platters of hotcakes, sausages, bacon or ham, eggs, and put them on the table. They had a marvelous time. They would sit around the table morning, noon, and night and tell fish stories until I practically had to chase them out of the kitchen. I'm sure the fishermen appreciated the meals in the kitchen as there were no restaurants around here that opened up early in the spring or stayed open that late in the fall.

"The cutthroats they would bring back in those days! Most of our fishermen were from Spokane and the surrounding area and many of them came back year after year. Then the Fish and Game Department decided we had more fish up here than we knew what do do with, so they set up traps on Gold Creek and other spawning creeks around the lake. They took out so much spawn they ruined our lake. To think of that beautiful fishing that is probably gone forever!

"When we started the resort it was very primitive. We had wells scattered among the 32 cabins and the tenants would get water from the pumps at the wells. We had little Lang woodburning ranges in the cabins. As the years went by the women didn't want all that inconvenience. There were not too many true nature lovers left and we had to start modernization. Thank heavens, that all came under son Al's regime after he got out of the service in 1954.

"I'll never forget the big stove we had in the resort kitchen; big ovens, big flat space for cooking hotcakes, bacon, ham, eggs, and fried potatoes. It was a real art to keep it stoked with wood so it wouldn't be too hot, or get too cold.

"Not too many years ago we had a big garbage pit up the road toward Nordman. The bears used to come in there by the dozens. One time one of our guests asked me what we did for entertainment. I told her we would swim, go hiking, boating, canoeing, sunbathe, play bridge, and when we got really bored we would go up to the garbage pit and watch the bears.

"I would make a point of taking our personal guests there. One evening I took a group up in my car and there were 8 big bears having a great time. They really entertained my friends. They were fun to watch. It took a lot away when it became necessary to take garbage to huge land fills. There are not many bears left around resort areas. There are too many people."

While Ike, Sue, and their children were operating the resort, Ike continued his logging business.

In 1954, when his son Al, took over the resort, Ike decided to begin retirement. But that was not to be. He took a big logging contract at Ruby. When that was completed he went into the mobile home business at Orofino and Kamiah, Idaho. He and Sue lived in that area for several years. At that time they began going to Florida for five or six months each winter. Ike bought swamp land and spent his time clearing and filling it for sale as housing lots. On one piece of property Ike bought, there was an old house which the Elkins completely remodeled for themselves.

Sue told the story of a trip she and Ike took to Tennessee in 1927. It was the first time Ike had been back home since he was 16 years old. She remembered it well, as it was the year the interstate bridge was built in Newport. The engineer on the bridge wanted a new sports model Buick with all the trimmings. He wanted it broken in before he bought it. In those days a car had to be broken in before you could drive fast. Ike, being in the garage business with the Buick agency, agreed to go to Detroit and pick up the car for the engineer.   On the way back to Detroit on the train, Sue and Ike decided to extend their trip and go back to Ike's old home. They drove the new Buick to Tennessee via Lake Erie, Niagara Falls, New York City, Washington, D.C., and down the Blue Ridge Mountains to Tennessee.

Sue described their visit, "When we drove up to Ike's sister's place she almost had a heart attack. Here was this kid who had run away from home when he was 16 with only 30 cents cash in his pocket, with this beautiful sports car and a wife. Ike never did tell why he was driving the Buick. We had a great time meeting and visiting with all of Ike's many relatives."

The first time Ike saw Priest Lake was in 1912. He drove up from Newport with a friend by the name of Stewart, in a buggy pulled by one horse. They went from Coolin to Granite Creek by boat. He recalled, "I never saw such fishing in my life, before or since. The holes were full of dollies and you could catch a sack full of cutthroats in a couple of hours.

"I never saw such a wild country in all my travels. I don't remember seeing many cabins on the lake in 1912. A little later Cougar Gus had sort of a houseboat on the lake. Huckleberry Finn had a boathouse on the little lake. Pete Chase had a cabin on Upper Priest where he made moonshine. He was still there in 1932 when the Federals went up there and caught him. They stayed at our resort overnight. They had Pete, two gunny sacks full of beaver hides, and a gallon of Pete's moonshine. They didn't do much to him as Pete was back in three or four days.

"In the logging business during prohibition, moonshine was very important. Every Saturday I would have to go out and rustle up a gallon or two, as I couldn't keep my loggers around unless they had some liquor to drink. If Pete and his friends were out of moonshine, Millie Ward was always a source, as she had connections in Montana. A lot of these old boys on my crew couldn't work the next week if they didn't get drunk on the weekend. They could and would drink anything!

"We used to do a lot of fly fishing on the little lake. The best spot was on the bay to the left of the mouth of Upper Priest River. Several times we would stay in the Gumaer cabin on the shore of the bay.

"Another time I was up on the lower West Branch where Fidelity had a logging camp. The cutthroats were coming up the creek so thick you could scoop them out with a bucket. We pulled water out of the creek right from the kitchen. What a place."

Ike was a big game hunter as well as an excellent fisherman. In spite of a very busy work schedule he found time to make several hunting trips to Alaska with his good friend Dr. C.P. Getzlaff, a Newport physician. When they made a trip in 1925, they went the inside passage on a passenger ship. They ran into a violent storm and everyone on the ship got sick, including most of the crew and Dr. Getzlaff. Ike and a couple of the nurses escaped. When Ike and Dr. Getzlaff boarded the ship, Getzlaff had signed the register, "Dr. C.P. Getzlaff and colleague, Ike Elkins." When Dr. Getzlaff took to the sack, the nurses, in sheer desperation, started calling for Doctor Elkins. Ike said, "I didn't really know what to do, so I asked C.P. how I should handle the situation. Dr. Getzlaff said, 'You're the only one who can walk. You check as best you can, and come back and report, and I'll tell you what to do.' For the remainder of the trip I was greeted with great respect as 'Doctor Elkins.'"

Ike knew a lot of the men who worked for Dalkena when they were logging the Caribou country in 1912. The camp was on Caribou Creek where the old dam is. It was on this operation that he first saw *sand monkeys* at work. They were a vital cog in getting logs to the creek during the winter.

The roads for the logging sleds were iced from water tanks that sprayed water down each sled runner rut. The water would freeze and the ruts were solid ice. When a driver came to a downhill section of the road, he would have to check the speed of the sled, as there was no brake system to keep the load of logs from running over the horses. If the ruts were slick from ice or new snow, he would holler "sand."

On each downhill stretch, there would be one or two men near a hot fire. Surrounding the fire would be several buckets filled with sand. If sand was needed to slow the speed of the sleds, the right amount of sand would have to be poured into each rut by the sand monkeys. If the sand was too hot, it would melt through the snow or ice and wouldn't hold the sled back. If too much sand was applied the horses would have to pull too hard and the driver would yell, "hold the sand." If the sled got to going too fast the skinner would yell, "more sand." If too much hot sand was in the ruts, it would stick to the sled runners and the driver would have to wait until the sand cooled.

There are still signs of the dam across Caribou Creek about two miles above the mouth of the creek, where the Dalkena Lumber Company stored water. When they got ready to move the logs down, they would blast a hole in the dam, float the logs down the creek into the Thorofare, and then into a big boom in Mosquito Bay. Tracks of the old sleigh haul are still visible on the east side of the creek.

Ike was well acquainted with Rose Hurst. He said, "The first time I saw Mrs. Hurst I thought she was a man. She came into the resort one day with a pack on her back, a fur cap, a big mackinaw, pants, and had on a pair of snowshoes. She was trapping beaver as far north as the Thorofare."

Ike knew Capt. Markham very well. He used to stop in at the resort to drop passengers, mail, and supplies. Ike said, "He came into the dock one evening to drop some passengers. His young son was standing on the bow trying to tell his dad exactly what to do. Capt. was an excellent pilot and knew how to handle the big boat. I think he hit the dock a little hard to teach his son a lesson. As he hit the dock, his son flew clear over the dock and into the water on the other side. Capt. Markham said, very matter of factly, 'Son, I told you to wait until I landed.'"

One of Ike's favorite characters was Millie, wife of Ward Adams. Ike went their bail several times during prohibition while they were operating Millie's Bar in Oldtown. Millie was a good Catholic, in her own way and on her own terms. She knew Father Flannigan of Boy's Town. Once in awhile when he came west, Millie would take him on a tour of Priest Lake in her big Steelcraft cruiser. One time when Father was visiting, Ike called her on the phone and said, "Is this Sister Millie? She recognized my voice and boy, did the blue smoke start to fly out of that phone!"

On another occasion Millie blew her stack at Ward because he got lost in the woods while on a hunting trip with Ike and R.D. Smith. Ike and R.D. had told Ward where to go and exactly what to do. He promptly got lost. This irritated Millie to no end. Ike and R.D. had to come back to get lanterns when they hadn't found him by dark.

R.D. finally found him about midnight. Ward was on his hands and knees, crawling in circles, praying, and crying all at the same time. He had lost his gun, was badly scratched, and completely exhausted. Ike went back to get the pickup and drove it to the end of the road about two miles from where R.D. had found him. He was a larger man than R.D., but R.D. carried him out because Ward was unable to walk. It was a long time before Millie would let him forget it.

Jack Rule worked for Ike from 1932 to 1936. Then he moved up to the little lake and lived in the Milwaukee Mine cabin near Plowboy Campground. The story was that Jack was a black sheep and an outcast from a blue blood family in England. Ike took him a bottle one day when he went up with a couple of guests to fly fish. Jack invited them in for lunch of venison mulligan stew. Ike said everyone ate it. After a few drinks, Jack got quite talkative and admitted the stew was beaver meat.

The first trip Ike and Sue's daughter, Janet, made to Priest Lake was when Ike was building the first log cabins at the resort. She remembers seeing Bert Winslow's boathouse on the lakeshore. Some of Ike's crew were living in it. Others were living in finished or partly finished cabins.

Her first memories of the north end of Priest and Upper Priest were picnics, swimming, and other trips in her Dad's Chris Craft cruiser. They generally came to Mosquito Bay or the sandspit Occasionally the family had the thrill of having Ike's trusted employee, Huey Eiler, bring them up in the "Silver Streak," a big, safe, inboard cruiser. The fishermen all preferred this boat for chartered trips to Upper Priest because several of them could stand on the big forward deck to fly fish.

Jan was born in Newport, graduated from Newport High School, and attended Whitman College where she was affiliated with Delta Delta Delta sorority. In 1944, she married R.D. Smith of Newport and Priest Lake.

In October, 1947, Jan, R.D., and his mother, Mrs. Pearl Smith, bought the Sam Byars' homestead property from Mrs. Grace Byars. In 1952, Jan and R.D. purchased Mrs. Smith's share. When Jan and R.D. started work on a summer home along the Thorofare, there were no roads to the property on either side of Priest Lake. The east side road ran from Coolin to Indian Creek. The only road on the west side was a logging road that turned off the Nordman-Metaline Falls road and went up over Granite Mountain and down Tango Creek to Bottle Bay. They brought a caterpillar and other heavy equipment over this route and barged it to Mosquito Bay. Normal supplies were transported by boat from Reeder Creek Bay.

To get lumber for the buildings, R.D. and Al Piper, their next-door neighbor on the Thorofare, brought in and set up a sawmill, which solved the problem of getting lumber on the job. It was 1960 before Jan and R.D. began living on their property. Until that time Jan worked in Newport for J.C. Penney's.

Jan said, "Diamond Match built a pretty good logging road to Camp 9 and on up the Caribou. R.D. and Al Piper put in a passable road to our property. Al was a lot of help to us and a grand fellow."

Not too long after Jan began living on the Thorofare, the Priest Lake Waterways Commission installed a CB radio in the Drift Inn for emergency communication, as was done at several other lake resorts. Jan became the chief northern CB contact for mobile units. She was on almost full time duty during the Sun Dance and Trapper Creek fires in 1968. She has covered lost person searches and innumerable messages, such as, "I'm out of gas," "Call my wife," "I'll be late,"Call the resort and tell them their motor conked out on me," "I chewed up my prop, call so-and-so and have them call my wife and have her bring up another prop."

Jan, by her own confession, was not a hunter, fisherman, or a rough-and-ready outdoors woman. She did enjoy the people who would stop by as they went up and down the Thorofare. Being an Elkins, she had to be doing something for people and ended up opening the Drift Inn. She built up a good business that lasted 8 years. Her hamburgers and pies became legendary to all Priest Lake visitors. History will bear out the fact that no establishment or business on Priest Lake, in such a short time, was as well-known or remembered with such affection as Jan's Drift Inn. Every tourist, boater, fisherman, or canoer that travelled the Thorofare stopped by for a hamburger, piece of pie, a soft drink, a beer, or waved a cheery hello.

After R.D.'s death in 1968, Jan closed the Drift Inn and lived for a time with Ike and Sue in Florida.

In April, 1970, Jan married Orville Bailey, a well-known Boise contractor, state government official, and owner of a marina on Lucky Peak Reservoir on the Snake River.

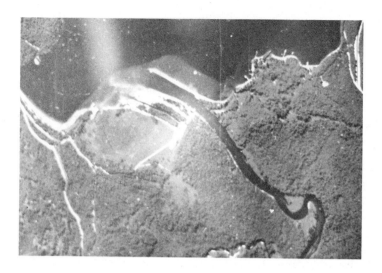

Fig. 80 Airview of the mouth of the Thorofare, Sandpiper Shores, Mosquito Bay, Beaver Creek area. (Courtesy Orville Bailey)

Fig. 81 The Jan Smith Drift Inn, 1960-1968.

The following summer they started on Jan's 20-year dream of a Sandpiper Shores Subdivision along the north shore of the Thorofare. The name was a natural selection, as sandpipers are regular summer inhabitants of the sandy shores of the Thorofare. The project became more than a dream when Northern Lights installed an underground electric service line to Sandpiper Shores from Indian Creek. The line was also extended across the Thorofare to the Beaver Creek Camp Association property.

The Sandpiper Shores Subdivision development was a large undertaking. First phase plans called for the development of 30 lots on the Thorofare and on a dug canal running parallel to the Thorofare frontage. Water, sewage, electricity hookups, and breakfront were installed on all lots. The next phase will start on sectioning the remaining 55 acres that are a part of Sandpiper Shores development.

One afternoon Orville was in their home when a well-known Spokane doctor walked in, sat down, and ordered a beer. Orville went along with the request as a courtesy and set him up a bottle of beer. When the good doctor went to pay for it, Orville told him he couldn't take money as the Drift Inn had not been in operation for the past five years. The doctor was so embarrassed he apologized all the way to his boat.

In Jan's words, "Isn't it a kick? A little world up here all by itself! It was real fun. I was young and brave, I guess. Without electricity it was probably a stupid venture, but I really had fun."

17

DOROTHY WINSLOW OVERMYER

Dorothy Winslow Overmyer, probably one of the prettiest and most talented second generation Priest Lakers, was born in Rambler, Minnesota, September 10, 1903. She came to Priest Lake in 1908 with her parents, Butler Bert Winslow and Pearly Mead Winslow. She attended the grade schools in Nordman and Priest River. Dot graduated from Priest River High School.

Dorothy, or Dot as she was always called, remembers her first trip up the Thorofare in 1908, on her way to her grandparent's home, Chauncy and Sara Mead. The Mead cabin was approximately one quarter of a mile up from the mouth of Upper Priest River.

In a personal letter Dot called attention to an incorrect statement that appeared in the local paper late in 1977. The story stated that Walter Slee transported Nell Shipman's crew, animals, and supplies to Mosquito Bay when she established her movie camp, Lionhead Lodge. Slee had sold the "W.W. Slee" to Dorothy's father several years before Nell Shipman set up her camp. Father Bert and brother Graydon were the pilots on the steamer at the time of the Shipman move to the north shores of Priest Lake.

Commenting on the Winslow family, Mrs. Rose Hurst remarked, "Bert Winslow was a fine man, he was a fixture around here for a long time. Graydon was a wonderful boy with a fine mind. Dorothy knew this lake like nobody else did. In fact, all the Winslows were well informed about this lake. Dorothy knew when it was a fittin' day to go out on the lake."

"The most exciting thing that happened to me during the years I spent on Priest Lake was co-starring with Nell Shipman in the film, *Light on Lookout*," commented Dot during a taped interview. In her modest way she explained that she was really supporting the star, as it was called in the days of silent movies.

Dot met Nell when she first arrived in 1921, with her production crew and animals. Dot's first trip to Lionhead Lodge was in January, 1923. She, Ralph, the leading man for the film, *Light on Lookout*, and Aubrey, her future husband, walked on the ice from Coolin to

Fig. 82 Left to right: Nell Shipman and Dot Overmyer at tree-line camp, Lookout Mountain, 1923. (Overmyer Collection)

Mosquito Bay driving the dog team loaded with supplies for the camp.

Several of the scenes for *Light on Lookout* were shot in six feet of snow while the party was camped for five days on the southwest slope of Lookout Mountain. It was located on the flat or bench at the base of the tree line near the steep pitch going up the trail to the top of the mountain. Water was obtained from the spring that is the headwater of Lucky Creek.

During the shooting Dorothy and Nell slept in a pup tent. The crew of Bobby Newhard, Barry Shipman, and Aubrey Overmyer, plus Ralph, the leading man, were housed in a big tent that also served as kitchen, dining room, and storehouse for supplies and production equipment.

Each day the crew would dog sled and hike to the tree line or above to film the required footage according to the script. "The one scene up there I really remember, was me standing on a steep ledge on the face of the mountain and the wind about blew me off. In the story I was Nell's cousin from the city, who had come visiting."

The movie was shown in Priest River and Spokane in early 1924. Dot never got to see herself play in the silent two-reel thriller. The film was shown throughout the U.S. and Canada.

Fig. 83 At Lionhead Movie Camp. Left to right: Nell Shipman, Dot
Overmyer, Bobby Newhard (photographer), Ralph leading man
for the film, *Light on Lookout*), Barry Shipman.
(Overmyer Collection)

Fig. 84 At Lionhead Movie Camp. Left to right: Daddy Duffill, Dot Overmyer, director Bert Van Tyle, Barry
Shipman, Nell Shipman, Bobby Newhard, leading
man, Ralph. (Overmyer Collection)

Dot remarked, "It wasn't all work, hardship, and struggling in deep snow while making movies. We had a lot of fun. There was a large cabin at Lionhead Lodge as well as many outbuildings on what is now called Shipman Point. I recently located the spot where cameraman Bobby Newhard lived with his wife, Edna, and their two girls, Betty and Joyce.

"There was a big living room with a dining room area and a large kitchen in the main lodge. We had a record player with lots of good records. We danced, played cards, read, studied scripts, and told stories by the hour.

"Nell was a very strong-minded person. At first I felt she was a little hard to get acquainted with. Once we got to know each other she was very warm and friendly. She and I got along exceptionally well. She was a topflight woman in every respect. I must admit she held the whip hand. She ran the place. She knew a lot more about picture taking than her director, Bert Van Tyle.

"Barry was the pet of the camp. He was the cutest boy, with great big brown eyes. He was 10 years old when I was there at age 18. We had a lot of fun together.

"Bobby Newhard was Nell's first photographer while at Lionhead. He was a talented, hardworking, likeable young man, and photographer for the films I was in. The last time I saw Bobby was in 1926, while I was living in Newport. He came to Newport looking for a location to make pictures. He had dinner and spent the evening with us. We had a good time talking about old times at the lake. It was wonderful to see him again."

Dorothy related three additional scenes from her movie career that have been prominent in her thoughts. The first scene was taken on the log that crosses Lion Creek on the east side trail. "The story involved my getting lost in the woods. I had to crawl across the log on my hands and knees and pretend that I was falling off the log and into the water that was rushing underneath. The boys had caught a procupine and had him in a cage. The scene called for Porky to come out of the woods and scare me. Nell said, 'When the porcupine walks up to you don't pretend to scream, really scream.' I gave a real scream and the next day Porky wouldn't come out of his cage.

"The shooting of the next scene was on Mosquito Bay. The script called for me to be wandering around in the woods as a lost girl from the city. A bear came out of the woods, we were working with Brownie on the loose, and he scared me. When I was scrambling across a foot log my skirt caught on a broken limb. I yelled at Nell that I couldn't get across the log as my skirt was caught. Nell told me

Fig. 85 Leading man Ralph, Dot Overmyer, Nell Shipman. (Overmyer Collection)

Fig. 86 On location near Lion Creek. Left to right: Dot Overmyer, Aubrey Overmyer, Barry Shipman, Nell Shipman, Ralph. (Overmyer Collection)

to keep going regardless of what happened. The camera ground away, the crew had a big laugh at my expense.

"Really, Nell's pet bear, Brownie, was so tame and so well-trained that you could put a stick of candy part way in your mouth, go up to Brownie, and he would take the candy out of your mouth!

"The third scene was filmed in a small cave over a rock ledge a short distance up Lion Creek. I was still lost and I took shelter in a small cave I'd found. I was sitting in the cave with my legs out on the ledge. Nell had brought her white wolf out to scare me by driving him through the cave. As he went by he ran across my legs. Nobody thought to check the other end of the cave and when the wolf saw the opening at the other end he kept right on going. Two days later some of the boys at a logging camp on Caribou Creek came down and told Nell that her wolf was at their camp. The animal trainer took his wolf cage up there and caught him.

"I could have reached out and touched that wolf as he went by me. I'll admit that I didn't have to act scared. I was, to say the least. The wolf scene was a most exciting incident. In fact, being in pictures and working with Nell is about the only excitement I ever had at Priest Lake."

Dorothy mentioned that she did not have a chance to meet and learn to know many of the old-timers around the upper end of the lake. She knew the Byars family, Daddy and Mary Duffill, the Geisingers, Gumaers, and the Angstadts.

"I was at the Angstadt's Lone Star Ranch many times. The main cabin was back a little way above Bear Creek. It sat up on a little hill on the north side of the meadow. The meadow was terrible. You took your life in your hands to try to walk across it, it was nothing but a bog most of the year. The Angstadts lived in a nice log cabin with a big living room, dining room, and a kitchen at the back. There were two bedrooms downstairs and three or four upstairs. It had a big front porch. There were two or three little log guest cabins nearby. I well remember the big rock that had the name, *Lone Star Ranch*, painted on it. The rock, as I remember, was fairly close to the house. Harry was dearly in love with Belle. He waited on her hand and foot.

"I also remember Lloyd Peters, his Dad, and Paul Jr. Father Paul was a tall man, perhaps 6 feet 4 inches. He was slender but very strong. He was more quiet than either of his sons. I think the father was as much in love with Nell as was his son Lloyd. I believe they were both movie-struck men. It was kind of a family affair. Paul Sr. worked hard building cabins, pens, and sets for the movies.

"I was well acquainted with Coyle Bowman because he worked for my Dad on the "W.W. Slee." Lloyd Peters mentioned Coyle in his book as 'Coil Anderson.'

"I also got well acquainted with Jesse Parsons during his visits to Priest Lake. He was a real character. During the bathing beauty contest I was in, Jesse had on a great big lady's hat and bathing suit with a bright colored scarf around his middle. The contestants paraded across a little artistic bridge over a strip of sand that was the bed of a little creek. The girls in the contest were unaware of Jesse following us. He purposely fell off the bridge to the delight of the audience. That was Jesse Parsons in all his glory."

According to the article written by editor Parsons that appeared in the *Priest River Times,* July, 1923, Dorothy won the beauty contest and was given a supporting role in another two-reel silent movie. The article included a detailed statement of the day's activities that has become known as Band Day on Priest Lake.

When Miss Shipman organized and presented a benefit show to raise money for band uniforms, one of the specialty acts was Dot Winslow leading a high kick can-can dance, choreographed by Nell. During interviews, several old-timers have mentioned Dorothy's talents and her photogenic qualities. One person commented that even as a small child, Dot was very pretty in the lovely clothes her mother made for her and she had a natural ability to pose for the camera.

While with Shipman Productions, Dot married Aubrey Overmyer in Spokane in June, 1923. Nell and Bert Van Tyle stood up with them at the wedding. Aubrey was a Newport boy. They became acquainted when Aubrey worked for Dot's Dad on the "W.W. Slee." He became an assistant cameraman for Bobby Newhard.

Late in 1923, Dot and Aubrey left Nell's movie camp and went to Newport. They lived in the Newport and Priest River area for several years. Dot's daughter, Janice, was born in Newport in 1926. Dot and Aubrey separated in 1929.

In 1929, she became bookkeeper and office girl for Tom and Bud Jarrett, who had bought Bert Winslow's fishing camp at Reeder Creek. When Ike and Sue Elkins took over the fishing camp in the late fall of 1931, Dot continued on the job for the next 12 years. During the winter months of 1932, '33, and '34, Dot's mother took care of daughter Janice while Dot took a bookkeeping and secretarial course at Kinman Business College in Spokane.

"For many years my Dad and Donald operated the "W.W. Slee" and th. Winslow fishing camp. Bert died in 1947. Donald passed away in 1956. Their ashes were scattered over Priest Lake. Mother died in 1961, and is buried in Spokane."

Dorothy continued her reminiscing, "I was at Elkins' Resort until 1943. When I left I worked as bookkeeper for Melcher's Tire Store in Spokane. When they sold out I went to work for the Big Mountain Ski Lodge at Whitefish, Montana. I was there for two national ski meets. In 1958, I was employed by the Great Northern Railway in Glacier Park until I retired, for the first time. In 1962, I moved to Spokane."

Retirement was not to Dot's liking, so she applied and got a Civil Service appointment with the U.S. Post Office. Her first assignment was at Shadle Park in Spokane. Later she was transferred to Harper, Washington. She stayed there until she retired a second time and permanently, in 1970. With a sly grin she remarked, "When I retired, they closed the post office."

She now lives in Port Orchard, Washington near her daughter and family. She continues to come often to Priest Lake to enjoy its beauty.

18

THE SHIPMAN SAGA

Nell Shipman, silent screen actress, writer, and producer, built a movie camp she named "Lionhead Lodge" on the south side of Mosquito Bay on Priest Lake during the winter months of 1921-22. For the following four years, the Lodge served as her headquarters, home, and office. Shelters were built for members of her crew, as well as for her two dog teams, several horses, and pens for zoo animals.

Prior to coming to the northern shores of Priest Lake, Miss Shipman and a sizeable staff moved to Spokane from Hollywood, California. They shot indoor scenes for Nell's feature length silent motion picture, *The Grubstake*. After work on the indoor scenes was completed, Nell and her director, Bert Van Tyle, spent a month visiting various areas in the Pacific northwest in an attempt to locate a suitable area for filming the outdoor scenes for the movie. When they returned to Spokane, Van Tyle announced to the film crew, "I have never seen anything to match the beauty we found at Priest Lake." The board of directors, a group of Spokane businessmen who backed the venture, asked Nell why she demanded such an out-of-the-way spot. She replied, "I want exteriors to match the true locale of the story I am filming, and to me Priest Lake is the loveliest, wildest, most perfect spot of all."

One of the chief organizers of the company backing the venture was the father of Dorothy Playter. Dorothy and Nell had become close friends during the filming of *Back to God's Country* at Great Slave Lake, Northwest Territory, Canada.

Nell's experience with on-location filming with nature as scenery began in 1919, on the shores of Great Slave Lake near the Arctic Circle. This background gave her a lot of confidence while selling the board the idea of moving her production company to Priest Lake for the outdoor scenes. She also had the advantage of using the experience from the James Oliver Curwood film *Back to God's Country* in which she starred and co-produced.

Dorothy and her husband, Wellington, ran a movie studio at Minnehaha Park in Spokane. Apparently Dorothy's father had put up the money to finance the production of some of their films. To recoup some of his losses, he conceived the idea of selling $180,000 worth of stock to finance *The Grubstake.*

Curwood's *Back to God's Country* had been a real financial bonanza. The backers of this production realized more than a 300% profit on their investment.

Miss Shipman's lack of experience as her own business agent, was overshadowed by confidence in herself. Her enthusiasm and courage, bordering stubborness, convinced the board they really couldn't lose money on the production.

The board approved the move to Priest Lake, perhaps with some reluctance, in spite of the fact a sizeable portion of the budget had been spent during the filming of indoor scenes at Minnehaha studios. A reduced crew and the entire zoo of more than 200 animals were transported by truck to Coolin, Idaho, at the south end of Priest Lake. At Coolin the crew and zoo were loaded onto Sam Byars' steamer and a large barge for the 21-mile trip north to Sam Byars' Forest Lodge, at the mouth of the famous Thorofare connecting big and little Priest Lakes.

The company leased the Byars' hotel and outbuildings for the fall and winter of 1921-22 while their permanent camp was being built in the Lionhead area on Mosquito Bay. Simultaneously work began on shooting outdoor scenes. The company added a few local men to their staff on a part or full-time basis, including Elmer Berg, William "Daddy" Duffill, Earl Geisinger, Joe Gumaer, Cougar Gus, Bob White, and others.

Fortunately for the film, but unfortunately for the crew and animals, the winters the company was on location, the weather was in a cold deep snow cycle. During the winter all materials and food for the crew and animals had to be transported by dog sled from Coolin to the north end of the lake. The distance by ice was 21 miles, when it was solid, and by shore trail almost 24 miles. The trip on the ice, when it was firm, was a relatively easy two-day trip. By shore trail the trip was a four-day struggle. The Halfway House, located in Bear Creek Bay just east of the mouth of Granite Creek, was a rest haven for tourists and local travelers. The Halfway House was the home of Harry and Aunt Belle Angstadt. It was a large rustic log cabin, also known as the Lone Star Ranch. Part of Nell's picture *Wolf Brush* was shot on this spot. Nell's crew would use Halfway House as an overnight stop, both going and coming. They had one overnight stop at Mrs. Handy's hotel in Coolin while they were loading supplies.

Kevin Brownlow, writing in *Parades Gone By* used Nell Shipman's Priest Lake venture as an example of "the most incredibly rigorous conditions endured by many early pioneer film makers — for the sake of the picture." The *Atlantic Monthly* of May, June, and July, 1925, serialized a story of the hardships of movie making in the rugged Kaniksu Forest in the Panhandle of Idaho.

Barry Shipman, Nell's son, spent a lot of time with the movie crew. He said, many years later, "To me the years there were one big lark." He did concede at the same time, that his mother had engaged in a real pioneering effort. He wrote in 1976, "We are a nation built by pioneers and the long-ago, outdoor movie making effort that established the movie industry had its pioneers too. My mother could well be included in that group. A brief description of how it was then might put some perspective on the long-ago, outdoor movie making effort. The company transported all materials and supplies by boat or dogsled, built their own cabins and other shelters, chopped their own wood, poached their own fish and game, read by lamplight, and taxied out by dog team during the winter months. They coped with handcranked motion picture cameras, struggled with cantankerous klieg lights (a carbon arc lamp), and managed with many other inconveniences that were common in the early 1920s. Today, I understand there is a road all the way up the eastern side of the lake. Cabins and vacation cottages abound, public parks are in use, and for all I know there may be electric lights and television."

Realizing what Nell went through, Tom Fulbright gave Nell her title, *Queen of the Dog Sleds*, in an article he wrote for the 1969 issue of the *Classic Film Collector*. He stated in the writeup, "She is the person we old fans associate with dog sleds, parkas, and canoes rushing toward rushing waterfalls. She is a beautiful girl who is so well able to take care of herself, and most times the hero also."

Miss Nell Shipman, the name she preferred for her professional life, did not keep a diary and as a result there is not an accurate record of the day to day activities, trials, and tribulations, the high and low spots of the four years on location at Lionhead Lodge. Lloyd Peters, Sr., author of the book, *Lionhead Lodge, Movie Land of the Northwest,* took and kept a large number of pictures of the Shipman era. Without Mr. Peters' pictures and a number of his personal remembrances, particularly of the activity during the first winter, not much remains of the true story except legend, and stories, of a few old-timers who worked for Nell, plus a few brief paragraphs in Nell's autobiography, *The Silent Screen and My Talking Heart.*

Without question the major problem was financial. No records are available on the total amount the Spokane backers put into the project. Mr. Peters reveals in his book that not all wages were paid to all crew members. He refers in particular to the trip Nell and Van Tyle took to New York to sell the film, *The Grubstake*. It took them so long to sell the film, that winter came to northern Idaho, ice froze to a depth of several inches, and snow began to pile up along the lake shore and in the mountains. When word came that the film had been sold and the money was in the bank in Spokane, huge quantities of winter supplies for man and beast were purchased in Spokane and Priest River and hauled by horse-drawn sleds to Coolin.

The company and the film got a lot of free publicity as many daily papers across the country printed pictures and ran stories of the struggle the movie crew and Bert Winslow had in getting the winter's supply of food and equipment to Forest Lodge.

Fig. 87 Cabins at Lionhead Lodge, 1923.

With a locally built ice-breaker made of logs, wide enough to make a channel for the barge, attached to the front of Bert Winslow's steamer, the "W.W. Slee," it took seven days to break the channel as far as Canoe Point. He was still two miles short of the Thorofare. The seven days included many trips to the shore along the way to cut and load tamarack cord wood needed to fire the Slee boilers. From Canoe Point the supplies were transported by dog sled across the ice to their headquarters at the Byars' resort.

With the supplies paid for and stored, work proceeded on building the permanent camp in Mosquito Bay. Late in the year the New York source of money began to dwindle to an insignificant amount. Nell made a trip to the coast with her pet bear and her parka and raised $1500 in Portland and like amounts in Seattle, Tacoma, and Spokane. She appeared personally with her bear at the premiere showing of *The Grubstake* in each city.

To further ease the financial burden, Nell wrote, produced, and starred in several "butter and breakfast" two-reel thrillers that were sold for a good sum. These included *The Love Tree, Wolf's Brush, White Water, The Light on the Lookout,* and *Trail of the Northwind.*

The final months of Nell's venture on Priest Lake were catastrophic and were undoubtedly frustrating and humiliating. It took all of her courage, ingenuity, as well as her mental and physical strength to cope with the problems. It became obvious to her that she had to give up. The mental breakdown of her director, Bert Van Tyle, was a severe crisis. He was having very serious problems with his feet, due to the many times they had been frost bitten. He refused to give up until gangrene set in and the pain was such that he went berserk and had to be taken to Spokane for treatment. Joe Gumaer, one of Nell's faithful friends, took things in hand and by force took Van Tyle to Priest River and put him on the train for Spokane.

Creditors were closing in on the operation. Several lawsuits were filed for wages and unpaid bills. There was no money for food for the animals and at times not too much for the few remaining crew members, or Barry and Nell. Nell, with her own hands, killed the last horse she had to feed her dogs and zoo animals. A near-by logging crew finished their operation and gave her a generous supply of hay and grain for her nonmeat-eating animals. However, some of the animals became so weak they had to be destroyed.

While Nell was out making a last desperate attempt to raise money, Elmer Berg and Daddy Duffill took care of the animals as best they could. Nell's trip was unsuccessful, but fortunately the San Diego Zoo agreed to take what was left of her animals and would pay the transportation costs from Priest River to California. A large number of Nell's friends volunteered their time and equipment to get the animals to Priest River.

In a letter, Nell told Olive Woods of Priest River, that two

Fig. 88 Daddy Duffill in midst of animal cages, Lionhead Lodge, 1924.
(Jan Bailey Collection)

circumstances led to the failure of the Priest Lake venture. One was the freight costs of $1.00 per pound for getting supplies from Priest River to Lionhead Lodge. The second circumstance, the immediate and biggest reason, was that the firm in New York that held foreign distribution rights for *The Grubstake*, American Release, went into bankruptcy on the day that a company in Great Britain paid American Release thousands of dollars for the foreign distribution rights.

Caught in the middle, Miss Shipman's dream went from sure success to what she called, "An absolute, total, and massive crash." One of her biographers said of her, "Undaunted, she picked up the pieces and turned to writing."

Another factor that could be mentioned is Nell's and Director Van Tyle's lack of experience in financing a venture as expensive as the filming of a feature-length silent movie. It was more a matter of not understanding the intricacies involved in peddling the rights for the film's circulation. After the showing in New York of *The Grubstake* before a large number of potential buyers, Nell was depressed because she was not immediately beseiged with offers. She was desperate and was willing to accept almost any amount of money under any conditions. She did not realize that the apparent indifference on the part of the buyers was all a part of the game. Each buyer was standing by waiting for someone else to make the first move toward an offer.

When the first buyer offered her a deal, she grabbed it within the next twenty-four hours. She received only a pittance toward an advance payment with little or no guarantee for additional income from the film. As soon as news of the deal leaked out, one buyer, whose name later became synonomous with film making in Hollywood, offered to advance Nell $10,000 for the rights with a promise of many such additional payments. She had already made a legal deal and could not accept the second offer.

The film was successful in the U.S., Canada, and several other countries throughout the world. At the premiere showing in Spokane, ticket holders queued up for four blocks at the threatre doors. The same experience was reported from Portland, Seattle, and Tacoma. There are only two known copies of the film today and these may be obtained at $750 per showing.

The following three stories that appeared in the *Priest River Times*, J.G. "Jesse" Parsons, Editor, the first in the March 8, 1923 issue and the next two in the March 22, 1923 issue set a historic record for a special premiere showing of a feature-length film in a small town.

"Manager George Nelson, announced that *The Grubstake*, Nell Shipman's famous picture which has been playing to packed houses in Spokane, Portland, Seattle, and Tacoma, is the attraction for the opening of the New Rex Theater, Sunday evening, March 18, at 7:00 o'clock. The entire house was reserved for the showing.

"Movie critics have stated that the techniques of the northern scenes in this picture are better than in any picture ever released."

"The Priest River Cultus Club held a luncheon in honor of Nell Shipman at the Charbonneau Hotel, Sunday, March 18, at 2:00 PM. The paper stated that it was one of the outstanding social events of the season.

"About 70 Cultus Club members and their guests, including a number of ladies from Coolin attended. The Cultus Club girls, Dorothea Van Winkle, Frieda Bunde, Mary Nelson, Catherine Van Valkenburg, Katherine Nelson, and Vivienne Beardmore assisted Mrs. Charbonneau in serving.

"Mrs. A.C. Van Valkenburg gave a short address in behalf of the club and extended an honorary membership in the club to Miss Shipman to which she replied in her charming manner and displayed her kindly feelings for Priest River people. Nell gave a reading she had composed, *We Can All be Stars at Home*. The members of the Cultus Club were Nell's guests at *The Grubstake* showing."

"Sunday evening, March 18, the Priest River Band started playing several selections at 6:15 in front of the Charbonneau Hotel, in honor of Miss Shipman. They marched to the Rex Theater where they played for the crowd while C.W. Herr took flash pictures of the band, the theater, and the crowd.

"Boy Scouts, Donald McCombs, Glen Brown, Norbert Treat, and James Parsons were ushers. Within several minutes after the doors were opened the house was packed. J.G. Parsons introduced Miss Shipman who charmed her audience in a few words about her picture. She then gave a reading of her own composition about the great northwest in which she extolled it as the finest land and the place she called home.

Nell's director, Bert Van Tyle, had as his guests the station agent, the postmaster, the village council, the marshall, the editor, and a number of his friends from Coolin and Priest Lake. William "Daddy" Duffill was one of them and had not been to Priest River for more than four years. Van Tyle announced that he would furnish a feature film, a two-reel comedy and two vaudeville acts for a benefit performance for the band."

Nell was born in Victoria, British Columbia, Canada, October 25, 1892. She was christened Helen Foster, by her parents, Arnold and Rose Barham who were both of English extraction. She had one brother, Maurice. Shortly after she was born, her parents moved to Seattle and lived there and on Bainbridge Island. She attended Seattle grade schools and at an early age was given piano lessons with the parents' fond hope that she would eventually become a concert pianist.

At the age of twelve, daughter Helen announced to her parents that she had theatrical ambitions. They reluctantly enrolled her in the Egan Dramatic School of Seattle. Near the end of her second year of study, she got her first professional engagement playing the ingenue in a touring company's production, *At Yale*. The show appeared in many large cities in the country and closed in New York late in 1906.

In 1907 she played the piano, danced, and sang in Jesse Lasky's production of *The Pianophiends*.

In 1908-09 at age 16, she was the leading lady for Charles A. Taylor's stock company that toured Alaska. The play, *The Girl from the Golden West* was the most popular show of the company. Taylor wrote a play for her, *Girl from Alaska* that opened in Portland, Oregon. She also toured with the company in Washington, Idaho, and Utah. She appeared in several stage plays at the Seattle Theater with the Baker Stock Company under her own name, Helen Barham. She appeared in Vancouver, B.C. in an operetta as well as in stock. For a short time she did vaudeville sketches on the Pantages circuit. In 1910, she starred as Necia in Ernest Shipman's play, *The Barrier*.

In 1911, she married Ernest Shipman, a long-time Shakespearian producer and theatrical manager. With his brothers, Fred and Joe, the Shipmans operated a world-wide film distribution service. Joe invented the system that is still used in studios for picture blow-ups.

While son Barry was on his way to being born, February 24, 1912, Nell began writing. She won two first prizes for scenarios. Both were made by Selig Productions starring her and Hobart Bosworth. During this period, Ernest Shipman made the film *100 Years of Mormonism*. Later he became an independent producer in Italy and Canada.

In 1914, Nell Shipman wrote *Shepherd of the Southern Cross* which was one of the first silent movies to be produced in Australia. She also wrote, *Under the Crescent,* published by Grosset & Dunlap and later made into a movie by Universal Studios as the first picture of a series starring Ola Humphrey. Also in 1914, she was hired by Universal to write three three-reelers starring Jack Kerigan to be filmed at Lake Tahoe. During the filming of the stories *Son of the Stars, Melody of Love,* and *Goodbye Summer,* the director and the leading lady quit and Nell took over both jobs. Son Barry started his acting career in one of the three-reelers. Somehow she found time to write *The Wreckers* and *The Gunman,* for Universal, as well as other titles lost or forgotten.

Vitagraph Studios co-featured Nell and Bill Duncan in James Oliver Curwood's *God's Country and the Woman.* This was the first of the big outdoor wild animal pictures. Part of it was made in three months of shooting in the Big Bear country in Canada. The remainder was shot in the company's Hollywood studios. It was a good moneymaker.

While under contract with Vitagraph in 1916-17, Nell starred in *Through the Wall* with Bill Duncan, appeared in *Wild Strain,*

Cavenaugh of the Forest Rangers, Gentleman's Agreement, Girl from Beyond, Baree, Son of Kazan, and six *Wolfville* shorts.

Under contract with Fox Studios, she had the lead in *Fires of Conscience* starring Bill Farnum. For Lasky-Famous Studios she played the lead in *The Black Wolf.* Frank Richter directed and James O'Neill played the father in this picture.

In 1920, Nell, as an independent producer completed *Saturday Off, Trail of the Arrow,* and *Something New.* She also obtained a divorce from Ernest Shipman.

From 1921-24, in Fulbright's words, "She made outdoor nature and wild animal shorts, played personal appearances over Blue Mouse Circuit, made a lot of history, front pages, features and shorts, got caught in two bankruptcies, (American and Louis Selznick) gave her animals to the San Diego zoo, lost the studio property and became seriously ill. Some of the story is told in *The Movie That Couldn't be Screened,* in the *Atlantic Monthly,* May, June and July, 1925."

In 1925, following the Priest Lake period, Nell married Charles Austin Ayers, a talented artist. They lived in France, England, and Spain for a short therapeutic interlude for Nell. May 3, 1926 twins, Charles Douglas and Daphne Ann, were born to the Ayers in La Caruna, Spain. While in Europe, Nell wrote a syndicated column for Florida papers, *The Tamiami Trail.*

Late in 1926, the Ayers moved back to Sarasota, Florida, and Nell made a silent film, *Queen of the Sarasota Fiesta,* under the sponsorship of John Ringling. She wrote and attempted to produce her pageant play of Florida. The land boom in the state collapsed and production ceased.

In 1928, she wrote and produced her first sound picture, *Are Screen Stars Dumb?* In 1919, she wrote *Get That Woman,* and *M'sipu Sweetheart* which was selected as the story for Clara Bow's comeback at 20th Century Fox. It was never completed as a film. Her children's fairy story, *Kerly Kew and the Tree Princess,* was well received. Nell was deep in her writing in the 1930s. She wrote and Dial Press published her novel, *Abandoned Trails. The Eyes of the Eagle,* written by Nell was produced by Arthur Hornblow under the title *Wings in the Dark.* The film starred Myrna Loy and Cary Grant.

One of Nell's major disappointments came when Will Rogers was killed in an airplane accident in 1935. He was to star in a story *Hot Oil* that she wrote in collaboration with G.P. Putnam. That same year she divorced Charles Ayers. The rumbles of WW II stopped production of Nell's story *Jungle Ship,* an outdoor wild animal picture to be produced in South America starring Nell, Martin Johnson, and Frank Buck.

From 1940 to 1958, Miss Shipman wrote commercials, enlistment films, documentaries, patriotic scripts, and an anti-communistic film, *The Fifth American.* From 1958, until her death in 1970, Nell wrote several books, did research, and completed her autobiography.

Tom Fulbright included a special note in his *Classic Film Collector* article to the effect that "emphasis in the later years seems to be upon writing, it was obvious (to him) that the objective has only been an attempt to come back to her own business — motion pictures."

In March 1923, while Nell was in Seattle appearing personally at a showing of *The Grubstake*, she read a story in a newspaper that the newly organized Priest River Band needed money for uniforms.

The Priest River Band was organized March 12, 1922. The band consisted of 4 clarinets, 8 cornets, 3 trombones, 2 baritones, 3 altos, a base, a tenor, and one snare and one bass drum. Prof. Ralph Sdao, the leader, was a former Italian Army officer and during the Fourth Liberty Loan Drive toured the U.S. as assistant leader of one of the finest Italian Military Bands.

George J. Naccarato was the first president of the organization. Each band member signed a note for $50 to be held as a bond that he would obey the rules and be faithful in attending practice. The leader had to sign a $100 note.

When Nell returned to Coolin, where she was spending part of her time that winter, she put together a benefit show for the band.

In a letter dated June 23, 1968, Nell asked Olive Woods if she knew, or could find, the names of the two girls who did the "Can-Can" act with Dorothy Winslow at the benefit performance for the band uniforms. She added, "The benefit show must have taken place after the roads opened up in the spring. This was not a showing of *The Grubstake*, but a vaudeville show rehearsed at Coolin during the winter prior to the band visit to Lionhead Lodge covered so completely in an article by J.G. Parsons, dated July 19, 1923.

"The show consisted of the following acts: Three local girls, led by Dorothy Winslow (she acted for us in some two-reelers, as did her brother, Donald) performed a dance I had taught them, a real old-time high kicker routine, which was a great success.

"Barry Shipman and his school chum, Donald Winslow sang *Gallagher and Shean* that lifted the roof off the hall. There was no living with them after their knockout performance. I was playing the

Sado's, Priest River Band

Fig. 89 The Priest River Band. First row, left to right: Ralph Sdao, band leader, Mike Bombino, Mike Lamanna, Pete Bombino, Pete Mauro, Ed Naccarato, Ernest Jachetta, John Contino, Romeo Mauro, George Copelli, Fred Simmons, manager. Second row: Gus Naccarato, Phil Naccarato, Charlie Naccarato, Frank Bombino, Herman Lartz, Joe Bombino, Joe Pagnotta. Top row: Tony Veltri, Mike Maio, Tony Moriniti, Frank Bassio, George J. Naccarato. (Courtesy Mr. and Mrs. Pete Mauro)

piano and I got to laughing so hard I fell off the piano stool. I added a single, something I had done in personal appearances, where I put on different hats and sang and recited. The show closed with my pretending to impersonate local celebrities like the chief of police, H.W. Brinkley, the mayor, the fire chief, etc. These appeared as 'still-lifes' framed. If the names of all these old-timers could be mentioned, that would be a piece of real reporting. The show as I've attempted to describe it, was put on in Priest River sometime in 1923, prior to the band trip up the lake to show me their new uniforms."

A story of the show appeared in the P.R.T., May 24, 1923. "Friday nite the Rex Theater had a larger crowd than even its opening night, when Nell Shipman, author, director, producer, and actress in moving pictures, of the Nell Shipman Production Company, which is located at Lion Creek on the north end of beautiful Priest Lake, gave a benefit performance for the Priest River Band. All the seats were sold, many were seated in chairs in the aisles and balcony and still many more stood up, and each and everybody got their money's worth.

"The performance opened with an overture by the band, which was followed by another piece by the band complimentary to Miss Shipman.

"Then came a dandy two-reel animal comedy, Brownie Bear in *Saturday Off*, which was a wonderful picture for the kiddies and enjoyed fully as much by grownups.

"Paul J. Peters sang, *When You Look in the Heart of a Rose*, and Miss Elizabeth played a piano solo, *Prelude in C Sharp Minor*, by Rachmaninoff.

"The Coolin Colleens, Dorothy Winslow, Mildred Kieth, and Ethel Bartges, then appeared in a dance specialty, and were encored until one of their number had to announce that their limit had been reached.

"The work of Donald Winslow and Barry Shipman, as Mr. Gallagher and Mr. Shean, respectively, then brought the heaviest applause of the evening, as these small boys portrayed these comic characters to perfection. Many remarks were heard that this number of the show alone was well worth the price of admission.

"The next and last number was the nine-reel Nell Shipman picture, *The Girl From God's Country*. This is a wonderful picture of the north woods and its wild life in the beginning and ends with some daredevil aviation stunts.

"Miss Shipman accompanied the vaudeville numbers and Mrs. A.C. Van Valkenburg accompanied the pictures. Beulah Crowell, Mary Huff, and James Parsons were the ushers.

"The receipts from the show were $206, which added to the amount already subscribed, makes enough to pay for their uniforms.

"The members of the band particularly wish to express their gratitude to Mr. Van Tyle and Miss Shipman and the members of their company, who came so far to give this benefit for them, to George Nelson for his assistance, to Stanley W. Jones for transportation, to Warden L. Fann for his services in measuring members for uniforms, to the Priest River Commercial Club for their putting on the drive for the uniform fund, to the *Priest River Times* for printing and its continual boosting for the band since it was first organized and to the firms and individuals who made cash subscriptions to their uniform fund."

Fortunately a marvelous story of the band's trip to Lionhead

Lodge was printed in the *Priest River Times* July 15, 1923. The story was written by editor and publisher, J.G. Parsons. With minor deletions the story is printed verbatim for its historical significance.

"Last Sunday is a day that will long be remembered by many Priest River and Coolin folk as well as many that came from different sections of the United States, the occasion being a visit to the Nell Shipman Camp at the head of beautiful Priest Lake.

"It all started as a band appreciation day for the benefit performance Nell organized to raise over $200 for band uniforms. The performance filled the Rex Theater to overflowing and some people had to be turned away.

"In planning for their entertainment, Miss Shipman decided to make it a big day and invite everybody in the Priest Lake and Coolin area and feed the bunch barbecued beef. So an invitation was issued through the *Times* and excursion rates were arranged with the Priest Lake Transportation Company to handle the people to Coolin from Priest River, and from Coolin to Lionhead Lodge up the lake with Bert Winslow and his steamers. Stanley Jones, the efficient manager of the Transportation Company handled a large number of people, at $1.00 per head, from here to the lake and many more went in their own cars. A number went up to Coolin the evening before so that they would be sure to be there to catch the boats.

"At Coolin over 200 merrymakers loaded on a barge towed between the steamer, 'The W. W. Slee' and the tug, 'The E. W. Harris,' and on both boats and the happy party started for the long trip to Mosquito Bay.

"The band, resplendent with new uniforms, played many times going up the lake and their music was fine, sounding better than ever on the water.

"On arriving at the camp, it was found that many had already arrived, and Miss Shipman and Bert Van Tyle were on the dock to welcome everyone. The first thing on the program was the inspection of the zoo containing many wild animals of North America as well as quite a number of dogs. After that everyone lined up and were served barbecued beef sandwiches, doughnuts, watermelon, and coffee.

"After lunch the sports were started in the water, and prizes were given for each event, each one being a picture of Miss Shipman framed by herself in some novel manner.

"Following are the winners of the events: 100 yard dash, Wayne Wright, Priest River; Evinrude race, Elmer Berg, Priest Lake; row boat race, Bill and Louie Whetsler, Priest River; girls' swimming race, Marion Manchester, Spokane; long distance swim, Frank

Hutchinson, Diamond Match; log paddling contest, first heat, Bill Whetsler; second heat, Louie Whetsler; third and final heat, Louie Whetsler; children's swimming race, Curtis Beardmore, Priest River; diving contest, George Beardmore, Priest River; bathing beauty parade, Dorothy Winslow, Coolin. The first prize, in addition to the photo of Nell in this event, was a part in Miss Shipman's next movie.

"In a special Evinrude race between Aunt Belle Angstadt and Elmer Berg, Belle broke one of the steering ropes on her boat and ran full speed into one of the steamboats. This furnished an extra thrill for the crowd, but fortunately no one was hurt, and she went on and won the race.

"Other events, with no winners listed were: motor boat race, Earl Geisinger, Harry Angstadt, Lloyd Peters and S. Sybelden; rowing race, Paul Peters, Daddy Duffill, Diamond Match crew; long distance swimming, Ray Peters, Barry Shipman, Diamond Match crew; 100 yard dash for men, Ray Peters, Lloyd Peters, Paul Peters, Diamond Match crew; high diving and fancy diving contest, Lloyd and Ray Peters, Diamond Match crew; water basketball, Lionhead Lodge and Diamond Match crews versus Priest River and Coolin.

"The band boys presented Miss Shipman with a large, fancy box of candy and a box of cigars for Mr. Van Tyle.

"After the contests Barry Shipman did some exhibition diving."

Vivienne Beardmore McAlexander reminisced about the big day during a conference with the author. "I remember so well the band trip to Nell Shipman's movie camp. A cousin of mine from Oshkosh, Wisconsin, and a friend of hers were visiting us at the time and father had his Cole-8 car with jump seats. Six or seven of us rode to Coolin in it. They were greatly impressed with Priest Lake and the animals in Nell's zoo. It was a memorable trip for them. The only thing that spoiled the weekend was the poisoning of one of Nell's prize sled dogs, Tysore.

"Everyone was in a happy mood. The band uniforms were so good looking, "I'm sure they had a great appeal to the young men who played in the band. They were a good bunch of musicians, if not, they really had their hearts in the music, under the direction of a wonderful leader, Ralph Sdao. The band played and people moved about on the barge and danced to the music of the band from time to time. Some of us had to sit on the back end of the barge. That's where the sparks from the steamer's smokestacks landed, as the tamarack wood very liberally gave off sparks. For the occasion my mother had made a beautiful white organdy hat for me. By the time we got back to Coolin it was so peppered with black holes that I had to discard it.

211

"It was a gala day! Jesse Parsons led the bathing beauty contest. What a character he was! He borrowed my two-yard long, bright red chiffon scarf, draped it around his waist and pranced before us like a majorette. Dorothy Winslow and I were in the contest with several other girls whose names I can't remember. Someday I want to give my prize picture of Nell to the Bonner County Historical Society."

During an interview with Inez Anselmo Fiedler, she said, "As a young mother of 17, I made the band trip to Mosquito Bay with my 15 month old son, Frank. We had a marvelous time, it was really a big deal! One of the highlights of my life. I'm not sure that Frank enjoyed the trip as I took along only a box of graham crackers for him to eat.

"We enjoyed seeing Nell's zoo, the barbecue, the sports and particularly the bathing beauties, Vivienne Beardmore, Agnes Peterson, Dorothy Winslow and several others.

"It was a 'slow boat to China' trip but we danced on the barge, sang songs, and made merry all the way up and back . . ."

Martha Aherns Jacky also made the trip. She remarked, "We had such a good time, I had almost forgotten that the band made the trip. I do recall, with vividness, colorful Captain Bert Winslow and the beautiful high dives made by Barry Shipman."

Elmer Berg had worked for Nell Shipman off and on while she was on location on Mosquito Bay. After the Shipman Productions folded, Elmer dismantled three of Nell's cabins and re-erected them on his property. They are still in use at BCCA. For many years foundations of some of the other buildings, a number of old wire cages, and the parquetry floor of the main lodge were distinguishable on the site of Shipman Productions. Years later when the Idaho Department of Parks and Recreation began work on the Lionhead unit of the Priest Lake Parks, the remaining cages were disposed of. Over the years the stories of Nell's venture remain legendary.

After WW II, when the land rush began along the shores of Priest Lakes, interest in the history of Nell Shipman's silent movie camp intensified. The increase in boat traffic, the Drift Inn venture of Jan Elkins Smith, and the increase in the number of people building summer homes around the lake, culminated in a continuous request for information about the early history of the area and about Nell Shipman. When she died in 1970, the *Priest River Times* featured a "Tribute to Nell Shipman."

By 1975, interest and curiosity led to many conversations and reminiscing about the area. A chance remark made by the author to Orville Bailey of Sandpiper Shores led to the naming of the area

Fig. 90 The last standing edifice at Lionhead Lodge, 1966. (Al Piper)

occupied by Nell Shipman's camp, Shipman Point. Orville, a personal friend of R.P. (Phil) Peterson, Deputy Director of the Department of Parks and Recreation and then Acting Director, suggested that the author make such a recommendation to Mr. Peterson. The suggestion was made and a reply was received from Phil requesting a resume be prepared of Nell and the "point" so he could present the recommendation to the Board of Directors of the Department. In October, 1975, a letter was received from Mr. Peterson confirming the fact that from that day on the land occupied by Nell Shipman's movie camp was to be known as "Nell Shipman Point."

The naming of the point led to an impressive ceremony dedicating the area in honor of Nell Shipman on August 31, 1977. The idea for the dedication involved four individuals over a period of several years, Janet Elkins Bailey, Lloyd Peters, former Governor Andrus, and Barry Shipman.

In 1964, Lloyd Peters, Sr. after visiting the site of Nell Shipman's movie camp, stopped by the Drift Inn for lunch. Among the items that decorated the walls of the inn was a photo of seven old-timers of

213

Fig. 91 Left to right: Don Bremer, Joe Walker, Mrs. Walker. Shipman Point. Plowboy Mountain in background. (Beulah Shipman)

Priest Lake. Mr. Peters recognized some of the men in the picture and began to tell stories of Nell Shipman, her crew, the zoo animals, and the fun and frustration of making silent movies in the 1920s. Jan enthusiastically encouraged Mr. Peters to put all of his stories into book form which was published in 1967. When author Peters learned the camp site had been named "Shipman Point" he contacted and received enthusiastic support from former Governor Cecil Andrus for his idea to officially dedicate the area in Nell Shipman's honor. Peters also contacted Nell's son, Barry Shipman. Barry not only approved of the dedication idea but put a lot of thought and energy into organizing the ceremony. His invitation idea titled, *Come to the Point* is just one of the several major contributions he made to the ceremony.

Governor Andrus had already won legislative support for a Priest Lake State Park and work was immediately started on the Lionhead Unit in preparation for the ceremonies originally set to be held in July, 1976. The appointment of Andrus as Secretary of the Interior

Come To The Point!

To all friends, fans, and movie nostalgia buffs — dedication ceremonies honoring silent film star and pioneer film maker, Nell Shipman, will take place August 31st, 1977, at Nell Shipman Point, Lionhead State Park, Priest Lake, Idaho.

Nell brought the great Northwest to the world's movie screens. See where it all began when Idaho and Hollywood pay tribute to a great lady.

Fig. 92 "Come to the Point" design by Barry Shipman.

slowed work on the project and it was not until Governor John Evans was briefed on the project that details were approved and progress was resumed. A great deal of special credit must be given to author Peters for his work on the details of the dedication project.

On the day set for the dedication, Governor Evans was attending a national conference at the request of President Carter. William J. Murphy, a native of north Idaho, and acting governor of the State of Idaho, made history by stating directly to the family of Nell Shipman, "In the name of the people of Idaho, I hereby dedicate this place as *Nell Shipman Point* in the Lionhead Division of Priest Lake State Park, to be a constant memorial to the courageous woman whom we honor today."

Lt. Governor Murphy praised Miss Shipman for her vision and confidence to begin the production of motion pictures in the northwest which gave people everywhere a chance to share the natural beauty of the state through the medium of motion pictures. He mentioned the fact that the hardships and the tragedies suffered by her production company served as the trailblazers for other movie companies and productions that would bring honor to Idaho. She was an early leader in filming outdoor scenes on location. Feature film and TV companies are now recognizing Idaho as a vertible gold mine for set locations.

Hollywood, like Nell Shipman, found Idaho! In 1931, MGM filmed *Northwest Passage* starring Spencer Tracy, Robert Young,

215

and Walter Brennan in Coeur d'Alene and McCall. In 1940, *It Happened in Sun Valley* starring Ronald Reagan and Claudette Colbert was filmed at that famous resort. In 1941, *Sun Valley Serenade* with Sonja Henie and Glenn Miller was filmed at the resort by 20th Century Fox. *The Wild North* starring Stewart Granger, Cyd Charisse, and Wendell Cory was filmed in 1951, by MGM in north Idaho. In 1956, *Bus Stop* with Marilyn Monroe was filmed near Sun Valley. *Idaho Transfer*, produced by Peter Ford, was filmed in southern Idaho in the early 1970s. *Breakheart Pass* starring Charles Bronson, Jill Ireland, and Ben Johnson was filmed in northern Idaho in 1975, by 20th Century Fox.

According to other remarks made by the Lt. Governor of Idaho, a policy will continue to welcome filmmakers to Idaho. As a result the state is enriched economically as approximately 40% of all production costs remain in the state. He also emphasized the point that important as the economics are, the state must look beyond them and realize that the creativity, the drive, and the intensity involved in movie-making offers an exhilarating and enriching experience to all citizens of the great state of Idaho.

Barry Shipman's response to Lt. Governor Murphy's dedication remarks was an emotional experience for him. In his words, "This kind of an experience doesn't happen every day. To come back after 55 years and find so many friends who felt so kindly and warmly about your mother, it kind of gets to you."

Among the guests Barry met was his school teacher at Coolin, Loui Turner Frasier. He reminisced about his grade school days in Coolin. "Everybody loved Loui. She let us bring carrots, potatoes, meat, and even onions, which we cooked on top of a big, round central heating stove. That was our hot lunch program. What a teacher! How I loved that woman!"

At the time Barry went to school in Coolin there were seven grades in the one-room school. He remarked that he felt he didn't have to go to school anymore because he had learned all there was to know from grade one through grade eight.

Barry stated that his memories were naturally very different than the incidents his mother wrote about. To him it was somewhat of a lark. He realized that there were a lot of problems, injuries and hardships, but it all was part of making movies. He told about one of his vivid memories, the making of a two-reeler that was trying to teach a boy about trapped bears.

Nell wrote the story with the Northwind as the villain and his grandson who was supposed to be taught a lesson in trapping bear.

Fig. 93 Coolin schoolhouse. Barry Shipman and Loue Turner, teacher 1923-25. (Beulah Shipman)

Daddy Duffill was the trapper, who got caught in one of his own bear traps. Nell and the grandson, Barry, were to go for help on a dogsled. "I'm on the back of the sled, as I could mush dogs and mom was riding. You know how the ice buckles and gets rough in places. We made it a little worse and I'm supposed to fall into the water. She gets out of the sled and comes back to pull me out and she falls in.

"We had one camera and it was on shore for the long shots and to see the big sled go by just before I fell in. That's all fine! We have one camera! Now we have to do it for the close-ups! The cameraman, Bobby Newhard at that time, didn't trust himself to crawl out on the ice after seeing us go through it. He put a bunch of boards down, like a raft. That took a little time. 'Alright,' says Nell, 'in you go!' When both of us were in the icy water I climbed out too fast two or three times and mom grabbed my belt to hold me in and she pulled my pants down." The audience was delighted with Barry's dramatization of the scene. In true trooper style Barry remarked, "Well, that was movie making on location." He did tell the audience that he was on the trail of a copy of the film and if he ever finds it he will dedicate it to Lionhead Park and have copies made so it could be shown to visitors that will be coming to The Point in the years ahead.

There are now four generations of Shipmans in the movie-making dynasty. Nell, who is in the silent movie "Hall of Fame," Barry who has more than 70 screen script credits for TV and motion pictures, Barry's daughter, Nina Shipman Bremer, has appeared in 12 feature length films as a contract actress for 20th Century Fox, and Nina and Don Bremer's daughter, Westerly, has already made her debut in the movies and on TV. Nina has made more than 80 TV guest show appearances and more than 125 TV commercials. In 1975, she published a book, *How to Become an Actor in TV Commercials*.

The film that got Barry the most attention was *Stranger at My Door*. It had a very successful run for Republic Studios and has appeared on TV at least 25 times. He was part of the team that wrote 11 serials. Among them were *The Lone Ranger, Dick Tracy, Hi-O Silver,* and *Flash Gordon Conquers the Universe*. He wrote the original *Death Valley Days*, in the days before Ronald Reagan, when Stanley Andrews played the old ranger. The *Writer's Index* carries on page 160 the impressive list of Barry's screen credits.

Barry married Beulah McDonald, a contract actress and dancer at Paramount. She was featured in many Paramount musicals in the 1940s. The couple had three children. Mike, an artist, is a graduate of UCLA; Noel, a law graduate of Princeton; and Nina who graduated from Pasadena Playhouse.

Nina, like her father, warmly thanked the audience for the many touching comments that individuals had said to her about her grandmother. "I've known and lived in fantasy at Priest Lake ever since I can remember. Each time I asked Nell or my dad to tell me

Fig. 94 Beulah Shipman.

about their experiences we always ended up at Priest Lake. Today, to have had the chance to walk on this very same place that I have heard about all my life is a real emotional experience.

"I tried to picture everything I had heard about this area and it has been almost like a flash-back, like a summer re-run of all the stories I have heard since I was a little girl. I'm telling you, in all sincerity it is quite a thrill!

"I am awfully proud to be the granddaughter of this courageous, vital, dedicated, and stubborn woman who went about the business of making movies in an age before anybody heard the words, women's lib. Nell never had to be liberated. She was just Nell, she did her thing! I'm proud of her and I'm proud of all of you who cared enough about what she did and where she did it that you would take the time and trouble to come here to honor her today."

Jack Dalton, Park Planner for Northern Idaho, responded for the

219

Fig. 95 Nina Shipman Bremer, Shipman Point Dedication, August 31, 1977. Seated left to right: Claude Simpson, Tom Tharp, Acting Governor William Murphy, State of Idaho, Barry Shipman, Jack Dalton, Art Thayer, Lloyd Peters, Sr.

Fig. 96 Shipman Dedication display arranged by Lloyd Peters, Sr. (Brad Steiner)

Department of Parks and Recreation by giving special recognition to Phil Peterson and Mike McElhatton, assistant Director of the Priest Lake State Parks for the work they had done in setting the stage for the dedication program.

He further stated, "This area will be retained in its natural state in perpetuity. I can assure you that Nell Shipman Point will never become a site for a condominium, but will remain much as Nell found it 57 years ago."

Representing the Priest Lake Chamber of Commerce, President Tom Tharp, indicated that the preservation of the area was a life-long dream that came true. He said, "The permanent display that will be erected on this beautiful piece of shoreline will give the thousands of visitors who come here the real story of what transpired on this spot almost 60 years ago. The Chamber of Commerce is proud to have been a part in the dedication of this beautiful spot to a great lady, Nell Shipman."

Mayor Art Thayer, representing the city of Priest River, said, "Miss Shipman spread the name of Priest River from Juneau, Alaska, to New York. The citizens of Priest River thought so highly of Nell Shipman that the Rex movie theater held its grand opening, March 18, 1923, by showing Nell's film, *The Grubstake*. We would like to add our praise and gratitude to this kind and gracious lady who still lives in the hearts of Priest Riverites."

Author Peters reminisced about his firsthand experiences as a member of Nell's movie crew. He told the audience of over 300 that he remembered well his two years with Nell Shipman. "Everyone did a little bit of everything and everyone, including Nell, did his act. We cared for the animals, fed them, cleaned the pens, built scenery, freighted our supplies by dog sled in the winter, cut wood, and shot outdoor scenes from here to the top of Lookout Mountain. I would do it all over again if I had the chance."

Practically no factual information remains of Nell's activities during the winter months of 1923-24. Her zoo was still intact and someone had to be at the movie camp to care for the animals. How much time Nell spent at the camp is largely conjecture.

Pete Peters, Lloyd's father, and Ray Peters did go back to work for Nell in March or April of 1924. Lloyd went back to work shortly after July 30, 1924. In early winter, possibly the month of November 1924, winter scenes were shot for the film *White Water*.

Piecing together stories from Nell's autobiography, Peters' book, Elmer Berg's recollections, Fern Geisinger's memory of the winter, and Sylvia Gumaer Burwell's story of the closing of their logging

Fig. 97 The "Gal from God's Country."

operation on Armstrong Meadow, the end of the Shipman Saga may be told.

Between mid-November and Christmas of 1924, Van Tyle began to lose control of himself as a result of pain in his infected foot and worry about the survival of the movie-making operation. In a fit of rage he fired Lloyd Peters over a trivial incident in the kitchen where

Lloyd was acting as cook. A day later Ray Peters and Van Tyle got into a violent argument over an insignificant incident and Ray quit. He joined Lloyd who had gone to the Geisinger fox farm at the mouth of Upper Priest Lake for a short visit before returning to Spokane.

Lloyd apparently held no animosity toward Van Tyle or Nell, as he stated on page 168 of his book, "I want folks to know that they just don't come any finer than Nell Shipman and Bert Van Tyle . . . We had so many thrilling and happy times making pictures, and I'm sorry to say, some sad ones too. After three action-packed years, the wheel of fortune came to a standstill on the wrong number! We had some bad breaks, but they could have happened to anyone."

The business stationery used by Nell in 1924, carried some significant information. The official title of the company was, The Nell Shipman Studio Camp, Lionhead Lodge, Priest Lake, Idaho. Home of the famous Nell Shipman animal zoo. Bert Van Tyle, manager. Producers of *The Grubstake, Something New, Saturday Off, Neeka of the Northland, The Trail of the Arrow, The Girl from God's Country, The Romance of Lost Valley*. Now in production, twelve two-reel dramas of the great northwest. In preparation, *Over the Last Ridge,* and *The Purple Trail.*

Among the many beautiful tributes to Nell Shipman after her death, January 23, 1970, at Cabazon, California, was the one written by Dick Diaz, a Shipman right-hand-man since 1929.

Nell was a star
Her brilliancy was seen by many
Now that Star has passed from view,
We feel the loss so much
because Nell gave so much
She gladdened the hearts of millions
not only because Nell was a star
but because she was a woman
from God's country
and they understood.

Nell talked to animals
a deer was her friend
and it understood.

I have followed our Star since 1929
I've seen its effect on people and places
wherever Nell went
Those of us who understood
we'll always remember
Now Nell's gone back to God's Country.

In 1974, the Canadian Film Institute held a Nell Shipman Festival. It was a special tribute to her as Canada's First Lady of Cinema.

The October-November 1977 issue of *Screen Thrills*, has a Shipman dedication article by Fulbright and Thompson. The concluding sentence honors the Shipman name. The formal dedication ". . . will remain a lasting tribute to a remarkable woman whose multi-faceted career was directly responsible for bringing the film industry to Idaho and for bringing the beauty of Idaho to millions of film fans."

One incident in tracing Nell's career happened in 1953, that may be of interest to Priest Lakers. At that time Dr. Wilson Compton was Director of the Voice of America. The Comptons had arranged a social hour at their penthouse apartment in New York for all people connected with the broadcasts.

One of the guests, after placing her wrap in the bedroom, asked Mrs. Compton where she got the picture of Priest Lake that was hanging on the wall. Mrs. Compton reported that her husband at one time owned the Elmer Berg Resort at Beaver Creek on Priest Lake and that was a picture of the area. The guest remarked, "I'm quite familiar with the area as I lived there almost four years in the early 1920s. I am Nell Shipman!"

The magazine, *Scenic Idaho*, October-November 1977, carried the story of the Shipman Dedication written by Just Hallin.

Moody Powell Cook has a by-line article in the *Hollywood Studio Magazine*, Vol. 11, No. 3, February 1977, entitled, *Queen of the Dog Sleds*. The article was written by Claude Simpson at the request of Phil Peterson, Deputy Director, Idaho Department of Parks and Recreation that was directly responsible for the naming of Shipman Point. The same issue of the publication carried a dedication story by Thomas Fulbright, a long-time and dedicated chronicler of the life of Nell Shipman.

Incredible Idaho, a magazine published by the Division of Tourism and Industrial Development of the State of Idaho, Vol. 9, No. 4, Spring 1978, carried an article by Claude Simpson detailing the Shipman Dedication. Acting as Master of Ceremonies for the event, he concluded the program with the following words: "Nell Shipman was a true trail blazer! She left her indelible mark on this strip of land. She was born 60 years too soon. What a splash she would have made on TV and in sound and color motion pictures of God's Country around Priest Lake! Nell Shipman, we thank you for the privilege of witnessing the dedication of all this in your honor."

19

SYLVIA

No history of Priest Lakes, north of the narrows, would be complete without an account of Sylvia Gumaer Burwell's experiences, fortunes, and misfortunes of her 44-year struggle to maintain private ownership of her first home.

Sylvia Fremming of Westbranch attended Priest River High school for two years and was graduated from Newport High school. She married Joseph M. Gumaer in Sandpoint, November 10, 1921. Her lifelong friend Vivienne Beardmore McAlexander was her bridesmaid. A dance followed at the St. Elmo Hotel in Priest River to honor Sylvia and Joe's wedding, with more than 500 people attending.

August 13, 1923, Sylvia and Joe bought the Schurr homestead at the head of Upper Priest Lake. A short time later they moved into the well-constructed two room log cabin on Long Beach Bay with their six-month-old son, Donald.

Remains of the cabin are still visible a few yards south, or left, of the mouth of Upper Priest River. Upper Priest originates in Canada and crosses the border in Sec. 11, T 65N and flows south. About two miles from the mouth, the river heads E SE and enters the lake in the NE corner of Sec. 19, T 63 N. The 84½ acres of the homestead extend along the west and north shore of the lake. Approximately 15 acres lie south of the river's mouth.

Wm. P. Schurr and his wife, Nelle, began their permanent residency along Long Beach Bay in 1912. They spent the first summer building their log cabin. The following spring, they started a large garden back of the cabin. Joe Hungate, an early summer vacationer on Priest Lake, bought vegetables from the Schurrs and remembered, in particular, the luscious strawberries that were grown in the Schurr garden.

During the tourist season, the Schurrs would load their rowboat with produce and ply the shores of Upper Priest Lake, the Thorofare, and bays of Priest Lake as far south as Canoe Point selling their berries and vegetables. The logging camps on Caribou Creek were good customers also.

October issues of the *Priest River Times*, 1914 and 1915, carried personal items of Mrs. Schurr coming to Priest River to shop for the first time in two years and going east for the winter. The 1915 article quoted Mr. Schurr to the effect that he had a poor opinion of his bachelor ways of housekeeping while Nelle was visiting her family.

The Schurr Homestead Patent was signed by President Woodrow Wilson, January 19, 1920. In one sense of the word, it is ironic that the Schurr homestead was later taken from the legal owner even though the signed patent stated, "NOW KNOW YE, That there is, therefore, granted by the UNITED STATES unto the said claimant (William P. Schurr) the tract of Land above described; TO HAVE AND TO HOLD the said tract of Land . . . unto the said claimant and to the heirs and assigns of the said claimant forever; . . ."

Sylvia mentioned in a personal letter, August 13, 1977, that Mr. Schurr was a hard-working honest man. He broadaxed the logs for his cabin and hewed the cornice blocks until they looked as though they had been cut with a circular saw.

During the summer months, Schurr worked for the Forest Service. Wife Nelle had the green thumb. She was also a very hard worker and an excellent cook and housekeeper. Sylvia stated that she knew from her own experiences the hardships Nelle had endured.

In September 1918, Nelle suffered a brain hemorrhage and died on the homestead. Mr. Schurr laid the body out in a boat and towed it behind his rowboat that he rowed to Coolin. He stopped overnight at the Fish family home on the big lake. Mr. and Mrs. Fish wanted to help pay for the funeral expenses but Mr. Schurr would not accept their help. He insisted he wanted to put her away with his own funds.

Sylvia said, "I have visualized, time and time again, Mr. Schurr rowing the Thorofare and both lakes with the body of his wife lying there. She was everything to him, just everything. They had no children and he was left alone. He put his place up for sale and for many years did not get any takers, until fools like ourselves came along. Schurr died in Spokane in 1926 at the age of 68."

Sylvia continued, "As far back as I can remember, my husband, Joe, talked about owning his own farm. We lived on the Schurr homestead for five years, got it paid for, and Joe wanted to give it away as he really didn't have any farming blood in his veins. Nobody wanted it anyway, but of course, old me, who loved property, for the sake of its security, wasn't about to give it away. I spent five of the best years of my youth paying for it and nobody was going to get it without paying a good price. In fact, in 1926 we bought the Wheatley homestead property from Dr. Marion Setters of Spokane to further fortify my desire for security.

"One winter we had a logging operation on Armstrong Meadows. We skidded the logs with two two-horse teams to the Thorofare down the small creek or slough that drains the meadow. We lived in a hastily-constructed cabin on the east side of the meadow where I cooked for the men. Our logging operation was closed down overnight by a Forest Ranger on the excuse that the manure behind the barn was a hazard to the environment. The snow was three or four feet deep, there wasn't another human being within miles of the place, the manure pile was frozen solid, there wasn't even a mosquito or fly around, and yet we had no recourse.

"We didn't have time to use up our food supply or our hay and grain. Nell Shipman bought our supplies and unfortunately for us she went broke before she could pay for the provisions. That's all over the grade now. She had a hard time and we had a hard time too. I have always had a warm spot in my heart for Nell.

"During the first year at the lake my mother took care of Don part of the time, as I had so much to do I couldn't really take good care of a year-old child. On one trip my mother was going down the lake with him on the Byars' steamer. Nell was also on the boat. She took off her jacket, wrapped him in it, and entertained him all the way to Coolin. Mother thought Nell had a real way with youngsters.

"We got Frank Algren to come up as a sawyer. He sawed our logs for $1.50 a thousand and he didn't have a chain saw! It was rugged going in those days. I don't know how many board feet of timber we got in the Thorofare, but it was a lot. I showed my daughter-in-law the letter the Forest Service wrote closing up our operation and she just howled. I still can't understand the rationale behind the letter written back in those days.

"We did make a little money that year. The rest of the time we lived on what Joe made by working for the Forest Service, helping Nell Shipman, and an occasional job proving up on a mining claim for someone.

"You didn't live in luxury in those days. I had one dress. I wore men's wool pants, a wool shirt, and logging boots. It was slim pickings. If it hadn't been for my sister-in-law, Mrs. Charles Mears, Joe's sister, I wouldn't even have had one dress or warm things for the baby. Charlie Mears started and ran the Corner Store in Priest River.

"One day Joe and the crew were down on the logs in the Thorofare when Nell Shipman sent her cameraman to get Joe because her director, Bert Van Tyle, was raving mad from his infected foot and had threatened everyone in camp. It was the strangest thing, he simply was out of his head with pain from gangrene in his foot that had previously been frozen."

Joe didn't take the time to return and tell Sylvia what was happening. He didn't return until the fourth day. The men did not know what the absence was all about but they did report that he had to go out with Nell's director. Van Tyle would not let Nell accompany him on the sled. She did go down the lake but stayed far enough behind the dog sled to be out of Van Tyle's sight.

Joe Gumaer was as strong as an ox, had a lot of courage, and he handled the trip with no difficulty with the exception of the dogs. As Sylvia remarked, "Joe had one heck of a time with the dog team. He was green as grass about sled dogs! Joe later made the comment, 'If those dogs were mules I would have had a fighting chance to get them to do what I wanted them to do. The dogs would sit down when they got tired and wouldn't go until they got ready.'

"When Joe got Van Tyle to the Lone Star Ranch on Bear Creek his brother, Fred, was there and helped him get Van Tyle and the dog team to Coolin."

The ice below the narrows was mushy and the team and sled broke through the ice twice the last day of the trip. Nell walked the entire distance and finally convinced Van Tyle that she should accompany him to Spokane.

"It was no wonder Joe was gone so long," remarked Sylvia. "He was not a dog trainer or a dog team driver. When he got the team back to Lionhead Lodge he was so frustrated it took him several days to get back to normal. Was he ever glad to get rid of those mutts.

"We got to know Nell and her crew very well. Of course, they truly lived in a world of their own. I still have a note from Nell. 'Dear Sylvia: Do come over some sunny day when we are making pictures. We will have someone take you home.' Somehow I never got around to go over for the visit. We did stop there frequently on our way out or back."

Other acquaintances of Joe and Sylvia's included the Gregorys who bought the Angstadt place on Bear Creek; Frank Brown, one of Pete Chase's partners, spent most of his time digging in Pete's mine on Trapper Creek. A man by the name of Whittaker from Spokane would visit Pete quite frequently and transport a few gallons of *Uncle Pete's Monogram* to Spokane. Aunt Belle was one of Sylvia's very favorite friends. In Sylvia's book, Aunt Belle was a "real doll."

The Gumaers and the Geisingers were neighbors on Upper Priest and have remained longtime friends. "I had heard of Fern's fame for the biscuits she could make before I got to Upper Priest," said Sylvia. "Boy, could she bake them! She was a remarkable person in so many ways." She remembered Fern saying one day, "We can't pay our taxes on time this year as we don't have any money on hand. We have our meat, eggs, water, wood, and a small supply of salt, sugar, and flour — what more could we have? We really don't lack for anything."

"Wm. Schurr was not much of a talker," commented Sylvia. "I do remember him telling me that Dorothy Winslow's maternal grandparents, the Meads, filed a homestead on the Schurr property but let it go without proving up on it. No record of this statement appears on the abstract I have for my property. It is possible, I presume, that the Meads squatted on the spot prior to the formation of the U.S. Forest Service."

Schurr also told Sylvia that the Meads built and lived in a cabin a short distance up the river from the mouth. The confidence Sylvia had in Mr. Schurr's statements convinced her that the Meads did live along Upper Priest River. Several individuals have reported that remains of a cabin can still be found about 1/3 of a mile from the mouth of the river.

The first year the Gumaers spent on Upper Priest was the roughest year they passed in their new home. When they moved in they had to dock the barge at the mouth of the Thorofare and transport their goods and supplies to the end of the little lake in a rowboat or by backpack on the 6-mile Navigation trail.

"In the days of putt-putt motors the lake trip got awfully tiresome. What a relief it used to be to get on land after an 8 or 10 hour trip to Coolin. My husband used to say that anyone with common sense couldn't drown in the lake. He had no fear of water. I would often walk halfway to Coolin to avoid the rough waters from storms that would come up. Cape Horn was always the worst spot. There is no way you can cut the waves by going crosswise. There wasn't a trail on the west side of the lake in those days, and for that matter, there wasn't much of a trail on the east side when you were carrying a baby in your arms. It was awful! I was lucky to get over the trail on foot.

"When my son went into the army he said to me, 'Now don't worry mother, I lived through all those trips up and down Priest

Lakes as a child and I'll live through this.'" He did, became a lawyer and served with distinction as Magistrate, First Judicial District, Wallace, Idaho. I'm sure he thought if he had been spared in those rough days he would be spared for the rest of his life."

The first homesteader on Priest Lake was Andrew Coolin, a lifelong friend to Sylvia. She was also his confidant. He had so much respect for her he willed to her his Priest Lake home at Outlet and all his private papers including thousands of shares of mining stock he had on hand when he died in Spokane, January 10, 1936. He was buried in the Priest River cemetery.

Andy was the first postmaster for Coolin, Idaho. The name of the original settlement was Williams, but when Andy got his appointment in 1894, the town was named after him. Many of the documents in Sylvia's possession include papers in connection with Andy's service as a notary public, some of which carry the heading of Williams, Idaho. Many of the mining stocks were signed in Andy's shaky signature.

"He had such faith in mines around Priest Lake. He was still promoting mining stock a few days before his death," said Sylvia.

Sylvia said that Andy had married a woman back east who claimed she had a lot of gold mines out west. "I guess she was the same breed as Andy. She came west but didn't like it. She took their three girls and went back east and left a boy for Andy to raise. About all she got out of it was the trip. She didn't think this country looked very promising."

Andy's son, Stewart, built a boat and contrary to advice of many men, put a big motor on it and during the first run it broke apart and sank. Andy said, "He bane smart enough but he don't seem to be well balanced."

A.J. Klockman, promoter of the Continental Mine, and Andy were very close friends. They spent their lives promoting mines in the Priest Lake area. Old-timer Ike Daugherty once remarked, "If these men would mine the country instead of the people we would all be better off." Ike was a frequent visitor at the Gumaer cabin and, like Joe, was a nonstop talker. "They were my main source of entertainment, as they never ran out of something to say," commented Sylvia. "Living around mining men all my life I have some of their faith in my system. I heard so many stories of the great possibilities of the many mines around the lakes that I soon developed a faith in the fortunes that lay under the surface. I was as enthusiastic about mines as Klockman, Andy, Granddad Gumaer,

Cecil H. Wheatley, Harry Handy, Charles Beardmore, and many others. I am convinced that someday profitable mineral is going to turn out big in Bonner County."

In 1978, a helicopter survey was made of the area surrounding Upper Priest Lake and the big lake north of Two Mouth Creek. It was an attempt to locate uranium deposits with a helicopter equipped with trailing sensors.

In 1977, 1978, and 1979, Dr. Fred Miller, of the U.S. Department of Interior's Geological Survey office conducted a ridge by ridge walking survey of possible mineral deposits in the same area as far north as the Canadian border. He will not complete the survey until late in 1980.

The mine that really intrigued Sylvia was her father-in-law's "Hawksnest." He located it by aiming at a line between the Continental Mine and the Mountain Chief and other mines up the trail toward Gold Creek. He was sure it was the same bed of ore. He had a good mental picture of the main veins of ore in Bonner County. The day that her father-in-law blew the Hawksnest, Sylvia rowed him to the southwest corner of the lakeshore where most of the miners docked their boats when they were on their way to the mines further up the trail toward the Gold Creek area. She had time to row back home before he set off the huge charge.

"It was a beautiful lead and silver vein. Just think of all the people who walked over this mine," said Sylvia. "Harry Handy of Coolin offered Granddad $10,000 for his share of the mine. Charles Beardmore who grubstaked Granddad wouldn't sell either because he didn't want to let go of a good thing. A year later the elder Gumaer developed diabetes and could no longer do heavy work. After the old man died the mine went to pot.

"There were so many stockholders involved in the mine that a consensus could not be reached on what to do with the mine and development was never seriously undertaken. Granddad never gave up hope for he lived out the remainder of his life at the Globe Hotel in Spokane, studying and dreaming mines. He was 87 years of age at his death."

A short distance from the hole where Granddad Gumaer blew the Hawksnest the remains of a cabin foundation is visible. Mrs. Burwell remembers the site. It could well be the same cabin foundation that Martha Ahrens Jacky remembers when her dad took her there in 1925. Her father told her it was a Hudson's Bay trapper cabin that was built in the early 1800s. A.J. Klockman also

232

referred to moss-covered stumps that were cut by early trappers to build a trapline shelter in the general area of Upper Priest Lake.

The remains of the Mitchell cabin may still be located a short distance off the Navigation trail toward Gold Creek. Ike Daugherty had a small cabin about halfway along the trail between the Hawksnest and the Mitchell cabin. The Mitchells were the major stockholders in the Mountain Chief Mine. Sylvia remembers a Mrs. Baker who died while hiking the trail to the Mountain Chief. The Bakers were stockholders in the mine.

Shortly after WWII the U.S. Forest Service and conservationists began intensive studies of the Upper Priest Lake region to make it a scenic or primitive area. By the early 1960s, the usual disagreements, controversy, and litigation between the Federal Government and the individual property owners was at a high pitch.

Mrs. Sylvia Gumaer Burwell, Dr. Kermit D. Peterson and Dr. Donald E. Babcock, and John J. and Mandy Long were the private property owners of 417.2 acres that the conservationists wanted to include in a scenic or primitive area. The area was to encircle Upper Priest Lake and the Thorofare as far south as the Al Piper and Beaver Creek Camp Association properties. Including the lake, the proposed area would cover approximately 8,500 acres.

On February 24, 1965, the Department of Agriculture submitted a report to Senator Henry M. Jackson, Chairman, Committee on Interior and Insular Affairs, recommending that Senate Bill 435 be enacted. The bill sponsored by Senators Church and Jordan of Idaho was to extend the "boundaries of the Kaniksu National Forest" that would include the 417.2 acres of private property on Upper Priest Lake.

The report indicated that it would be "highly desirable that Upper Priest Lake and its immediate environs be kept free of habitation and commercial developments" . . . Owners of some of the privately owned lands . . . have made tentative preparations to subdivide their properties into lake front lots and sell these for private recreation homesites."

SB 435 granted the Department of Agriculture the right to acquire the private property "at a fair market value, and these lands may be managed under the principles of multiple use and sustained yield."

House Resolution 5798 is similar to SB 435 with a statement that acquisition "will involve an expenditure of $500,000 from the land and water conservation fund."

PROPOSED UPPER PRIEST LAKE AIRPO

Fig. 98 Proposed Upper Priest Lake Airpo

234

RECREATION AREA AT PRIEST RIVER

apper Creek Subdivision.

PROPOSED UPPER PRIEST LAKE RESORT

Fig. 99 Proposed Upper Priest Lake Reso

236

d Recreation Area, Trapper Creek Subdivision.

June 14, 1965, Public Law 89-39; 79 Stat. 129 (SB 435) was enacted by the Senate and the House of Representatives. It was "an act to extend the boundaries of the Kaniksu National Forest in the State of Idaho, and for other purposes." Sec. 2 of the act made it clear that the Secretary of Agriculture " . . . should make every reasonable effort to acquire the property by negotiated purchase." And that "the property should be appraised at its fair and market value . . ."

The act, under Sec. 3, described the real property to be purchased as follows:

(The act as printed spelled each descriptive word. To save space initials are used.)

Township 63 north, Range 4 west, Boise Meridian: Sec. 18, SE qr SE qr; Sec. 19, NE qr NE qr; lot 3 (SE qr NE qr); Sec. 20, SW qr NW qr; Sec. 33 lot 1 (NE qr NW qr), lot 2 (SE qr NW qr), lot 3 (NE qr SE qr), lot 6 (SE qr SW qr), W½ SW qr NE qr, W½ NW qr SE qr SW qr SE qr.

Township 63 north, range 5 west, Boise Meridian:
Sec. 24, NE qr NE qr, E½ NW qr NE qr, NE qr NE qr SW qr NE qr, NW qr SE qr NE qr, lot 2 (NE qr SE qr NE qr), lot 3 (NE qr SE qr SE qr NE qr).

As is the case, litigation is involved when valuable private property is wanted by a sovereignty. There are always two sides to the question as to what is the "fair and market value" or just compensation. This is true in most cases of similar nature. Under the law, federal and state governments have the right to take private property for public use (Claudius O. Johnson, *Government in the United States*, First edition 1953, pp 123-4). Johnson further states that the V Amendment of the Federal Constitution prohibits the government from taking property for public use without just compensation. The due process and equal protection clauses of the XIV Amendment are further limitations on the power of governments to exercise the power of eminent domain.

The *World Book Encyclopedia* succinctly states eminent domain is the inherent right of the state to force a property owner to sell his property when it is needed for public use. The publication further states that "Federal, state, and local governments have the right of eminent domain."

As the pressure mounted from the Department of Agriculture (U.S. Forest Service) to acquire the private property on Upper Priest Lake, Mrs. Burwell, owner of the Wheatley homestead property and the Schurr homestead became very concerned. She constructed a large steel building just west of Trapper Creek and during the summer of 1965, operated the Trapper Creek Trading Post. She also platted the Trapper Creek Subdivision into 176 lots. The subdivision extended from ¼ mile east of the mouth of Trapper Creek in Sec. 20 along the shore in a NW direction to Wheatley Point. It extended N along both sides of Trapper Creek for ¼ of a mile, more or less, in Secs. 19 and 20.

On August 14, 1964 the subdivision plat was signed by Sylvia Gumaer Burwell, Donald F. Gumaer, and Mary Eileen Gumaer. The engineer's certificate was signed by Chester V. Adams of Adams Engineering Company, Spokane. The plat was filed for record in Bonner County September 2, 1964. The total cost of the platting was in excess of $5,000.

Drs. Babcock and Peterson of Spokane had purchased, as an investment, the original 141-acre Geisinger-Malcolm property in Sec. 33, at the head of the Thorofare. They purchased the property from P.E. Jacobs' sisters who had inherited the property from their brother. Mr. Jacobs acquired the property in 1936 for $159.95 on a tax sale. During the summer of 1965, Babcock and Peterson brought in a bulldozer and knocked down and burned the cabin and outbuildings. The shoreline was leveled and divided into lots. According to the records on file in the Bonner County Auditor's office, Dr. Peterson et al, platted the shoreline for housing units. A sign was erected, "Lots For Sale."

Jack Swanson, *Spokesman-Review* staff writer, reported that, "Dr. Kermit Peterson . . . announced that he would have to sell his land for private development in 30 days.

"To forestall the Peterson sale . . . Nature Conservancy loaned (a committee) $30,000 without interest, to pay Dr. Peterson."

John J. and Mandy Long purchased their 30.75 acres along the north border of Sec. 33, T 63 from the N.P. Railway in 1936. John J. Long received a warranty deed for the property May 15, 1963.

The private property owners rejected the Department of Agriculture's final offer under an attempt to acquire the property by negotiated purchase and filed a complaint in the U.S. District Court, Bonner County, Sandpoint, Idaho.

The trial, Civil (case) No. 2-65-64, U.S. of America Plaintiff vs. 417.2 acres of land in Bonner County, State of Idaho, Kermit D. Peterson, *et al* defendants, was ruled in favor of the plaintiff by Judge Fred M. Taylor, October 14, 1965. He based his judgment on the following points:

The case of the Plaintiff was to the 'satisfaction of the Court.'
The United States of America is entitled to acquire property by eminent domain.
The Department of Agriculture is empowered by law to acquire land for the "purpose of protecting and conserving the outstanding scenic values and natural environment of Upper Priest Lake."

The Attorney General of the U.S. has the authority to direct the institution of such condemnation proceedings; that the lands taken is the fee simple title; the sum of money is $400,600 and is a fair price.

The above was ordered, judged, and decreed that the U.S. is entitled to possession of the 417.2 acres of lands so described.

Judge Taylor further ruled that a certified copy of the judgment be posted and a copy served upon any defendant as of October 15, 1965.

Sylvia Burwell said, "We had to put up a real fight to get what little we got out of the property on Upper Priest Lake. I had paid taxes on that property for 42 years. I had planned all those years to get enough out of my hard-earned investment to have a good nest egg for my retirement years.

"They dangled a few dollars in front of me and said, 'You will just have to sell it.' We didn't have a prayer. But that is all water under the bridge. Life is too short to cry over a shattered dream."

Dr. Babcock said, "We made 10% on our investment. I was disgusted with the entire proceedings."

Sylvia's daughter-in-law, Mrs. M.E. Gumaer, is very bitter over the results of the trial. In her judgment it was a miscarriage of justice and a downright affront to a hard-working honest citizen like her mother-in-law to be cheated out of a rightful inheritance.

Neither John nor Mandy Long could be reached for their reaction.

The late Lloyd Bennett made the comment about the trial, "The lawyers probably got most of the money. That was the biggest graft I've ever seen." Lloyd wasn't feeling too kindly toward the Forest Service as he had received word that his lease on his cabin lot in Tule Bay was being cancelled in 1978. If anyone really got left out it was the Geisinger family who lost their first home on a delinquent tax sale.

During WW II Sylvia worked at the Trentwood Rolling Mill in Spokane. In 1946, she started to work, temporarily, in the men's department of the Palace department store (now Bon Marche) and retired from the Bon 23 years later.

In June 1946, Sylvia married Carl Burwell. Carl died in 1951. During her very active retirement years she has resided at the Altameda Apartments in Spokane when not traveling.

20

WHEATLEY, IDAHO
THE TOWN THAT ALMOST WAS

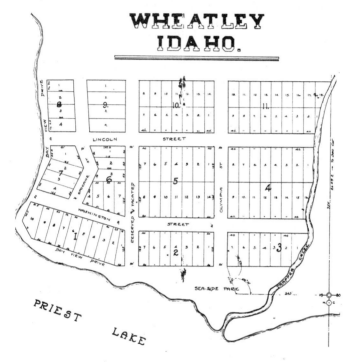

Fig. 100 Wheatley Townsite, Upper Priest Lake, 1914.

The center spread of a 5"x6" pamphlet published during or after WW I under the signature of M. F. Setters, Secretary, Wheatley Townsite Co., 415 Chamber of Commerce Bldg., Spokane, Washington, carries the plat of Wheatley, Idaho.

The platted townsite was located on the Wheatley homestead

bordering the west side of Trapper Creek in the SE corner of Sec. 18, and the NE corner of Sec. 19, T 63 N. The Wheatley Homestead Patent was signed by President Theodore Roosevelt, March 2, 1908.

Cecil Hutchinson Wheatley, born July 13, 1872 in India, of English-Scottish parents, came to the U.S. as a young man, and was for many years a machinist for the Great Northern Railroad. According to a letter from his daughter, Bonnie C. Wheatley, of Spokane, her dad spent the last years of his life panning creeks for gold, his lifelong hobby, near Oroville, California. Bonnie said he found enough gold to keep him happy. He died December 1, 1950, in Oroville.

According to the brochure, "The upper stretches and the land surrounding Wheatley was thrown into the forest reserve and the townsite is the only patented land on the upper stretches of Priest Lake, and the most beautiful spot on earth for a summer resort. It lies practically level, covered with shady pines and now and then a tall tamarack or fir with Trapper Creek on one side, a deep bay on the other, a sloping gravelly beach in front and towering mountains behind, ending the Continental range.

"One half mile up Trapper Creek is the gorge where the creek comes tumbling and roaring down, falling from two to three hundred feet in about one fourth of a mile. In the pools above and below the falls the gamey rainbow trout or speckled beauties make their home.

"Four miles farther up Trapper Creek is the upper falls and between these stretches are many fine pools for fishing. Often deer may be seen scurrying away through the brush or drinking at the stream. Three miles away, over a road that is practically level and is shaded at all hours of the day by tall trees, is Gold Creek, a fisherman's paradise, a creek from 50 to 73 feet wide, which can be waded at all points, and behind each rock, in proper season, there lies a hungry fish, from one to four pounds, to grab the tempting bait.

"Upper Priest River, Cedar Creek, the Continental Mine and numerous creeks emptying into upper Priest River can be reached from here over well-built government trails and many are virgin streams to the fisherman and hunter, while the lake itself offers good fishing during the season."

Now comes the three paragraphs that are the real pitch and purpose of the pamphlet, PRIEST LAKE IDAHO, HOW TO GO AND WHERE TO GO — FOR YOUR MIDSUMMER OUTING. The cover also included the following:

It offers more beauty of landscape,
More variety of rock sculpture,

242

More sublimity of mountain peak and cliff,
More fascination of forest, stream and lake,
More enjoyment for the sportsman in trout pools and
    streams of pure water
And more beauty of the wild and aboriginal than any
    section of the great west.

The publication incorporates additional sales arguments:

1.   The homestead has been platted into lots and placed on such terms that they are within the reach of everyone, and a limited number only have been placed on the market at this time.

2.   The company will sell you a lot at low value on monthly terms of $10 down and then $10 a month. In their liberal contract which we agree to give you back, at any time you wish, all the money you have invested, reserving only the first $10 you paid, which must necessarily be applied toward the expenses of getting out the contract, postage, and other incidentals connected with your sale, and they will loan you, at any time, ninety percent of all moneys paid in, excepting the first payment.

3.   They will also allow you to exchange your lot at any time for any other unsold lot in the plat. Their purpose being either to please you or return your money — hence you have nothing to lose and everything to gain.

The writer of the brochure offered a few additional inducements to encourage people to invest money in Wheatley. It was stated that the government has sold 500,000,000 feet of timber surrounding the lake. This would insure the coming of a railroad in the near future. When the road was completed and the timber logged, the geographical location of Wheatley would be the base for supplies for the various operations and a good-sized town would undoubtedly spring up.

Wheatley would also be the natural outlet for the Idaho, Continental, and other mines in the country already beyond the prospect stage and only waiting the advent of a railroad to prove that the mineral deposits in this country will be a close second to the Coeur d'Alenes. Hence lots must increase many, many times in value in the next few years. In the meantime they have afforded purchasers their full value in the pleasures derived from vacations, and the company is always willing to take the chances in valuation if a purchaser is not.

Trapper Creek offers plenty of power and a waterfall

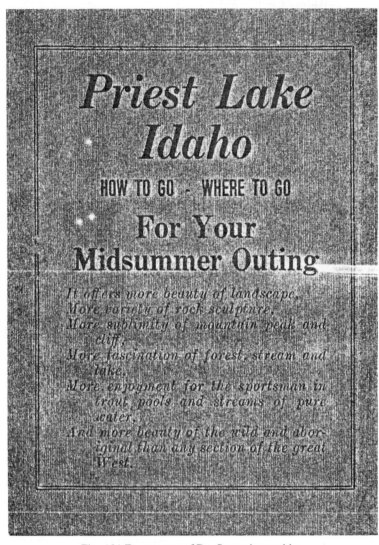

Priest Lake
Idaho

HOW TO GO - WHERE TO GO

For Your
Midsummer Outing

It offers more beauty of landscape,
More variety of rock sculpture,
More sublimity of mountain peak and
cliff,
More fascination of forest, stream and
lake.
More enjoyment for the sportsman in
trout pools and streams of pure
water.
And more beauty of the wild and abor-
iginal than any section of the great
West.

Fig. 101 Front cover of Dr. Setters' pamphlet

244

Fig. 101A Back cover of Dr. Setters' pamphlet

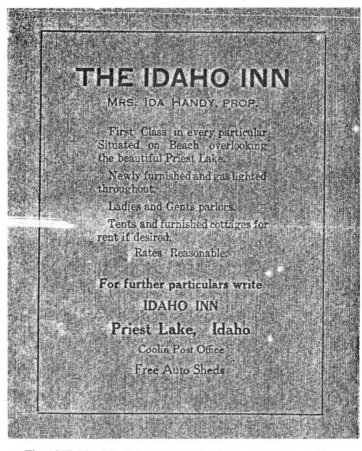

Fig. 101B Mrs. Handy's advertisement in Dr. Setters' pamphlet.

Fig. 102 W. W. Slee's advertisement in Dr. Setters' pamphlet.

to furnish all the electricity that can be used and will allow every lot to be thoroughly supplied with water.

The lots range in price from about one-fourth of what is asked at other lakes, besides the natural advantages that other lakes do not offer and the certainty of a profitable investment.

Groceries, supplies, and mail can now be delivered daily, and telephone connections with Spokane can be made by going across the lake to Navigation Ranger Station or at the mouth of the Thorofare.

The "why" is answered in the following paragraph quoted from page 10. "You may ask us why, if we are so sure of increased demand on valuation, that we do not hold them." We answer by asking, "Where would Spokane, Portland, or Seattle be if owned by a corporation?" We want co-operation. We are willing to carry all the risk and have your contract certified by a responsible bank or trust company, if you wish, to show our good will and that this is not a lot-selling boom, but a sure, safe, and profitable investment. For further information address Secretary Setters."

The following business organizations carried advertisements in the booklet: The Idaho Inn, Mrs. Ida Handy, proprietor; Leonard Paul's Store; The Northern Hotel, A.M. Carsline, manager; the Priest Lake Navigation Company, Captain W.W. Slee; and John T. Little and Company, Spokane. Edward T. "Dad" Moulton, Wheatley, advertised the fact that he had rowboats and a motorboat for hire. He specialized in taking parties around the lake in a motor launch.

The publication had a special message for citizens of Spokane. The introduction or preface emphasized the answers as to where to spend a vacation and how to get there. "The ideal place for a vacation, of course, would be a lake. None of the lakes around Spokane, except Priest Lake, the gem of lakes, could offer all the advantages for a perfect vacation. The most beautiful spot on this picturesque lake, is situated at Wheatley at the head of Upper Priest Lake."

To get there it was proposed that you take the Great Northern train to Priest River, Idaho. Take an automobile stage for the 24-mile journey through "tall timber, over rushing mountain streams, over hill and across valley, a new picture at every turn, until you arrive at the lower end of the lake at a town called Coolin."

At Coolin, a vacationer had the choice of taking a steamboat or a fast motor launch for the trip to Wheatley. The trip up the lake was described as the "Thousand Isles of the West" in beauty and scenery.

Fig. 103 Mrs. C. H. Wheatley and children, Bonnie, C. H. Jr., and
William (on rail) aboard the "S. S. Banshee," 1907.

Fig. 104 Lean-to, Wheatley, Idaho. C. H. Wheatley, Sr., daughter
Bonnie, and son William, 1904.

Fig. 105 First building erected at Wheatley, Idaho, Upper Priest Lake, 1905.

Fig. 106 Last of the "S. S. Banshee," August 6, 1916.

The lake is three to six miles wide and is dotted with islands, bays, and promontories, alternating abrupt shores and sandy beaches, tributary mountain streams and virgin forests, remaining practically unimpaired in all its primeval glory. On the west, ranges of mountains covered with timber, and on the east the watchdogs of nature, their heads towering skyward, rugged and barren of all vegetation and capped with snow or their peaks hidden in veiled mists of clouds." Passing through the Thorofare between the two lakes, "at any time of the year, thousands of fish, from 6 to 24 inches in length can be seen scurrying away from the boat."

The message stated in the last paragraph, "After the two-mile journey you enter Upper Priest Lake with lofty mountains on each side, snow-capped in the distance, and here you will exclaim, Oh, how beautiful! . . . "

This paragraph, in part, is as true today as it was during the first several decades of the 20th century.

When Sylvia Gumaer Burwell was reminiscing about the Wheatley homestead she mentioned that Mr. Wheatley was a miner at heart. His one business venture involved a boat. He inherited some money from his mother and decided to buy a boat to run round trips from Wheatley to Coolin to carry prospective buyers of lots. The first trip he made, "He hit the only rock on the lake, the one off Indian Rock in Kalispel Bay, and smashed his boat beyond repair." What was left of the hull of the boat ended up in the graveyard for old boats and docks on the south shore of Priest Lake.

Sylvia said she never learned the true story of how Dr. Setters acquired the Wheatley property but thinks there is some truth to the rumor that Dr. Setters got the property in return for an unpaid doctor bill.

"For a long time Mrs. Wheatley refused to sign over the papers in a final settlement. I'm pretty sure there was also a cash settlement in favor of the Wheatleys. The title was clear when we bought the property.

"After the Wheatleys left, Pete Chase burned the homestead cabin. Pete also burned Dad Moulton's cabin in the small beautiful bay around the rock bluff, known locally as Wheatley Point, about one-half mile up the lake from Trapper Creek. About the only reason Pete didn't burn our cabin after we left was because Bob White lived in it for a time."

The area is now a part of the scenic area in the Kaniksu National Forest.

21

EDWARD "DAD" MOULTON, MAN-ABOUT-PRIEST LAKE

Edward "Dad" Moulton accumulated a number of firsts during his 19 years on Priest Lake. He was the first, if not the only, General Custer Scout to settle in the Priest Lake country.

Dad was, in the words of Leonard Paul, "The first true host" for the Priest Lake area. Dad was also the first and only, mayor of Wheatley, Idaho. He undoubtedly was the first individual to advertise in a publication that he operated a launch service from Wheatley to Coolin to transport prospective lot buyers to Upper Priest Lake.

If not a first, he was among the first characters to enliven the pages of the *Priest River Times* from its origin through the 1950s. The September 3, 1914 issue told of Dad setting a bear trap in the early spring on Armstrong Meadow. Late in the summer he was the guide for a hiking party from Navigation to Beaver Creek and being so close to his bear trap he thought he might as well check it. To his great surprise, caught by his front toes, was a huge black bear, that had not been in the trap more than 10 minutes. Dad said, "It don't pay to pull up your traps too often nohow."

The next week another story appeared about the Irishman. "We heard the other day that Dad Moulton was a flirt. So we checked into the matter and after seeing Dad scouting around in his 20-foot launch with anywhere from 2 to 3 of the female gender, the pick of the season, we came right out face to face and asked him about it. Dad looked as innocent and honest as a newborn babe and said, 'I don't know about the flirt part but I always did believe in going it while you're young, and that is what I'm doing.' By the way, Dad is 72. Go to it Dad, we're with you to the finish."

The October 1915 issue of the *Times,* carried the personal item that characterizes Dad's popularity, "Dad Moulton moved to Coolin for the winter. The town of Wheatley is the loser for all the winter inhabitants will miss him."

A *PRT* article, May 14, 1914, apparently aimed at Dad's Irish luck and the good neighborliness of Priest Lakers told about Dad

Fig. 107 Edward "Dad" Moulton, copied from a John
Peterson portrait. (Marjorie Paul Roberts
Collection)

paddling his 20-foot launch from Eight Mile Island to the Lone Star
Ranch on the warmest day of the year. The reporter chided him for
being so worn out that he had to stay all night at Angstadts. The next
day Harry Angstadt had to "harness up his launch and tow Dad to
the head of the little lake."

The A.J. Klockman diary, pp 31-32, dated about 1905,
corroborates the general friendliness of Ed Moulton as the following
quote indicates: "We were on our way from the Continental Mine to
Andy Coolin's and we stopped at the cabin of an elderly Irishman,
Dad Moulton, who said he had heard about us many times, and
received us with open arms, insisting even that we sleep in his bed,
while he slept on the floor, and who took us the next day in his boat to
Andy Coolin's, where we parted with him, very reluctantly . . . "

In addition to being the host for visitors to Priest Lake, Dad
Moulton was a hunting, hiking, and fishing guide, a trapper, a
hunter, and a prospector. He came west the first time as a guide for

253

General Custer. In 1898, he came to Priest Lake and stayed on the two lakes the rest of his life.

Ed, like most of the early prospectors, was a firm believer in the mineral possibilities of Bonner County. He admitted that prospecting in his time was a grim life. He said that many mornings it was "fish or no breakfast."

The March, 1916 issue of the *PRT* had a mining news item, "Dad Moulton from the Priest Lake mining district passed through here last week on his way to Spokane, where he expects to transfer his mining interests to Spokane capitalists, who will develop them.

"It comes from good authority that from 10 to 12 thousand dollars will be expended in the development of the Washington group of claims at Binarch Creek . . . They have a 16-foot ledge of silver-lead ore on the claim."

"Dad Moulton was one of the genuine old-timers," said Vivienne Beardmore McAlexander. "I can't remember what he did specifically for a living. He was always handy to have around as he could do almost anything. I'm sure my father grubstaked Dad a time or two on mining claims. He also built a couple of buildings for my dad near the Hawksnest Mine on the little lake."

During his first years on the lake, Dad had two camps in the Coolin area. He soon moved north as the southern end of Priest Lake became too populated for his Irish temperament. He set one camp at Canoe Point and a short time later he put one on the Thorofare. He built a log cabin at the Kootenai No. 2 mine on Upper Priest Lake and lived there the remainder of his life. No record could be found when Dad built his cabin on the little lake. Fred Bailor of Spokane stated, in a personal letter that Dad Moulton lived on Upper Priest in 1909. After his death Pete Chase burned the cabin.

Very little is known of Ed Moulton's life before he came to Priest Lake. He loved people yet he cherished his solitude, an Irishman to the core. We do have his interesting face and his Irish eyes still with us through the eyes of Artist John L. Peterson of Spokane, Chicago, and Coolin.

Marjorie Paul Roberts of Coolin has a Peterson portrait of Dad Moulton in her home at Coolin. Artist Peterson was a personal friend of Dad Moulton.

A final tribute to Dad Moulton appeared in 1957, in the 40 years ago column of the *PRT.* "Dad Moulton for about 20 years a guide, trapper, hunter, and prospector on Priest Lake, accidentally shot himself and died within a few minutes. Most everyone in Priest River and all living around the lake knew and loved Dad Moulton. He was

Fig. 108 "Dad" Moulton in front of his cabin on Upper Priest Lake.

truly a man from the West, always having a hearty greeting for everyone, and a personality that made him friends by the score. He was 74 years of age."

It is tragic irony that Dad, a man who had spent his life with a rifle in his hand, in an unguarded moment, would inadvertently pull his gun barrel first out of his boat, which resulted in his death.

"It has always been a real delight to me to have known Dad Moulton almost as a member of our family, through the many, many stories I've heard my dad tell of this remarkable man," said Marjorie Paul Roberts. The list is long of those second and third generations of Priest Lakers who knew Dad from the stories told about a wild west Irishman.

The 1977-78 winter issue of *Incredible Idaho* has a feature article on Dad Moulton and his artist friend, John L. Peterson. The magazine was published by the Idaho Division of Tourism and Industrial Development.

22

SIX SHOOTER JACK

The colorful, romantic, and legendary stories that surrounded John ("Jack") Mayer's life would make a first-rate fictional narrative. He was better known as Six Shooter Jack, because he really did wear a pair of 38s on his hips when he appeared outside his home. Just why he wore them was known only to Jack. His wife of eight years, Pearl Kerr, never learned from him why he wore the two six shooters.

Jack Mayer was a prospector and miner who spent his entire life working in mines and roaming the hills of the west in search of ore. His wife, Pearl, said during an interview in 1977, "Jack told me that he grew up following a burro in the hills of California. In fact, that's about all he would talk about."

The rumors that became accepted as facts about Jack revolved for some reason around the color black. From three well-respected Priest Lake old-timers, one legend was pieced together. It was said that Six Shooter Jack always came to Nordman riding a big black horse with a black tooled leather saddle beautifully decorated with silver. He wore a big black Stetson hat, a black shirt, and his two six shooters strapped around his hips.

Pearl said, that the only truth in the story was the two six shooters. "In fact, Jack didn't own a horse, let alone a saddle in all the eight years I was married to him. He never had a black hat or a black shirt either." The usual stories of prospectors finding valuable ore and frittering away the proceeds or getting the raw end of deals when ore had been found were, as far as Pearl knew, nothing but hearsay.

Jack Mayer was superintendent of the Nickleplate Mine during the time that Pearl Kerr was married to him. The couple lived in a lovely log cabin they built a short distance north of the old Nordman store and near the Nordman school house.

Pearl Kerr's father, Thomas Kerr, brought his family to the Nordman area in 1909, at which time he filed on a homestead that included the beautiful deep lake that still carries the name, Kerr Lake. Before the days of modern refrigeration Kerr Lake furnished most of the ice for the local residents and resorts.

One summer when the Nickleplate mine was not running, Pearl

cooked for John Nordman's haying crew. She said she would never forget the Swedish expletives when John discovered she had scoured his coffee pot. John was convinced that a coffee pot had to be coated black inside before you could make a good pot of coffee.

When the Nickleplate was operating, Pearl cooked for the men on the job. She enjoyed the big cabin near the mine for it had a good kitchen at one end and a nice long table in the middle where the men could eat and play cards. It had a lean-to bedroom on one side. She also recalled the beautiful clear spring that furnished water for the camp.

Mrs. Henry Hampton told a story of the time she and Mrs. Roy Kenyon took some flowers to Six Shooter Jack when he was in the hospital at Priest River. "The girls at the hospital arranged the flowers in a big container and we took them to his room. We hardly got through the door when he yelled, 'I'm not dead yet, get those out of here as fast as you can!' He was a good old rascal and after we cheered him up a little he seemed to appreciate our visit even though he kicked up a lot of fuss."

Six Shooter Jack drifted into the Idaho Panhandle during the first decade of the 20th century. He did some prospecting in Bonner County and in 1910 or 1911 went to work for the Nickleplate Mine.

In 1916 he married Pearl Kerr. The couple divorced in 1924. Jack went to Lewiston, Idaho and prospected and mined in the Clearwater and Salmon River country the remainder of his life. He died in Lewiston.

At the time of the interview, 1977, Pearl was living with a sister in Priest River, Idaho.

23

MATCHLESS ADA MAE MARTIN

There are few people who have ever come to the Priest Lake-Nordman area, who have not come to know and appreciate Ada Mae Martin. The effort that Ada Mae and her husband, Russ, put into making Nordman the hub of activity for tourists and local summer residents, as well as the permanent residents, deserves a lot of praise. Ada Mae as postmaster, was most efficient in handling temporary, semi-permanent, and permanent mailing addresses by the hundreds. At times she went far beyond the call of duty to be accommodating.

Ada Mae arrived in Spokane from Nebraska in 1917 with her parents, James Arthur and Frances Fred Beard. Father Art, a taxidermist, had a friend, Jim Collins who thought Art should see the natural habitats of the animals he prepared for exhibits. Jim arranged a trip to take his own family, Mr. and Mrs. Beard, Ada Mae, and her sister Mary to Priest Lake.

Ada Mae recalls that the roads between Spokane and Priest Lake were in horrible shape. They were so bad that the first day they got only as far as the Grange Hall near Diamond Lake, where they spent the night. Early the next morning Jim took Art on a deer run on the hill south of Diamond Lake where Art saw his first deer in the wild.

It rained hard during breakfast and Ada Mae remembers hearing the rain drops hit the tin plates they were eating from. The roads from Priest River to Coolin were worse and by the time the group reached Coolin Flats, the kids had given up hope of ever reaching Priest Lake.

They did arrive at Coolin where they rented two boats from Leonard Paul. The men lashed the two boats together and fastened a little motor in the middle. With four people in each boat they went to Indian Creek.

"As an excited 10 year old, I thought I had come to the end of the world," exclaimed Ada Mae. "I was so thrilled and excited at the beauty of it all."

The entourage found the hunter's cabin where they were to stay. The floor was dirt and sand. The boats were unloaded and the mothers settled into the cabin. The oldest Collins boy was elected to return to Coolin to get the supplies that were left behind on the first trip. The men and the other Collins boy went fishing. "In no time at all, it seemed," said Ada Mae, "they came in with the most wonderful catch of fish you ever saw. We ate them for supper. After the meal Jim took all of us up to a falls on Indian Creek. Coming from Nebraska where the creeks run flat as a floor, we didn't know what to think of it. From that day on, my father and mother became great lovers of the outdoors.

"The big event of the trip," said Ada Mae, "was the trip up the lake to see Nell Shipman's movie camp." Del Gerson, a friend of the family and a former chauffeur for Nell when she was filming at Minnehaha Park in Spokane, picked them up at Indian Creek in one of Nell's boats. "I can remember the trip through the zoo and around the camp. Mr. Gerson had free run of the place. I did not get to meet Miss Shipman for she was away on a business trip. I will forever remember standing on the point and looking out over the lake to the mountains surrounding that end of the country. What a wonderful spot!

"I had the same excited feeling while at Nell's zoo that I would get when my n.other would take us older kids to Minnehaha Park to see the animals there. I remember that sometimes we would walk to the park from our home in the 1800 block on east Springfield. When we were flush, we would take the streetcar."

An interesting sidelight story was told by Ada Mae. While attending high school, she worked part-time for the August Bettinger family. Mr. Bettinger had a beautiful German police dog that had papers a mile long, in the words of Ada Mae. The dog, Bessie, was taken to Priest Lake and bred to Nell's famous lead dog, Tysore. It was one of Ada Mae's jobs to feed the puppies. She had to feed each pup in a different plate. She couldn't remember how many puppies were in the litter, but she could recall the big stack of pie tins that it took to feed them.

The first trip Ada Mae made up the west side of the lake to Nordman was with her dad who was doing some work for Johnny Marquette. The old road to Nordman began near the site of the Falls Ranger Station and followed a continual winding northerly course west of Four Corners. The dust made a cloud and the ruts were so deep a touring car would high center every few miles. They eventually got a peek of the lake at Outlet and were happy when they finally reached Nordman where the Marquettes lived.

The highlight of the trip for Ada Mae was the deer steaks and hotcakes they had for breakfast. Johnny Marquette, like most everyone that her father did taxidermy work for, made a special effort to show Mr. Beard the natural habitat of the wild animals. Johnny took the family to Kerr Lake, a short distance north of Nordman. Ada Mae remembered Mrs. Kerr's home being filled with dozens of beautiful flowers and potted plants. They also visited Bert Winslow's Resort on Reeder Bay.

After that trip it was 15 years before Ada Mae got back to Priest Lake. During the intervening years she married Russ Martin, July 3, 1929. They bought and operated a furniture store in Spokane.

In 1945, Ada Mae and Russ bought the Cedars from Bud Thompson and ran it for a year. "It was a lovely winter vacation," remarked Ada Mae. "We had an electric light plant, but most of the time we used kerosene lamps. Along with Elkins and Bud Thompson who had just built Linger Longer, we all got ice from Kerr Lake. The ice house was across the road, and each morning it was Russ' job to get a chunk of ice to put in our icebox, an old Coca Cola ice chest. In spite of the inconveniences, we loved this country. I probably got it in my blood from the first time I came to the lake. Russ came to love the whole area from his experiences at the Cedars.

"When we ran the Cedars we also had the telephone exchange. It was understood that after 10:00 PM, no calls would be put through to Priest River. One evening nothing much was going on so we decided to retire early. Before we put out the light we heard a chug, chug, chug of a tractor. We looked out and saw a big logging sled behind a tractor. It was Marty and Skeeter Vandervort, Earl Ferris, and several other men. They yelled at us to get our coats and come along with them as they were on their way to Lamb Creek for a party.

"We went along with them and had a good time singing, dancing, and drinking a bit. On the way back they all decided to stay awhile at our place. Earl always was the one who wanted to leave early so he took off with the sled and left two of Hill's guests behind. The snow was too deep to walk so they stayed the night with us.

"One of the men ran Kendall's Clothing Store in Spokane, and the other was a railroad man. The bunch had come to Hill's for a stag weekend. The next morning I got them a good breakfast.

"A few days later I received a hostess gift. It was a miniature of the dog that was, for many years, in the window of the Kendall Clothing Store. Most older citizens around Spokane will remember the dog advertising Kendall ties.

"When we were at the Cedars, the bar was in the shape of a horseshoe. Ward and Millie Adams bought the store from us and changed it to a right angle. They continued the tradition we had started of leaving a dollar in a round slot, so if you ever came back to the Cedars and were broke you always had a dollar on deposit with your name under it with which to buy a drink."

According to the story, the State of Idaho filed a claim on the silver dollars when Ward and Millie died without a will. Ward's half brother, Louie, finally won custody of the silver dollars.

In May of 1946, after Russ and Ada Mae had sold the Cedars, they went back to Spokane to go into the retail furniture business. In 1956, they learned that Dot and Deke Burns wanted to sell the Nordman store and bar. The Burns had started the business in the old Nordman store. They had the present log building built by the master log cabin builder, Tom Jarret.

In 1957, Russ and Ada Mae bought the business and building. They operated the grocery store, bar, restaurant, and post office until it was sold to Esther and Russell Haugen in May, 1966. Russ Martin had died in February. The year of 1966 was traumatic for Ada Mae. Not only had she lost her husband, but her bartender Mary Peterson, a good friend, Jim Burns, and Russ Haugen all died from heart attacks. Ada Mae remarked, "Everything happened that year. It got so I was scared to go up to that building."

Mrs. Haugen had never cared much for the business venture and in January, 1967, she sold the place to Nelda and Lem Lemburg.

Of all the characters that were regular customers during Ada Mae's years in the store and post office, Rastus Reed was her favorite. She thought of him as a natural born comedian, a jester, a clown, zany, but a good handyman. He had a heart of gold. She said, "If something needed to be done and if he was sober, he could do it. He liked his beer and when the spirit moved him, he could pull some of the darndest stunts that were ever created."

One day Louise, Ada Mae's sister-in-law, who worked in the store, sold Rastus a half case of Rainier beer which was his favorite brand at the time. He put it under his arm and headed for home. The next day he came back with the carton with two bottles missing. He put it on the floor and said, "Louise, don't you dare drink that beer. It is spoiled! It foams and has a funny taste." Louise checked it but could find nothing wrong with the taste, and told Rastus so. He blew up and stomped out the door. Later in the day he came back with a sheepish grin on his face and said, "Louise, I want my beer back."

Louise, trying to do the right thing, explained to him that if he thought it was spoiled he shouldn't drink it. He said, "No, I found out what it was that made it foam so much and taste so queer. I poured it out of the bottle into my shaving mug!"

Ada Mae continued, "One day Rastus got very angry with Russ when he wouldn't let him buy beer for everyone in the house. He had only his Social Security check to live on and we sorta took him under our wing and looked out for him.

"Another time he had had about all he could hold and Russ wouldn't serve him any more. He stomped out and went into the store, got his supply of groceries, and asked Louise for a case of beer. She knew why he had left the bar, and wouldn't give him the beer. He got so mad that he put all his groceries back on the shelves and stomped out."

Ada Mae feels that when you get into some of these remote places and get acquainted, you run into characters of all types. Such individuals seem to stay in areas like Nordman because they are accepted for what they are and are treated as human beings. Rastus was one of these and part of the local environment.

Mary, a sister of Ada Mae's, was a talented piano and organ player. She would come to Nordman on weekends to play the organ and Jim Burns would play the guitar for Saturday night dancing and entertainment. Mary always played with a large mirror in front of her so that she could watch the crowd behind her. One night Rastus was sitting at the bar and while looking into the bar mirror said, "Russ, you have two organ players down there." Russ tried to explain to him why it looked that way. Rastus got off his stool, went down to Mary and asked, "Which one is you?"

Many times Rastus would get feeling good, and get his limber body going in a tap dance. Ada Mae said, "Many people would bring friends along just to see Rastus. One night some Priest Lakers from Seattle brought all their house guests to Nordman to see the 'floor show.' It was Rastus. He was a talented, natural entertainer in anyone's book."

One act in particular always brought the house down. Rastus had an old hunting coat with a game pocket in the back where he carried his beer. During an act he would stop, open a bottle of beer and gurgle it down. Mary would imitate the gurgle on the organ and encore after encore would be called for until Rastus had had enough beer. Nostalgically Ada Mae remarked, "We don't have that kind of entertainment anymore. Too much civilization has ruined the local amateur talent."

Another character that fascinated Ada Mae was Millie Adams. "When we sold the Cedars to the Wards I met her for the first time," said Ada Mae. "Bud Thompson's wife, Ella, told me that Millie would either like you immediately or not like you just as quickly. I was about half scared of her as I had never been in this kind of business. It kinda went along with the country and I finally got into the swing of it.

"She came into The Cedars one day during the sale negotiations and discussed the details in language of a kind that I was not used to at that time. No lumberjack could get ahead of her in barroom language. I looked at her and figured that it was mostly show. But yet she was a wonderful, kind, and sincere person. She was one swell gal!

"I'll never forget the morning she came walking up the road with only a dress on that looked like a nightgown. She wasn't a very good driver and had run her car into Lamb Creek above Outlet. She was mad, looked like death and destruction, and swearing every step.

"When the sale papers were signed, Millie and Ward gave us a going away party and a welcoming party for them as the new owners coming in. For the occasion Millie had gone to a beauty parlor and had her hair and face fixed up. She had bought a new pair of slacks and all her other clothes were perfectly matched. She was really a good-looking woman. Ward and Millie had a big white Steelcraft boat on the lake. They took us on several trips, including one to Elmer Berg's Shady Rest Resort."

In the early days, before wheel transportation to Beaver Creek Camp, Ada Mae and Russ kept the members of the association in food and supplies. They let each BCCA'er have a charge account for the summer so that other members coming in could stop at Nordman, pick up any grocery orders, mail and messages, and take them to the camp by boat.

Ada Mae retired as postmaster on May 8, 1976. On Saturday evening, May 2, 1976, hundreds of friends and acquaintances around Nordman, Priest Lake, Priest River, Sandpoint, and Spokane, gathered at Nordman for a potluck testimonial dinner. More than a dozen people expressed sincerely and humorously the significant contributions she and her late husband, Russ, made to Nordman and the surrounding community.

Ada Mae is spending her retirement years at her home on the Barriers-Jim Lowe-Kaniksu road, Priest Lake. She is classifying her more than 200 dog figurines and taking care of her faithful and only live dog, Hairy, who was 13 years old, May 5, 1979.

24

MARTHA AHRENS JACKY

Martha Jacky personifies a summer Priest Lake old-timer. She has spent her summers at Priest Lake since 1911 when she made her first trip with her parents, Mr. and Mrs. Ralph D. Ahrens.

From 1911 to 1918, the family stayed at Mrs. Handys' Hotel or camped across from Eight Mile Island. In 1918, the Ahrens bought a log cabin that stood next to the Coolin schoolhouse. Mr. Ahrens retired in 1925 and built a house in Coolin that is still home base for family summer vacations.

Martha was graduated in 1923 from North Central High School, Spokane. In 1927, she received a degree from WSC. She married Lawrence Jacky in Coolin, August 21, 1928. Two children, William "Bill" and Joie were born to the union. Both are graduates of Washington State University.

In 1940, Martha and her husband bought the McCroskey cabin on the beach at the south end of Tule Bay. From this base, son Bill spent endless hours alone and with hiking companions tramping the trails and roaming the surrounding mountains locating and identifying old trappers and miners' cabins. He is one of the best authorities on this subject.

In the early 1970s, Mrs. Jacky was notified by the Forest Service that her lease on the land for her cabin was being cancelled, June 1, 1978. On or before that date the cabin had to be moved or destroyed.

About the time the family received the lease cancellation notice, the rumor was circulating that the Forest Service was planning to erect a 54-unit trailer campground along Tule Bay. "We were very lucky to have had a summer home here all these years," said Mrs. Jacky. "I do hope the Forest Service will leave the spot in its original state."

Joie expressed the feeling of the family when the lease was cancelled and remarked, "It is going to be very hard to leave this spot so dear to us. We have been lucky to have had this beautiful area for so long. I hope the Forest Service will let nature heal the scar of the cabin site and hold the bay as a scenic area for future generations."

In November 1977, Bill Jacky and his neighbor Clark Miller, both

Fig. 109 Martha Jacky, daughter Joie, and her
daughters on Tule Bay beach,
September 1977. (G. King)

Fig. 110 Bill Jacky and Clark Miller's amphibian,
with a player piano and a 25,000 watt generator
aboard, 1977.

wheat ranchers near Reardon, Washington constructed an amphibian vehicle to salvage the important items from the Jacky cabin as well as the Lloyd Bennett family summer home that joined them to the south. The Bennetts had their lease cancelled at the same time.

The salvage, in addition to the cabin furnishings, was a player piano and a 25,000 watt generator that weighed in excess of two tons.

In checking with officials at the Priest Lake Ranger station as to the future use of the property, a senior member of the Forest Service said, "And you may quote me, the cancellation of the leases was not to erect a trailer camp. Furthermore, there are no plans for appurtenances to or for the property on or near the site of the cancelled leases."

The site at this time, 1979, is being healed by nature. Many hiking, canoe, and boat campers are enjoying one of the loveliest beaches on Priest Lake.

25

THE HUNGATES

The Joseph W. and Winona Hungate family epitomizes the eternal Priest Lake vacationing families that have come to the shores of Priest Lake north of Granite Creek and to Upper Priest Lake.

Maude Hungate, a sister to Joseph W., affectionately called Chief by members of the family, predates by nine years her brother's first visit in 1912. Maude married an internationally known botanist, Charles Piper, who was sent by the USDA, in 1903, to study and classify the flora of the Priest Lake region. His book on flora of Washington included a great deal of information about Priest Lake flora and is still among the best published.

Prior to the construction of the first unit of the Hungate cabin in 1924, the family set up their main camp along Squaw Bay. They camped each year on Upper Priest Lake and other areas between the Thorofare and Coolin. The cabin stands east of Canoe Point along the most beautiful bay on either lake. It has been the central meeting spot of the Hungate clan for almost 60 continuous years. Son Richard holds the record for the largest number of consecutive years of vacationing on Priest Lakes north of the narrows. Claire Luby Patterson of Spokane holds the Priest Lake record of 69 years of continued vacations at Priest Lake. Dick's record, with the exception of 1943, when gas wasn't available, is a close second with 68 years to his credit.

Claire's father, Michael J. Luby, a Spokane attorney, selected a lot on a bay and brought his family to the spot in 1911. The bay was later officially named Luby Bay in honor of Claire's father.

Chief and Winona Hungate were lured to Priest Lake for the first time in 1912. They had heard Dr. Piper praise the beauty and tranquility of the two lakes as well as the mountains in northern Idaho. At that time the elder Hungate was teaching biology at Cheney Normal, now Eastern Washington University. He justified his first trip as a means of collecting specimens of fauna and flora for class demonstrations and study.

Until the family purchased their first Model T Ford in 1916 they would travel to Spokane by train from Cheney, then catch the train to Priest River where they stayed overnight. From Priest River the family was transported by stage to Coolin where they again stayed overnight. At Coolin they purchased groceries from Leonard Paul for a two-week camping trip and rented a two-man rowboat from Mr. Slee. In the morning they would climb aboard a wood-fired steamboat, piloted by Mr. Slee's son, and head for Mosquito Bay, towing their rowboat. Pilot Slee operated the first regular passenger run around Priest Lake.

Travel from Mosquito Bay was by rowboat with Chief manning the oars. The trip up the Thorofare to Upper Priest Lake ended at Trapper Creek. They made camp and spent a week of hiking, fishing, and swimming.

The first stop on the return trip to Coolin was at Squaw Bay. The family rowed back to Coolin in easy daily stages, stopping at Granite Creek, the Tonnetts in Luby Bay, and finally Coolin.

During the years after WW I, when the Hungate family camped along Squaw Bay, they became well acquainted with Diamond Match timber cruiser Barren. It was through Mr. Barren that they got permission from Diamond Match to build a cabin on Canoe Point.

The first unit wasn't much more than a storage shed. The first major addition to the storehouse, in 1924, was a 20' x 20' hip-roofed structure designed and supervised by Mrs. Hungate's father, Charles S. Terpening.

Mr. Terpening was a farmer until an accident caused almost total blindness. After the accident he studied for a chiropractic license and was for many years a very successful Doctor of Chiropractic.

The unusual construction of the cabin with its hip-roof and unpeeled split cedar logs that stand on end, makes it one of the few such designs in the northwest. The fireplace chimney was constructed with native stone built around wooden orange crates standing on end. The mortar was sand and blue clay dug from the banks of the Thorofare. When the fireplace was finished, the first fire burned the wooden crates leaving the chimney as it stands today.

The second addition was another 20' x 20' structure that remains standing with its original handsplit shakes repelling the weather. As far as can be determined, the cabin is the second oldest standing structure at the north end of Priest Lake; the oldest being the "homestead" cabin of Elmer Berg's, now a part of BCCA and owned by the Schreiber family of Malibu Beach, California.

Four of the five sons born to Joseph and Winona Hungate were present at the first reunion of the family in August, 1977: Richard,

Los Angeles, California; John, Vancouver, Washington; Robert, Davis, California, and Frank, Richland, Washington. Joseph, the eldest son, passed away several years ago. The central meeting spot was the Hungate cabin on Canoe Point which held considerable nostalgia for all of them.

Winona was a lovely, soft-spoken, kind but firm, mother. She was the queen of her brood and ruled the roost. She had a practical philosophy for raising her sons. As an example, she taught them to take care of their own belongings and share in the chores around the cabin. She explained to them that the area around the cabin had been the home of mice, ants, and packrats long before the Indians or white men came.

The cabin was not mouse and ant proof, but by stuffing cracks and openings, rats were held at bay. She explained to all her boys and later to the grandchildren, that if they did not want to share their goodies with the mice and ants, they would have to be responsible for putting them where they could not be reached. On each open ceiling joist she arranged a row of nails and assigned each one a nail on which they could hang their tin bucket, with a tight-fitting lid. They used 5 pound lard pails and most of them are still hanging on nails and are being used by the third generation. If anyone left his bucket open on the the nail, or open on the floor or table, the object lesson was soon learned. She, as well as the daughters-in-law, kept all foodstuffs in mouse-proof containers.

Her favorite annual excursion in the early days was to gather as many of the clan together and lead them to Lion Creek to watch the whitefish run. One hundred yards or so before she reached the creek she would stop and order everyone to keep quiet and listen for the sounds of the whitefish on their way up the creek to spawn. The sound was similar to pigs drinking milk from a trough.

"The run of whitefish was very heavy in those days," she remarked, "It seemed possible to walk across the creek on the backs of the fish, they were so thick." Many of her grandchildren still remember the sights and sounds of the run.

Chief took charge of the outdoor activities, particularly the hikes. Remaining true to the hiking patterns set by Chief Hungate, 23 family members, ranging in age from 7 to 72, hiked the 15-mile round trip to the top of Lookout Mountain during the family reunion in 1977.

In the late 1930s, Diamond Match offered to give J.W. and Winona Hungate an unencumbered deed to the lot where the cabin was built. Mrs. Hungate refused the offer as she felt that the

Diamond Match Company had been so kind to the family by permitting them to live there for almost 50 years with no strings attached that she could not, in good conscience, accept the offer.

Son Robert related a few nostalgic experiences of his early vacation trips to Priest Lake.

"We took the old electric car from Cheney to Spokane. We weren't allowed to take our dog, Tip, and I remember how he ran behind the car until he played out. Joe and I were crying our eyes out.

"The road from Priest River to Coolin was full of ruts and the old one-lunger stage couldn't make it up some of the hills and all the kids and men had to pile out and walk to the top of the grade.

"Father and Leonard Paul dickering over the price of everything — each trying to get the best bargain.

"My first experience with a teller of tall tales was Dad Moulton, a real campfire entertainer. In 1913, my brothers Joe, Dick, John, and I went over to Dad's cabin on Wheatley Point and he gave us a chunk of cooked bear meat. John, who was only three years old, announced after the first helping, 'Me want mo' bear meat.'

"We asked Dad how he got the bear meat. 'I just don't know how I got it. I had a deadfall up in the woods but I hadn't baited it or anything. There was a string there, but some fool young bear came along and pulled on it and got himself killed. All I could do then was to skin him and bring him down to my cabin.'

"One night Dad told us that he was picking huckleberries on Plowboy and a bear came running down the hill so fast that he couldn't stop when he saw him. Dad said, 'He jumped clear over my head.'

"We were always so excited about being out in the wilds. I caught my first fish in Lion Creek. The Thorofare was just beautiful. My father got disgusted with Joe, mother, and me the first time we rowed to the little lake, when we thought we were seeing deer behind every tree.

"We didn't have to fish much in those days to get our meat. Most of our time was spent hiking, huckleberrying, and gathering specimens for my father's biology classes."

"In the early days there was a cabin on the tip of Canoe Point. I don't know who built it. From time to time when it rained we would stay in it. It finally burned.

"For many years, Nig Borleske, the football and baseball coach at Whitman College, camped on the north side of the mouth of Lion Creek. You could always tell when Nig was going or coming as he had a motor on his boat that had a high whine that you could hear long before you could see him. He was an excellent fly fisherman. I know he camped there as late as 1936. Mrs. Borleske would gather wild ginger leaves and scatter them on the paths around the camp and on the floor of their tent shelter. The crushed leaves gave off a delightful aroma.

"There was a teacher from Lewis and Clark high school that camped where Diamond Match Camp 9 now stands. He had an old windup phonograph and every morning, rain or shine, he played the record, *It's Nice to Get Up in the Morning.*"

Son Richard recalled some of his cherished memories of Priest Lake, the beautiful primitive nature of the country, without roads, hoards of people, cars, and boats. The country stayed that way until after WW II.

"I remember on many cross country hikes with my father, we would never see another human. The streams before roads and logging were beautiful. Fishing was fantastic. My favorite spot was Lion Creek. The fish were larger and more firm than those in the lake and other streams."

Cougar Gus was Dick's favorite character. According to Dick, Gus was one of the few old-timers who was never involved in moonshining or rum running. One thing all the old-timers had in common, in Dick's judgment, was their closed mouths when outsiders were around.

"We really don't know too much about them, as they just didn't say much about their lives before coming to the Priest Lake area.

"I remember Cougar Gus better than all the rest. Once in a while we would run across him on the trail or he would just happen to find us, always at meal time. He carried a huge pack in the summer, because his home was wherever he decided to stop."

Dick said he asked Gus one day if he ever knew of a cougar attacking a human. "Yes, once! A cougar came into my tent, but he really was after my dog, not me. I shot him for his effort."

Elton Baldwin, a track star from Cheney Normal, was Nell Shipman's stunt man. Dick said that he was usually the man hanging on a cliff. Another boy by the name of Forest Swank, a summertime smoke-chaser from Two Mouth Ranger Station also appeared in several of Nell Shipman's two-reel thrillers. Baldwin is remembered for the 45-minute record he set going from Mosquito Bay to the top of Lookout Mountain. He ran the old five-mile trail up Lion and Lucky creeks to the top.

Dick remembers a Mr. Heberling who had a cabin just west of the spring on the site of BCRS. The story that Heberling did not have a

272

living relative and deeded the property to the Forest Service is not true. He had only squatted on the site. Some of the foundation blocks of the cabin are still visible.

Two of the Hungate brothers own property on Mosquito Bay and two own cabins at BCCA.

26

COUGAR GUS

Gustav "Cougar Gus" Johnson was, in the words of Dick Hungate, "one of the true woodsmen of the old school." Very little is known of his life prior to his arrival in the Idaho Panhandle.

Fern Geisinger said when she knew Gus he lived most of the time in a little lean-to thing behind Mosquito Bay. She said, "He had a good mind. In the cold weather he would read all night long. If he didn't, he would have frozen to death. He had to keep his wood fire going. In the daytime, when it would warm up, he would go to bed and sleep the rest of the day. His wants weren't many but I really don't know what he lived on. During the summer when the Forest Service was maintaining trails, and during fire season, the employees would discard their excess food and Gus would find it, salvage what he could, and bury it for use later. Once he found some canned cheese and gave it to me.

"One bad fire season all the natives lived pretty well as food for the firefighters had to be abandoned now and then for lack of manpower and pack trains to take it out of the woods. One time we found a half slab of bacon and a whole ham! What a treat!"

Mary and George Duffill gave a vivid description of Cougar Gus' living quarters, his life on the lake, and his habits. "We would say that in our time at Priest Lake, Gus was the oldest, if not the only real old-time mountaineer that ever hit the country. He lived the year around in a bark shanty on Mosquito Bay. His cats and dogs didn't have to go through the door, they could get out and in through the gaps in the bark almost anywhere.

"He did all his work and transporting with a canoe he called his "war boat." He could paddle a half-ton of supplies in that canoe from Coolin to the little lake between sunrise and sunset and never stop, except to take a drink.

"It was a strange thing and one we could never understand, Len Paul would not trust Gus for a nickle's worth of credit. Nobody could bring supplies to Gus unless they paid cash for everything they got for him.

"Cougar Gus was one of the group of people that no longer exist around Priest Lake," commented Joie Soper, daughter of Martha Ahrens Jacky. "They built and lived in an atmosphere they created for themselves."

Martha related a story of a canoe trip she and her college roommate, Eleanor Jackson, made to Upper Priest Lake in 1923, that reveals some interesting sidelights of Gus' life.

"We had our camp set up on the north shore of the little lake and Cougar Gus dropped by. He said he would like to go to Coolin with us. We weren't too keen on the idea, so we told him we weren't going until 8:00 o'clock that night. He said, 'That's fine with me.'

"When we started out, he took the paddle and, like the machine he was, paddled us all the way to Coolin on that beautiful moonlight night. All the way he kept us entertained by explaining many of the stars and constellations. He told us several stories from French novels he had read, some that were written only in French.

"It was a memorable experience I shall always remember, and to think that we almost missed it!"

Harold Branyan referred to Gus as a real character. "In spite of his love of solitude, he was a beautiful person. What I know of life in the woods I learned from Gus. He could bake bannock over an open fire that would touch your heart like a letter from home. For days on end he could live off the land with a sack of salt and a few pounds of flour. On the trail Gus was slow, steady, and determined. When things got moving too fast, he would remark, 'Vot's the hurry, hell's not that far away.'

"Gus taught me how to trap bear. We trapped together and we caught a number of black and brown bears but I never got a silver tip that Gus always said we would trap.

"On one of our rounds of the trapline we got caught in a storm and holed up at the Gold Creek cabin. I think it was on the Yakima claim at one time. Bob White used it for his home camp during the winter of 1928-29.

"I remember there was a whipsaw on the north wall. In the cabin there were several rifles in scabbards, three or four pack saddles, various tools, and several hand carved toys. Bob could probably tell you some great yarns about the cabin. Ike Daugherty and Cougar used to refer to it as the Gustason (sic) cabin."

"The cabin was always a good camp. Everybody left something, beans, rice, coffee, tea, sugar, etc. The many times I stopped by the cabin during my three years in the Kaniksu, I never saw it when it was not well stocked. It had two double beds, blankets and springs, which were rare in those days, plenty of firewood, and even Bull Durham which was always hung on a piece of hay wire from the ceiling on account of the rodents.

"There was a small cookstove and a heater standing in the middle of a box of sand in the center of the cabin. Stubby, my dog, always slept with me. Cougar liked dogs, but he didn't seem to think they belonged in bed. In the morning when we shook out the blankets to hang them on a wire, Gus would always say, 'Shake hell out of your blankets, the next guy might not like dog hair in his bed.'

"I met Gus during the first winter I spent at Geisingers. Earl, Scully, and I were on our way to hunt on Wheatley Hill when Earl decided to stop at Gus's for a cup of coffee. At the time Gus was living in someone's houseboat on Upper Priest Lake. Before we went in Earl warned me not to gawk or laugh at anything we might see or hear. Earl said, 'However, take a good look at his rocking chair and bed.'

"The first thing that really hit me was his rocking chair. It was built like a throne. The construction was basically natural curves and angles split from saplings. Hand whittled dowels were inserted in holes that were drilled with a brace and bit.

"The back was 5 feet high and the seat was at least 3 feet from the floor. The rockers extended 2 feet from the front legs and 2 feet from the back of the chair. It was balanced by at least 100 pounds of drill steel laid across the rockers, in front and back. A goat skin hung from the top of the back. Tanned deer skins, with the hair side up were on the seat. A tanned black bear hide was on the floor in front of the throne.

"Cougar was sitting there like a king. He was reading a National Geographic. After I got over the initial shock, Earl introduced me.

"Gus' bed was a very early American style, also made from pieces of natural limb bends. Fastened under each bed post was a single spring from a bear trap. Each spring was pegged to the floor and each post was pegged to the top of the spring. I couldn't really believe what I saw. Earl apparently noticed that I was dumbfounded, because he then called my attention to Cougar's rifles.

"Hanging on the wall were five 30-06 guns. Underneath was a hand carved 10-inch wooden trolling lure that looked like a whitefish. Under it, extending to the corners of the room were hundreds of stacked magazines.

"Not too many people knew it, but Gus had a good sense of humor. He used to get a good belly laugh everytime he told me the story about the time Al Geisinger told him he should be arrested for disturbing the peace. Apparently Gus had stopped at Elmer Berg's or

Sam Byars' on his way back from Coolin. When he got a snoot full he loved to yodel and he was pretty good at it. Coming up the Thorofare he was yodelling lustfully in good form. He stopped at Geisingers to leave the mail. Al was awakened by the singing and came down to the dock madder than a wet hen.

"About the last time I saw Gus, I had gone to the upper end of the little lake to see if anyone had mail to send out as I was going to Granite Creek. I stopped at Cougar's last. He was playing *Jolly Copper Schmidt* on his mouth organ. Billy Duffill was dancing, Frank Brown was singing, and Bob White was pouring drinks. I was a little late in getting started for the post office.

"Cougar Gus was very accommodating to most of his friends. He could be firm if he thought someone was taking advantage of him. One day Warren Upham and a man by the name of Herrick stopped by his float house and tried to talk him into baking bannock at a sportsman show in Spokane. Cougar refused. Later he told Upham, 'They must think I'm a damn fool, messing around with an open fire, when just around the corner they have new camp stoves.'

"Cougar was well along in years when I was at Priest Lake but he could set a good pace and keep it up for five or six hours at a stretch. He never seemed to get hungry. My stomach would get to rubbing my backbone and I would munch on dry oatmeal and raisins that I always carried in my pack. He used to call me the garbage can, because I always ate everything at the end of a meal. No leftovers was my motto.

"In 1933 or 1934, I wrote to Gus, but the letter was returned, marked 'Not delivered on account of death.' He had some fine guns and an exceptionally nice 44 Colt Frontier revolver. I guess the state or county got his goodies."

27

KATHLEEN STEVENS

Kathleen Stevens Stevens, a true daughter of Priest Lake, was born January 13, 1931. She was the only child of Priest Lake pioneers, W.E. and Carrie O'Brien Stevens. At a few months of age she began her lifelong love of the Granite Creek area, the narrows of big Priest Lake.

In 1931, Kathy's father purchased from the Dalkena Lumber Company, the first 20 acres of what is now the Granite Creek Moorage. The property extended from Granite Creek south to Jim Low's property that is now the Kaniksu Resort. A few years later he bought three additional pieces of property, totaling 80 acres along the south side of Granite Creek and extended beyond the property now owned by Jimmy and Nellie Shea.

For the next several years, 40 acres of the property, purchased from Mrs. Wheeler of Sandpoint, was contested in the state courts. "Dad spent a lot of time and money proving that he had bought the land from Mrs. Wheeler, but the state claimed it and had put the property up for a 'tax sale,'" reminisced Kathy. "I so distinctly remember Governor Smylie[2] falling asleep during one of the hearings. It was a real battle!" Mrs. Violet Hampton testified that Steve had bought the property in good faith and did get a deed from Wheeler.

In the early days there was only a footpath to the mouth of Granite Creek. There was a skid road between Jim Low's and the Stevens' property. It was about 1934, before a road was constructed to the bay that is now the boat storage area.

Kathy said, "I remember a little shed or shack on the beach near the mouth of the creek. I found a nicely carved paddle in the building. It was years later, when I attended the University of Idaho that I learned it was a fraternity initiation paddle. I often wondered who had left it there."

Willard E. Stevens, Kathy's father, was born in California and as a youngster attended school in Spokane. In his early teens he began working in local sawmills. He later became in turn, a scaler, timekeeper, and bookkeeper for the Dalkena Lumber Company. "In fact, I still have his scaling stick which I treasure," commented Kathy.

"I remember my mother telling me how she used to play mood music and sing for the silent motion picture houses in Bonners Ferry and Sandpoint."

When Kathy was asked to relate some of her early memories of Priest Lake she talked for several hours. Among the many stories of her childhood days the following incidents were selected for this biographical account.

"With some amusement and a bit of the tragic I remember the Roy Gregory family that lived on the farm that was previously owned by Harry and Belle Angstadt. It is on the east side of the swamp directly across the lake from Granite Creek and the Kaniksu Resort. Mr. Gregory was a disabled World War I veteran.

"The dairy farm that the family attempted to establish along Bear Creek was something of a disaster. He spent most of his time attending auction sales. He brought home loads of farm equipment, machinery, milk cans, feeders, and gadgets of all kinds. But it just wasn't a practical area for a dairy. I remember that they lost several cows in the bog.

"Mrs. Gregory struggled desperately to keep the dairy going. Mr. Gregory would leave his family over there for days at a time. They had no way to get out as he would leave the boat on this side of the lake. I went to school at Nordman with their son, Gary.

"An incident that I remember was just before World War II started. We had some Japanese people come in with huge baskets five or six feet high. They rented boats from us, loaded the baskets into the boats, and made three trips up the lake before the last of the baskets were loaded. Later, after the start of the war, radio equipment was found in several cabins on the upper part of the lakes.

"Not too long after this operation we had two young, good looking men rent one of our cabins for the entire winter. I was so impressed with their beautiful equipment and gear; the kind you would buy at L.L. Bean's. One of the men went by the name of Barney Oldfield. He wore a racoon skin cap. The other man had a cap made from a skunk skin with a long tail down the back. They were spectacular. They would go up the lake from time to time and return with bags that resembled bags of ore samples. We never knew exactly what was in the bags, nor have we heard from them since.

"I got well acquainted with both men as I was going to high school in Newport and I would ride home with them on Fridays, which was usually their mail and shopping day. The natives did a lot of speculating about them, they might have been with the FBI, the CIA, etc. For all we really knew they may have been geologists on a routine job. They always seemed to be having a good time and enjoying what they were doing. It could have been in 1944-45 as I was living with my aunt in Newport while attending high school. They took good care of the bags as I don't ever recall seeing any of them lying around in a boat or on the dock.

"During World War II, we had Italian and German prisoners-of-war come into the store from time to time to buy tobacco, cigarettes, or candy. They were stationed up north and as near as we could guess they were at Beaver Creek and Navigation Ranger Stations. I don't remember seeing an armed guard with them but someone that could have been a Forest Service employee, would accompany four or five of them on the trip down the lake. The men spoke very little English. At least they didn't speak it to us. They were exceptionally well-mannered and seemed to be very nice people. I couldn't think of a better place to be a prisoner of war than at Priest Lake.

"I have heard the rumor that one of the Italian men brought his family to America specifically to visit Priest Lake where he had spent considerable time from 1943 to 1945."

Kathy's remembrances of the Italian and German WW II internees or prisoners of war was confirmed by John K. Dompier of Spokane. During the summer of 1942-43, and 1945, the Dompier family vacationed at Shady Rest Resort, Beaver Creek, and made several trips to Navigation Ranger Station.

Mr. Dompier reported that he understood the men were from ships docked in Seattle and Portland and were being held by the army for the duration.

"The men seemed to be having a ball. I so well remember seeing supply boats at Navigation, loaded with hams, bacon, sugar, and other food items that were not available to the general public. It's no wonder that at least one of the internees brought his family to Priest Lake to see where he had spent his 'prisoner-of-war' days.

"I don't remember too many of the old, old-timers like Pete Chase, Capt. Markham, Cougar Gus, or Dad Moulton, but I have heard stories about them all my life. I don't believe I ever met Capt. Markham, even though he ran his boat, the 'Tyee,' up and down the lake in the 1930s. I do know that he is buried in the Seneacquoteen Cemetery which is on the south side of the Pend Oreille River, 15 miles east of Priest River near Hoodoo Creek on the Dufort road to Sandpoint. His grave is marked with a ship's wheel on the tombstone. The cemetery is maintained by a local group of interested persons. It is kept in excellent condition and is interesting to visit.

"I also remember our first telephone line. Bud Thompson's wife,

Ella, was our first telephone operator. The line went through the Ranger Station at Bismark, just to the west of the present Nordman store. Mrs. Thompson relayed the call to the General line. Mrs. Thompson was a very pleasant lady with a good voice for a telephone operator.

"It was a fun experience to have had the opportunity to listen to the lookouts talking to one another in the evening. It was an accepted pastime for them. It wasn't so pleasant, however, when lightning flashes would jump halfway across the room from the telephone speaker during bad electrical storms. Then the lines were busy reporting fires.

"One of the most colorful persons we had plying the lake from time to time in her cabin cruiser was Millie. Her last name was Adams, but only her close friends ever knew she had a last name.

"The first thing I remember about Millie was her bar in Oldtown, Idaho. The bar was an old converted railroad car, or perhaps a remodeled boxcar. I distinctly remember hearing how she came to marry Ward Adams.

"Ward, who was a lot older than Millie, was riding a boxcar during the Big Depression. In the same car was a young kid who Ward thought really looked as if 'he' needed help. Ward said, 'Hey kid, at the next town let's get off, get you a haircut, and get you cleaned up.' It turned out that the kid was Millie!

"The last time I can recall seeing her, and I still picture her in my mind, she came to our place with a boy named Snyder from Kalispel Bay. No one ever knew for sure, but this young man may have been her son. Millie was wearing only a pair of jeans and a bra, that's all! In those days people just didn't go around dressed that way. Her hair just stuck out every which way. It looked as though she had had a permanent but never combed it.

"I knew she drank a lot but she was like all these ladies, they had 'hearts of gold.' Millie and Ward spent their last days at The Cedars. She gave my cousin her lovely diamond that she had worn for years with a great deal of pride. She always liked him and out of the goodness of her heart she gave it to him. That was Millie!

"I heard the story of one of her trips to the north end of the lake in her big cabin cruiser. She apparently had a financial interest in the Shady Rest Resort that was purchased from Elmer Berg by Bill Muhle. She decided to visit the place and someone got her headed toward Beaver Creek in her boat. As she came to the long dock that Elmer had built for the resort, she couldn't get the cruiser slowed down enough to get it docked. After several passes, Bill yelled to her to drive by close enough for him to jump into her boat. After a couple more passes, Bill managed to leap into the boat, then docked it for her. Millie climbed out of the boat swearing with words that could be used only by someone connected with the logging world, stomped up the dock vowing with appropriate expletives that she would never get into that damn boat again as long as she lived. After several belts at Bill's bar she later took off for the southern end of the lake. True to her threat, she sold the boat a few days later.

"This past summer, 1974, I walked the old road from our place on the lake to Nordman. It used to go up over the hill back of Jimmy Shea's place. The hill is steep and it took a good Model T to make it. One of my aunts would never ride in a car going up or down the hill, she always got out and walked."

After graduating from Newport High School, Kathy enrolled at the University of Idaho. She was a member of Alpha Chi Omega sorority and majored in Elementary Education. She received her Bachelor's Degree in 1952, and Master's in Education in 1957.

While attending the U of I she met her husband, Dean Stevens. They were married September 6, 1951. They had two children, Matthew and Melissa.

Kathy taught two years at Edward's Air Force Base in California and 12 years in the Priest River Elementary School. She passed away May 17, 1977 and was buried in the Newport Cemetery.

Kathy's father-in-law, Herbert Stevens, wrote the following passage in her memory:

KATHY

None knew her, but to love her
None named her but to praise
She was a wonderful daughter
  A perfect wife
    A loving mother
      A devoted teacher
And a good neighbor and citizen
We love her,
  And we will all miss her.

28

PIONEER ARTHUR HAGMAN

Arthur E. Hagman, logger, river rat, filer, Priest River business man, carpenter, contractor, and now retired, was born May 5, 1896 on his father's homestead, Snow Valley Farm, 12 miles north of Priest River and one mile south of what is today called Four Corners. He now lives in a house he designed and built at Hagman's Resort on Priest Lake.

As a young man he sawed logs for 65 cents a thousand and paid 90 cents a day for room and board. "Big money," Art commented, "was the $3.00 a day we got when we drove logs for Fidelity Lumber Co., White Lumber Co., and Beardmore Lumber Co. down Priest River."

He was fortunate enough to talk Gladys May Hill into marrying him in 1917. In 1918, they moved to Laclede where Art learned the saw filing trade. Later the same year he bought the Priest River City Transfer from Mrs. Robinson as her husband Ray had died from flu during the influenza epidemic that swept the world.

Art operated the City Transfer until 1934. In the early 20s his trucks hauled supplies to Coolin. Among his customers were Nell Shipman and the Nickleplate Mine that was located one mile northwest of Nordman. Before there was a west side road to Nordman the route was to Coolin, then by the steamer 'Slee' to Reeder Bay, from there by truck to the mine. Later when a west side road was opened to Outlet Bay, supplies for the mine were picked up there by boat and moved to Reeder Bay.

"Every trip to Outlet we had to let the air out of the tires of our truck because we had to drive out on the sand bar that extended into the lake to where the water was deep enough for the 'Slee' to land. I must have pumped 100,000 pounds of air into those tires, by hand pump," said Art.

By 1934, the depression had caused a standstill to practically all business in the town of Priest River. Art decided he would take a job building warehouses, bunk houses, and other buildings for the CCCs. He worked on CCC construction at Cavanaugh Bay, Troy, Ahsaka, and Pierce City, Idaho, until WW II called a halt to the program.

Because construction work caused a lot of moving from place to place, Art and Gladys decided they would establish a home in Moscow, Idaho, because their son, Jim, was ready to enter the university. In the fall of 1936, the move was made and Jim entered college as a freshman and brother Frank started his freshman year at Moscow High School.

To help the war effort, Art turned his talents to carpenter work for the government. He helped construct the Armed Forces Supply Depot on East Trent in Spokane Valley. He also worked with the Western Housing Company who built houses for the government in Medford, Oregon, Spokane, and Seattle. On his way to Seattle for another Western Housing project he stopped in Wenatchee to visit a carpenter friend and was talked into contracting to build houses in Chelan. When he finished this job he moved back to Spokane and went into contracting partnership with his son Jim, who had just finished more than four years of service in WW II.

The father and son partnership, which lasted more than 30 years, built 20 homes in Spokane and during slack times three apartment buildings near Gonzaga High School were built. Mrs. Hagman managed the apartment buildings until Art retired in 1973.

When son Jim decided to develop the property he had bought with the money he made peddling papers in Priest River, the partnership continued to build for what is now Hagman's Resort. They also built 20 other cabins and houses on Priest Lake that include those of Jack Friel, Richard Hungate, Claude Simpson, Tom Moore, Tom Helfry, Mrs. Jean Whitney, and Floyd Ochs.

During his spare time from 1928 to 1969, Art and Gladys built, remodeled, and spent many weekends and an occasional vacation at their summer home in Ledgewood Bay, Priest Lake. The property was a 99-year lease from the U.S. Forest Service. In 1959, the Forest Service notified Art that the lease was to be broken in 1969, and he had until that date to remove his cabin.

"When I built the cabin I was assured by Forest Ranger Clarence Sutliff that the cheapest and best plan for obtaining a lot on Priest Lake was a lease from the government," commented Art. "The only real disappointment I had in my life was the loss of my only permanent home. I might add that it was truly more than a disappointment as I really resent having been pushed off my leased lot. About all I can add is, I've worked hard, enjoyed my work, and now I look forward to a lot of restful and peaceful years in the future."

Art's ever present sense of humor and wry wit which truly characterized him as an individual was demonstrated by the following remark he made after the lady of the house had carefully explained to him how she wanted a series of narrow slots built in her kitchen cabinet to enable her to stand on end big plates, platters, pie, and cake pans. Without a change in the expression on his face Art said, "That's good, but I don't like pie tins standing on end. I like them flat in my hand with apple pie in them." (He got his apple pie when the job was finished.)

29

HAGMAN'S RESORT

In June, 1957, James "Jim" Hagman and his wife, Elizabeth ("Betty,") began construction of Jim's boyhood dream of developing a resort on Priest Lake. When Jim was in high school in Priest River he bought the land from the Northern Pacific Railway Company. It is in Sec. 16, a short distance north of Granite Creek. He had earned the money for the purchase by delivering the *Spokesman-Review* and the *Chronicle* newspapers in Priest River.

After graduating from high school in Priest River, Jim enrolled at the University of Idaho in the fall term, 1936. In 1941, he was graduated from the university with a degree in business administration and accounting.

During WW II, Jim served with the Third Division of the Army throughout Africa and Europe.

He was discharged from the army in August, 1945. A short time later he, his father, and brother Frank started a construction business in Moscow, Chelan, and Spokane.

Jim met Betty Boughter when she was a senior nursing student at Sacred Heart Hospital in Spokane. She graduated with an R.N. degree in May, 1946. November 1, 1947, Jim and Betty were married in Seattle, where Betty was working.

The first building at the Hagman Resort was a two-story house on the beach near the southern line of their property. Throughout the years 20 units were built. All but seven units, which now comprise the resort, were sold to private parties. The resort also has a launch ramp, boathouse and moorage, and several docks.

In addition to raising their three children, Arlie Sue, Ken, and Gary, Betty has been the tireless, faithful "community-appointed" first aid nurse of the Priest Lake-Nordman area. Betty is called to render first aid assistance, medical advice, and the use of her personal station wagon as an ambulance to transport injured and ill people to Newport or Spokane. In her *spare time*, Betty is the day to day manager of the resort.

30

MOUNTAIN VIEW RESORT

Harry and Freida Groop bought the Young's Camp and renamed it Mountain View Resort. Ben Noonan purchased the resort from the Groops and divided the property into lots.

Jack Powers bought the lake frontage, the boathouse, and a lot on top of the hill. The remainder of the lots were sold to other individuals.

The boathouse is still in use and stands between Tillicum and Hagman's Resorts.

31

PERL SMITH RESORT

In 1945, Perl and Adalyn ("Addie") Smith bought a 9-acre tract of land on the shore of Priest Lake, a short distance north of Granite Creek. The property is now (1981) called Tillicum Resort. Soon after their purchase, the Smiths started construction of their dream, the Perl Smith Resort.

The property was originally school land and at one time owned by the Schaefer-Hitchcock Lumber Company. The Smiths purchased the plot from Porter Young.

"When we bought it," said Mrs. Smith, "the beach was a mass of rock with woods surrounding it. We had to build a road from the Granite Creek bridge to the resort area. The county later took over the road."

By the fall of 1946, the Perl Smith Resort was in operation. They retired in October, 1966, and sold the resort to Chris Wilkinson who renamed it Tillicum Resort. At the time of the sale, the resort had six rental cabins, a store, docks, and boat storage sheds. The resort is now owned and operated by Bob Sterling.

During the ownership of the Smiths and Wilkinsons, the resort was a popular takeoff point to areas north on Priest Lakes. Many summer residents north of Granite Creek stored their boats at Perl Smiths. He was a good boat and motor man and a most courteous and accommodating businessman.

Perl was born in River Falls, Minnesota in 1902. He came to St. Maries, Idaho, as a child and when he was 17 the family moved to Spokane. While working in Spokane he met his future wife, Adalyn Schomer.

Adalyn was born in 1913, in Kalispel, Montana, and came to Spokane at the age of 4. Since Perl's death in 1967, Mrs. Smith has resided in the family home at E. 8908 Knox, Spokane.

32

BEAVER CREEK CAMP ASSOCIATION, INC.

Why did people from Washington State College want to come, in the late 40s, to an undeveloped area on Priest Lake, has been a question asked by visitors many, many times. The property from 1921 to 1945 was known as Shady Rest Resort, owned and operated by Elmer Berg. It is located at the north end of Priest Lake in an area that was without roads, electricity, phones, or running water. The reasons are many but the enthusiasm and foresight of one couple, Wilson and Helen Compton, is the basic reason. Credit must also be given to several other courageous staff members of WSC.

During the exciting, and at times frustrating, years following WW II, Dr. Compton's vision came to pass, for a place where WSC administrators, staff, and faculty members could hide away for a few days for R and R in surroundings that provided all the benefits for "rest and recuperation." At an informal gathering of deans and department chairmen, President Compton made reference to the need of such a retreat for overworked administrators. Victor Burke, chairman of the Department of Bacteriology, told Dr. Compton that he knew of such a spot on Priest Lake in the Panhandle of Idaho. Compton suggested that Dr. Burke get a bill of particulars and report back. The place was the 52.72 acres owned at the time by William Muehle and known as Shady Rest Resort.

Bill Muehle had bought the property from Elmer Berg in 1945 for $15,000. Bill built a bar in the front room of the main cabin as he had his sights set on a profit-making operation in the bar business because Diamond Match Lumber Company had 150 men working out of Camp 9 across the lake from the resort. As soon as Diamond heard about the bar, the resort was ruled off limits for their employees. Bill immediately lost interest in the bar operation as well as the resort as a means of making money. He put the property up for sale.

President Compton looked at the property in the summer of 1947, and told Dr. Burke he was definitely interested in it. On January 2, 1948, Muehle flew to Pullman and notified Dr. Burke he would sell the property for $50,000. Dr. Burke notified Dr. Compton, who replied, "Offer him $25,000." Burke told Muehle of Compton's offer and Bill said, "I'll take it." The same day Compton gave Muehle a receipt that was filed in the clerk's office of Bonner County of his intent to purchase the property for $25,000. On March 3, 1948, William Muehle et ux granted to Wilson Compton a warranty deed for the 52.72 acres.

Soon after the Comptons bought the property they started developing the tract as a WSC staff and faculty recreation area. The idea soon stirred the interest of 22 faculty and staff members and led to the development of "The Beaver Creek Camp Association, A Family Plan for Vacation Happiness." The plan was announced in a sales brochure written by Robert A. Sandberg. The leaflet was sent to faculty and staff members.

In general, the pitch included such questions and answers as: Would you like to have a summer home in the cool forest on a clear lake? Do you like to swim, loll on a sandy beach, fish, hike, boat, canoe, camp in the great out of doors, hunt, or vacation with your children?

Page 2 of the brochure stated: "If these appeal to you perhaps Beaver Creek Camp is your answer. The camp is located on the north shore of Priest Lake in the heart of the Kaniksu National Forest . . . Priest Lake is one of the cleanest fresh water lakes in the west. Its white sandy beaches are set amidst beautiful mountain ranges (the Selkirk Mountains) in the largest primitive area left in this region."

In 1948, Wilson and Helen Compton leased, as an experiment, the resort for $1.00 to the newly-formed Beaver Creek Camp Association. The members as listed on page six of the brochure are as follows:

E.L. Avery	G. Brooks King	Charles G. Shaw
M.M. Bundy	S.B. Locke	C. Simpson
Victor Burke	M.A. Maxwell	R.L. Soule
Wilson Compton	D.F. McCall	R. Sprague
J.A. Guthrie	Ellen Moline	J.G. Watkins
K. Hobson	H.C. Weller	G. Nyland
R.E. Hungate	O.E. Osborn	H. Wood
B.J. Pointon		

During 1948, the camp was used by 131 individuals for 1300 days. This exciting and unexpected success led to the formation of the Beaver Creek Camp Association, Inc. By the time the brochure was published, during the late winter of 1948-49, six cabins and ten lots had been purchased by WSC staff members; twenty-three choice lots were available on either the lake, Beaver Creek, or the Thorofare. The sale price of the lots with cabins was $2,250 to $3,000 and the lots ranged from $300 to $1,000. Page 3 of the leaflet showed a plot plan developed under the direction of Harry Weller and Tom Hansen with the possibility of 60 lots which could be offered for sale prior to June 1, 1949, the date set for acceptance of the Compton's proposal.

The proposal included, in part, the sale to individual members of BCCA all lots as shown on the plat. All cottages except the old lodge (often referred to as the Homestead) and the new lodge (now the Batey cabin), to be held as a community center.

The proposal further included sale to the association all lands needed either as commons or as wilderness areas, physical equipment, including boats, all service buildings except the combined shed and cabin behind the Homestead, and the cellar building. All sales at owner's option to be contingent on total purchases of property aggregating $25,000. As soon as the owner (Dr. Compton) received from the association the amount of $25,000 plus four per cent interest on the unpaid balance, the owner would assign to the BCCA his remaining interest in all property in Beaver Creek Camp offered for sale and all unpaid contracts.

On February 28, 1950, Wilson Compton granted BCCA, Inc. a warranty deed and on the same date BCCA mortgaged the property to Wilson M. Compton.

On the date of the acceptance of Dr. Compton's proposal the Constitution and By-laws of the association included the following interesting and important statements: The membership fee is $40 (later changed to $100), payable in full or in four consecutive monthly payments; upon retiring from the association the membership fee shall be returned by the Treasurer; . . . each member has one vote; special assessments may be levied against the association only by the vote of three-fourths of the members; by-laws and the constitution may be amended by two-thirds vote of the membership; resale of lots may be made to members of the association only; Forest Service regulations shall in general be maintained.

Eight families of the original group that composed the membership of the first loosely organized BCCA purchased lots or a lot with a cabin prior to the date of the publication of the brochure extolling the virtues of the exotic area on Priest Lake. This group formed the nucleus of the BCCA, Inc. The members of the group were: E. Avery, M. Bundy, W. Compton, J. Guthrie, K. Hobson, R. Hungate, D. McCall, and H. Wood.

291

When individuals of this group were asked why they were attracted to this isolated spot, the replies were varied, but all expressed enthusiasm for the experiment of a communal effort. One member reported that his family had vacationed for 15 years at different lakes in Washington and Idaho and when he was invited by Dr. Compton to come to Priest Lake he came to fish with three other invited colleagues. In four days of intermittent fishing, the party caught 66 beautiful cutthroats. When he returned home he reported to his wife that Priest Lake was the most beautiful spot he had ever seen!

Another staunch supporter of the BCCA experiment said, it gave his family an opportunity to have a portion of a beautiful lake to share with others. It gave the family a chance to create a home in the wilderness. There also seemed to be a chance for permanent roots as a community project. The prospects looked good as a place for the boys of the family to learn to use tools and to do hard manual labor.

Another individual said he and several colleagues were aced out of a piece of surplus property at Farragut Training Base when the State of Idaho took the entire base for a park area. The BCCA idea developed soon after and it just looked too good to turn down. He made the additional comment that there were not many places left that had such a combination of everything a family could want for a vacation home.

A second generation lot purchaser commented, "I came to Priest Lake when I was in high school and college and I vowed I would spend my honeymoon at Elmer Berg's Resort. I did this! My husband fell in love with the place. My oldest son at the age of eight and his sister at six years of age planted their feet on the sands of the sandspit in 1946. In 1948, my second son at 20 months, got his baptism in the blue waters of Priest."

From 1948 to 1953, by selling cabins and lots, renting cabins and boats, charging $7.00 a launch trip to and from Stevens Moorage at Granite Creek, money from additional membership fees, annual assessments, and money loaned to BCCA by several individuals, Dr. Compton was paid the $25,000 plus 4% interest for the property. January 22, 1953, Dr. Compton granted BCCA a mortgage release. The Board of Commissioners of Bonner County, May 31, 1966, granted BCCA a resolution which ". . . Resolved that each and every of the roads as platted and dedicated in that plat of Beaver Creek Subdivision be vacated as public roads and that the re-located roadways be used as private roads for the use and benefit of the owners of the property only."

A great deal of credit and gratitude must be given to Wilson

292

Compton's wife, Helen. She practically conned the Navy out of two surplus ship-to-shore landing craft that were called the launches. They were open boats with good marine engines and strong hulls. They looked more like scows than boats, but they were sturdy and could haul and tow tremendous loads. The launches for many years transported passengers, food, lumber, cement, building supplies of all types, and were real work horses for the development of the tract.

Mrs. Compton talked Diamond Match into driving piling, building a big dock, snaking logs to the shoreline, and many other tasks that required machinery, man, and horsepower. She also twisted arms to get lots purchased and kept the place humming with activity, essential and otherwise.

Special credit must be given to Dr. and Mrs. Harry Marshall. They purchased the Homestead and took an option on the cabin that was called the Lodge because no one from WSC who was interested had $5,000 to buy the lot and cabin.

The Marshalls were natives of Iowa and became interested in Priest Lake because their daughter Katherine and her husband Harry Batey were quite taken with the primitive area at Beaver Creek. It is almost beyond belief that anyone would cast their lot with a group of *college profs* in a venture that could have ended up a financial disaster. The $5,000 cash for Elmer's main cabin put the association in a financial position to complete the purchase of the Beaver Creek property.

One of Mrs. Marshall's favorite stories was the midnight ride she and Harry Batey had on the last tow-trip made by the tug 'Tyee.' "It was an exciting experience," she said. "It began when Harry B. blew into my room just as I pulled my last toe under the covers, and said breathlessly, 'Hey, mother, wouldn't you like to go see the 'Tyee' take its last boom of logs down the lake?' I said yes, I would, but wait for me to dress. Harry suggested I pull on a pair of slacks over my p.j.'s because it would be cold riding out to the 'Tyee' in our Lone Star boat that is now called the 'Tin Bucket.' Well, that is what I did and we were off for an adventure.

"I had not realized how far it would be from our boat up onto the deck of the 'Tyee,' but with the help of the fellows on deck giving me a hand and Harry B. boosting me from below, I made it!

"The men were very gracious when we asked if we could come on deck. It was just midnight and they were getting dinner. The smell of steak, potatoes frying, and the aroma of coffee were tantalizing after our chilly ride. They offered us coffee but we declined knowing the difficulty they had getting the food on the boat.

"It was a beautiful moon and starlit night and we watched the logs slowly change their position in the boom. The lake was quiet and the boom of logs traveled easily but slowly. We must have stayed with them at least an hour. I don't remember just the distance we travelled, but I think we were not far from Twin Islands.

"We left them there and boarded the 'Lone Star' for a delightful trip back home. It was a memorable trip for me and I have had some heart pangs on seeing the 'Tyee' half buried in Mosquito Bay for so many years, but maybe that is the way old boats like it!"

Several of the original supporters and lot purchasers became disillusioned with the prospects of a successful venture for BCCA and others through no fault of their own had to sell their lots before cabins were built. One individual went so far as to purchase a lot, construct a cabin on it and sold it at cost, minus his labor to attract more members for the association. He built another cabin, at cost minus labor, for a lot owner who could not afford to build a cabin at that time.

In general, it can be said, the families that remained loyal to BCCA were courageous, resourceful, had faith in a communal effort, and had the desire and willingness to create something from a wilderness setting. They had the gumption to do a lot of hard manual work and enjoy it. A great deal of credit must be given to the members of the original group who lent moral support to the project and kept a few people in the fold who became discouraged with the future of the project.

Dr. Compton's long association with forests and the forest industry as secretary and manager for 26 years of the National Lumber Manufacturer's Association, gave him the background to envision the tremendous potential of the Elmer Berg resort property. His contributions to the industry were recognized in 1948, when he was elected as an honorary member to the Society of American Foresters.

In a personal letter, H.K. Steen, Associate Director of the Forest History Society, Inc., wrote in August, 1977:

"Compton was a forceful, articulate, and prolific spokesman for the forest industries. Beginning with publication of his doctoral dissertation in 1916, *The Organization of the Lumber Industry*, he compiled an impressive list of over 160 speeches and articles on a range of topics pertinent to forestry and the forest industries. Testimony to congressional committees and voluminous correspondence to business and professional associates was another way in which he effectively supported and advanced his beliefs.

Clearly, his contribution to the forest industries was one of leadership and substance. He has few equals."

In the early years of the communal experiment, there was an enthusiastic, warm, and distinctive special cooperation that existed among the first generation of BCCAers. There was deep concern for the protection of the native state of the local environment, helping one another when unexpected guests arrived, sharing food, medicines, tools, physical brawn, fish catches, berry patches, and caring for a neighbor's property when the owners were away.

From the middle of the 1940s to the late 1960s, it was not an easy trip from Pullman to Beaver Creek. The road from Pullman to Priest River, Idaho was crooked and rough. It was an ordeal trying to get through Spokane during a weekend and the road from Priest River to Granite Creek was just plain hell on wheels; dust, ruts, rocks, stumps, and muddy logging roads. Supplies had to be packed with extreme care if you expected a 50% survival rate for eggs and other perishables.

At Granite Creek, you might have a launch waiting for you and just as likely not. Mrs. Compton may have decided to take the one launch that was running at the time, to Upper Priest Lake for a community picnic or a pleasure trip unmindful that the launch had been ordered weeks in advance. At least the membership and guests had ample opportunity to get well acquainted with W.E. (Steve) and Carrie Stevens, proprietors of Granite Creek Resort and Moorage. In fact, the association was Steve's best customer for more than a decade.

Upon arrival at Granite Creek, you transferred your gear and supplies by wheelbarrow to the launch, rounded up your guests and family, and chugged 7½ miles up the lake, likely as not in waves two to four feet high. At the other end you unloaded the boat onto a wheelbarrow to get the stuff to a cabin. You built a fire in a wood stove, carried water from the lake, and went to the spring at BCRS with a gallon jug to get drinking water. If you wanted ice for your war surplus icebox you went to the ice house, dug out a chunk of ice from under two or three feet of sawdust, cut it, weighed it, and carried it back to your cabin.

In the evenings, when someone was around that could start the cantankerous Delco generator, you had electric lights from one or two bulbs hanging from the ceiling. More than likely you had to be satisfied with no electricity. You lit a coal oil lamp or two. If you were an experienced Beaver Creeker, you brought along your own Coleman lantern. The worst ordeal for most urbanites was taking a

Fig. 111 Elmer Berg's original cabin, kitchen, and bedroom, 1978. (M. Rutherford)

flashlight to go out the back trail to the privy in the woods that was inhabited by thousands of mosquitoes, flies, yellow jackets, hoot owls, or an occasional bear. Such was life at BCCA on a two-week vacation. All this was forgotten when the sun came up over Lion Creek canyon and cast its rays over the placid, beautiful, glass smooth, blue waters of Priest Lake, except when it rained!

ELMER BERG

In the minds of many BCCA members, Elmer Berg was an integral part of BCCA. So closely attached to the association was Elmer that it seemed logical and necessary to include him in the BCCA chapter.

Elmer Berg was born in Sweden in 1886. He came to the United States as a young man to work in the lumber industry. On May 4, 1921, he received a deed from the Clearwater Timber Company for the 52.72 acres of land he purchased from them. He developed the area and named it Shady Rest Resort. The tract is part of the grant by the United States Government to the Northern Pacific Railway Company dated December 9, 1901.

In 1936, Elmer Berg's cabins were those that are now called Gustho, The Homestead, Elders, Hiltys, McCalls, Bundys, and Averys. Elmer called the Avery cabin the Honeymoon Cabin because

Fig. 112 Hank standing in front of living room and porch addition to Elmer Berg's cabin, 1934. (H. Diener Collection)

it was more isolated from the rest of the resort. It was referred to by a *Spokesman-Review* columnist, Margaret Bean, as "one room and a path."

Rumor has it that Elmer buried a lot of money on his resort property. Carrie Stevens also believed it although Elmer never said anything to her about it. He did not bury any of the $15,000 he got when he sold out. The money was impounded by the State of Idaho on Elmer's death as he listed no known relatives. Carrie Stevens, bless her heart, wasn't about to let the state get the money. She remembered Elmer talking, from time to time, about a niece of his he had left in Sweden.

Then too, Carrie and Steve were not feeling too kindly toward the State of Idaho, as the state had filed suit in an attempt to get their valuable property on Granite Creek from the lake shore to the

Granite Creek bridge. At the trial, the Stevens proved they had clear title to the property. They were never compensated for the tremendous expense they incurred while opposing the state's claim.

Carrie wrote to the Swedish Consulate in Seattle and in due time the consulate located Elmer's niece and the $15,000 was duly and legally awarded to the rightful owner.

The fabricated yarn, commonly accepted as truth, was that Bill Muehle got Elmer drunk many times during his attempt to buy the resort. It was not true. It was during one of the rounds with the bottle that the story was created that Elmer, in a drunken stupor, signed a sales agreement. The truth was as Elmer confided to his trusted friend, Carrie Stevens, that he had suffered three heart attacks long before Bill Muehle appeared on the scene, one as early as 1942. The attack he had in 1944 was rather severe and he had a fear of dying alone at Shady Rest Resort. He talked to Carrie many times of the trips he had made down the lake with the bodies of his friends. He had a horror of his body being frozen and treated as if it were a frozen chunk of wood.

Elmer had discussed with Steve the potential sale of his resort to Muehle prior to the signing of the papers. Elmer helped Muehle finish building the Lodge during the winter and spring of 1946-47. The final rumor that Elmer died of a broken heart over the loss of his resort has no factual base whatever. It was Carrie Stevens' opinion that Elmer enjoyed building his new cabin at Granite Creek and loved to meet and talk to people while helping Steve during busy times around the marina. He died in his sleep April 2, 1947 at the age of 61. Carrie and Elmer's niece were responsible for having a lovely headstone erected over his grave in the Priest River cemetery.

It is doubtful that Elmer ever had enough money at any one time while operating his resort to bother about burying it. The record shows that R.D. Ahrens held a mortgage on the property from May 19, 1929 to July 25, 1946. The $20 or $25 a week he got for renting his cabins, rental fees on a few boats, and the money he earned working for the Forest Service was not a substantial sum. He had the usual running expenses, upkeep and the purchase of his diesel-powered electric plant and his launch, "The Elmer Berg," which he used in the early 1940s to transport his guests to and from Granite Creek.

Elmer was a fine old Swede and a wonderful host. Small but powerful; kind but stubborn; thoughtful and most accommodating to his guests; loved to tell stories when he was in a talkative mood; always whistled a tune when he came up the path with ice, wood, or a message, as he approached the honeymoon cabin. He would usually

Fig. 113 Left to right: "Old Man Chief," Elmer Berg,
Stan Spurgeon, 1934. (H. Diener Collection)

conclude his evening conversation with the comment, "I've waited
ever since I came to Priest Lake for a Flathead Indian maiden to
come over Squawman Mountain to do my cooking, so I'd better go
and see if she has come!"

As one Forest Service employee commented, "Elmer was a typical
old bachelor. Tempermental as a Jersey bull. He was a pretty shrewd

old Swede. During the early days he developed a good business for his resort, but it was rugged going.

"It was a remote area in the 20s and 30s and Elmer made it very comfortable for his guests in spite of wood stoves, coal oil lamps, back porch sawdust iceboxes, outdoor toilets, water carried from the lake, and a half-mile trail hike to the ranger station for a jug of drinking water."

The Hilty cabin as it stands today (1979) has been unchanged from Elmer's day, except that the homemade sawdust-lined icebox is gone from the back porch. Elmer kept the iceboxes full of ice from his ice house. The kindling and woodboxes were replenished every day. He would inquire each day if there was something you needed from down the lake. If you were out on the lake in a boat during the evening, he always kept the light on the dock until you returned. What a spot to spend a vacation!

The area was similar to Elmer's birthplace in Sweden. There is every reason to believe that he was shrewd enough to visualize his Shady Rest Resort when he purchased the tract in 1921. Soon after he became the owner he began building cabins. He built his own cabin on the point first and the next was the Elder cabin.

It is difficult to prove or disprove whether or not Elmer dismantled three or more cabins that were constructed by the Nell Shipman crew when she was on location making silent movies on Mosquito Bay from 1921-25. Close examination of several photographs of the cabins of the Shipman era and the Hilty and Bundy cabins as they stand today, do indicate a resemblance as to size, design, and corner cuts of the logs.

Elmer worked off and on for Shipman Productions from 1921 to 1925. During the winter of 1925-26, with the help of Billy Duffill, Elmer kept a lot of the zoo animals alive by rustling food for them when Nell had a nervous breakdown and had to leave her animals. For all the work Elmer did for the Shipman project, he certainly deserved whatever he was able to salvage when the buildings were abandoned.

The wife of a second generation Beaver Creeker made the remark during a casual conversation that when she thought of Priest Lake in 1921 she didn't think in terms of resorts. She thought that people in those days worked for a living and didn't come to a lake for a vacation. But they did both. People did come for a vacation and Elmer worked hard at making a living through his Shady Rest Resort. He had a lot of competition. Sam Byars' Forest Lodge was

Fig. 114 Madlyn Byars Gillis, son John, Elmer Berg, 1933.

just across the Thorofare. Resorts below the narrows were many, large, and well-known, to say nothing of the hotels in Coolin.

Elmer had a one-man operation. He never envisioned a Sandpiper Shores Development or a BCCA community. He liked to have people around him as long as they didn't pry into his personal affairs. When he launched his project the road ended at Coolin. It was a 20-mile trip up the lake to Shady Rest Resort. He relied on Bert Winslow's steamer, the 'W.W. Slee,' and Capt. Markham's 'Tyee I.' A few people had an outboard motor and could rent a boat at Coolin to transport themselves to Beaver Creek.

By 1936, the road had reached Reeder Creek and Elkins' Resort had a sleek Chris Craft that transported many of Elmer's guests under the piloting of Hughie Eilers. Elmer finally went to the expense of buying a launch to meet his guests.

In the early years, Elmer financed his venture by building one or two cabins a year for people around Coolin. He trapped in the winter and took care of the BCRS. He hunted cougars for the bounty. During a bad fire season he would work for the Forest Service, hauling supplies to Upper Priest Lake for fire fighting crews and hay for the pack animals.

During his span of time at Priest lake, Elmer saw the dwindling of the fur trappers, lived there during the heyday of the loggers, saw many mine ventures come and go, and the beginning of a steady stream of bigger and bigger pleasure boats roaring up and down the lake.

The changes that took place during his 25-year development can be equalled or surpassed by the changes that have taken place since Dr. Compton purchased Shady Rest Resort.

What happened to Dr. Compton's dream of a communal enterprise with the Lodge and the adjacent area? What happened to the buildings for group activities and the meadow for a common playground for the young and old? Also what happened to the tool house, the ice house, the Delco plant, the tools, the launches, the row-boats? All that is left that is shared by the BCCA membership is the sawdust insulated cellar and a common mail box.

What has happened to the custom of letting everyone know when a trip was planned to Nordman, Priest River, Sandpoint, or Spokane and the offer to bring anything that anyone needed in the way of supplies? In the years gone by it was not possible to leave the camp without one to a half-dozen supply lists.

The major factor that is responsible for the social and technological changes is the mode of transportation to the area. The development at BCCA can be compared to the development all over the U.S., if not all over the world.

Until the spruce beetle hit the timber in the Blacktail Mountain area in the 1950s, the only way to reach BCCA property was by boat or trail. To salvage the timber infected by the spruce beetle, roads were built from the Nordman-Metaline Falls road over Blacktail Mountain to a log dump just south of BCRS. At the same time a road was bulldozed to the ranger station. Agitation soon started to build a road from one end of BCCA property to the Thorofare. Within a year or two, more than half the people who came to BCCA used the logging road over Blacktail. The need for and the interest in the association launches dropped drastically.

Another major factor that contributed to the rapid changes in the basic tenants of the BCCA charter was the affluency of the membership. By the late 1950s, every BCCA member had his own boat, his own tools, and many urban necessities. With the construction of the Forest Service blacktop road from Granite Creek to the junction of the Blacktail logging road came propane gas, an excellent road to haul supplies and guests, and a great increase in automobile traffic to Beaver Creek.

These factors, and others not as noticeable, resulted in a change from interdependence to independence among the members of BCCA. Resistance and problems arose within the association. Some members still avow that showers, running water, indoor toilets, roads, electricity, gas, cars, ad infinitum, have spoiled the wilderness atmosphere.

The opposition to change among the older members of the association has decreased. Some of the second generation members are not sure they like the changes that have taken place, but changes will continue for better or for worse. The option is still here for those who don't want running water, gas, electricity, CB's or TV.

Nancy Hobson presented the case of some of the second generation members of BCCA in the following words: "Some of us have been searching for a reversion ahead. A search backward for a kind of community that relies on an interdependence of participants. We are looking for a sense of belonging. The more we progress the farther we seem to get from the basic sources of survival.

"When I first came up here I felt that sense of belonging. In 15 years it has all changed. The members of the group that made BCCA function were the type that were willing to cooperate. You look at their background and you can understand why it has been a successful venture, even though its character has changed drastically in 30 years. It is still important to some people and to others a lot of nonsense.

"The future of BCCA will depend a lot on how good a job the original membership did in passing on to their heirs the philosophy, purpose, and hopes of and for BCCA. The real meaning of the association with its communal background is too dear to lose. It would be a sad day in my life if this place ever became a typical resort with people, dust, beer busts, big boats, tennis courts, and all the rest of the urban necessities for a vacation."

The heirs of the generation that guided BCCA for the first three decades could be asked the questions; Do you feel the original goals are lost? Do you long for the return of the nostalgic days gone by? Would you love to work for the return of the days when you had to depend on each other for survival and progress? If so, will you assume the responsibility to work toward those basic goals and watch the rest of the membership sit by and go along for the ride?

A first generation BCCA member, Mollie Hammarlund, responded optimistically on the future turn of events for the association . . . "My own belief is that Priest Lake still represents the best of all possible places. People are still good-hearted and willing to help one another. We share common memories which unite most of us. Most of the second generation who have grown up at Priest Lake consider their experience here the best part of their childhood. There is a strong sense of camaraderie among them and a realization that the communal efforts of their parents created an exemplary environment which they want to continue.

"Perhaps it is because we live in an urban setting the rest of the year that we long for the simpler life at Priest and the close contact with friends we made when we were young. I find it remarkable that half of the BCCA members no longer live in Pullman; yet, they, their children, and grandchildren return from as far away as Hawaii, California, Florida, even Africa, nearly each year. As long as we solve major policy decisions in a democratic fashion via the association meetings, we will survive as an organization. But even without BCCA, as a group of friends and neighbors we exist as a unique community."

At the present time, two paths are open. One, to continue to solve the problems and to work under the original plan. Two, sell off everything for building lots, except the Wilson and Helen Compton Wilderness Area, to anyone who has the money, regardless of his interest in the original goals. If the second path is chosen, the communal effort of BCCA is doomed. Ten years ago BCCA, Inc. appeared to be secure. At this date problems have risen and will continue to rise as lots are transferred to heirs and other lots are sold. If there is no solution to some of these major problems, BCCA will cease to exist.

It all may be for naught if the present trend continues to take private property for public use under the state's power of eminent domain. This power of the Federal Government of the United States, in 1967, took 418 acres of private property on Upper Priest Lake and turned it over to the U.S. Forest Service for public use. It could happen here!

Jane Elder Wulff wrote the following as a tribute to Wilson and Helen Compton when Mrs. Compton last visited Priest Lake in June, 1975.

IT BEGAN WITH YOU
AND IT GOES ON AND ON — — —

Watching Lookout reflect the pink of the western sky
  Wondering what lies beyond Lion Creek valley
    Hearing the slap of a beaver tail on a quiet evening
     Waiting for a bite
       in the middle of a great peacefulness
    Bringing up the children
     Who bring up their children
    I could sing all my life and
      never pass the beginning
    Trying to live gratefully in the midst of plenty
     But it begins
     It began with you
     And it goes on and on

INDEX

FOOTNOTES

[1] Also referred to as Sears.

[2] At the time Governor Smylie was the Attorney General.

NOTES